Park Street

by

Sid Robertson

A Life in Aberdeen

PlashMill Press

Published in Scotland and the United Kingdom in 2008 by
PlashMill Press

First Edition

A CIP catalogue record for this book is available
from the British Library.

ISBN-13: 978-0-9554535-4-0

Printed and bound by CPI Antony Rowe, Eastbourne

PlashMill Press
The Plash Mill
Friockheim
Angus DD11 4SH
Scotland.

This book is not only for my family but also for anyone I have ever known; for it is all of them who have inspired me to write it.

Contents

Foreword

Poverty may not be something you can touch but it can reach out and touch you; hunger pains in an empty stomach, homelessness in hard times, tears of anger at a hard, cruel world. I was to be blessed and never know such poverty, but my father certainly did. My mother was third youngest of one of those huge families of the twenties and thirties. Fifteen brothers and sisters! Now there was an exercise in the survival of the fittest.

My father, Sidney Robertson, had been touched by poverty and my mother, Gladys Thomson, had been its next door neighbour. Their struggle through married life together was, like millions of others of their generation, a roller coaster of the best and more often the worst of times. In the end I believe it was a triumph, a triumph I never got the chance to praise my mother for and a triumph I pray I may yet be able to thank my father for.

My father was the son of Annie Nicholson, a hard working Shetland girl who followed the fishing fleets before settling in Aberdeen. Life and love had been unkind to her and the male lineage on my father's side was and still is a bit of a mystery to me. My grandmother, who died when I was eight years old, remains in my memory and my heart as one of the warmest, most gentle, most loving human beings I have ever known.

William 'Spud' Thomson and his wife Christina, 'Teenie,' were my mother's parents. He and my own grandchildren stretch my tangible links to this world from the First World War, in which he fought, to Bratz dolls and Gameboys. My grandmother who lived well into her eighties could blow a mean tune on a mouth organ all her days, a strong woman full of life. How could they, in those hard times, have achieved more than bring twelve of those fifteen children to healthy adulthood?

Life is and is nothing without our memories.

We mostly all live lives quite ordinary,
Our days filled with small things.
Yet each hour may be extraordinary.
Each second life's wonder brings.

Days of Heaven in Big Hell

Crisis was the bookmark for my entry on history's pages. I doubt however if Sidney and Gladys Robertson were overly interested in the trouble that was brewing in the Abadan oilfields of Persia on Friday the 24th of August 1951, when the latest addition to their young family was born at the Queen's Cross Maternity Hospital in Aberdeen. Was there and will there ever be a time when trouble does not stir in that ill-fated region of the world?

Sidney and Gladys were little more than children themselves, already with a two and a half year old daughter, Annie, and struggling to make a life in the harsh, black and white world of the early Fifties. Married as teenagers and yet to have a home of their own, a long struggle lay ahead of them. My father was an unskilled man, struggling to find a decent job after two years of National Service in the Royal Air Force. My mother was just a girl looking for a home to put her stamp on as a wife and mother, as was the norm in those days.

In 1951 the world was still recovering from the ravages of World War Two and had sunk into the Cold War. Prophets of Armageddon were everywhere! Rationing still applied to some goods and there was still a 'bombed hoosie' here and there to explore. The Aberdeen I was born into was a majestic city of grey granite, hewn from its own, world famous, quarry at Rubislaw. Hall Russell's, where my father had worked as a boy as a rivet catcher, and John Lewis and Son were famous shipbuilding yards at the mouth of the River Dee. You could walk the length of Albert Quay to Pointlaw across the decks of countless trawlers; Aberdeen was a major fishing port and a market and export centre for its fertile hinterlands of Buchan and the Mearns.

Several great paper mills operated in and around the city, engineering works like John M Henderson on West North Street, timber yards like Fleming's on Baltic Place, the Torry fish houses, textile mills, a comb works, the city was a hive of industry. A thriving seaport and LNER and LMR running passenger and freight rail services in and out of Joint Station confirmed the city's position as a great trading centre.

The world and Aberdeen were recovering from war and rebuilding for the future. Bruce's and Hall's were two of the city's largest building firms but I bet no-one at the former ever dreamed that quarter of a century later they'd

1

be responsible for the biggest architectural monstrosity ever to darken the Silver City's skyline, Norco House!

My first re-collection of this world was one of great expectation! I was approaching my third birthday, for which my father had promised me, as my present, a pair of 'Oor Wullie' dungarees. Me a man at last, and he assured me that Mum could never give me into trouble for getting them dirty. It is from that moment that all my memories of life stem.

My world then was an attic flat in an old tenement building at 74 Park Street. The first five months of my life had been spent at my father's mother's house at 66 Virginia Street, deep in the heart of the city's dockland area. At last, the Corporation had allocated mother and father a home of their own and it was there that my world began.

Number 74 stood at the junction of Park Street and Constitution Street just where the tram lines turned down to the Corporation depot in the beach area of the city. A building that could have sprung from the pages of a Dickens novel, it backed on to a smaller, equally dingy tenement that was entered up a flight of stairs off Constitution Street. There were three floors topped by our attic flat and a basement flat too, so eight families dreamt their dreams and held high hopes within its walls. There was no electricity; the lighting was by gas mantles. I never recall entering the front doorway and finding the stairway other than dark but I never recall feeling anything but safe in that place, safe with my mother, father and sister.

Next to the front entrance a flight of stairs led down to a drying green of sorts, where I can recall my mother hanging out her washing. A dilapidated old washhouse and several cellars ran the length of the green but I don't think they were ever used for any purpose. It was certainly not a place where kids could play either. There were no toilets in the building but a small brown wooden door set in the wall, ten yards from the street entrance concealed the one toilet, meant for the use of all the tenants. The door was as often as not kicked in; my mother always blamed drunken Teddy Boys, probably wrongly, heading home after closing time from the nearby Eastern Star, so I'll leave it to the imagination as to how all the families made other 'arrangements' for their personal needs!

My father was a small man, just less than five feet four inches tall. I always remember him as being sun-tanned in those days but the reality was that he was simply weather-beaten from long hard hours of manual labour, performed outdoors in all climates. His pride and joy was his shock of black hair, usually well plastered down with Brylcreem. It would trouble him greatly when it started to recede at a fair rate of knots in his late twenties! We cuddled often and he was so hard to touch, his body honed by hard work, but his voice and his heart were always soft. To my mother he was a dead-ringer for Dirk Bogarde in 'The Spanish Gardener.' As the years passed and my father and I grew up and grew older together I would always see in him a touch of James Dean's 'Rebel Without A Cause', not in any visual sense but for that edge that was always about him, that 'me against the world' edge. It had worn into him from a darker, harder time in his life and would never leave him in this world.

My mother was equally small in stature, almost two inches shorter than he was. She also had jet-black hair, which was shoulder length, deep dark eyes and a pale skin, which was highlighted by the bright red lipstick that was the mandatory fashion extra of the day. They each had plain grey Sunday best suits and when the occasion arose could cut a smart picture as a young couple of their time. My sister Annie and I were both growing and changing as kids do and the best description of us then was that we were noisy, messy, curious and mainly to our mother, deaf.

We are all explorers in this life and for children a world can be contained in no more than a few hundred yards. My world in those austere days of the Fifties was just that, small, busy, exciting and always with a new secret to offer any intrepid three year old about to make his first, almost solo, trip to the shops with his 'big,' five year old sister. You could stand at the front door of our tenement and see a Co-op grocer and baker at the top of Constitution Street. A short walk up Park Street would take you past Mrs Fyvie's paper shop and Barrack's the baker which simply oozed delicious smells into the air; you could actually see the baking being done at the back of the shop counter. A few yards on I seem to recall the tiny fishmonger's shop where I would stand spellbound as I watched the water stream down the window-pane, forming magical patterns as it ran. This of course was the cooling system of the day as was the way all the fish on display lay buried in deep trays of ice. A few more steps took you past the British Fish and Chip Shop, across the top of South Constitution Street, past Gammie's the hairdresser and on to Mr Suttie, the grocer at the corner of Wales Street. My mother did a lot of her shopping there; he was a tall bald-headed man always dressed in a grey jacket and white apron. He often gave you a wee sweet when mum had finished shopping and would smile as he scribbled down the total when she whispered, "Can I pay on Friday?"

On the other side of the street was our favourite chipper, 'The Golden Chipper.' Then you could head for home past Tommy Neri's sweet and ice cream shop on the corner of Frederick Street, the 'Saltoun Arms' pub on the other corner, Wood's the paper shop, Michie's the chemist and post office, then just opposite our front door the old second-hand shop. Just a stone's throw further down the street was Willie Reid's, a sort of repair shop. There you could buy paraffin, blue, pink or green and in a year or two, when I got bigger and stronger, my father would let me carry the accumulator battery for our radio across the road to have it topped up. Mr Willox the grocer was on the corner of Summerfield Terrace and he seemed to be at the outer limits of my world. It amazes me to look at this, now much changed, stretch of street and see that all this was within the length of a few hundred yards. All a family could need, right on their doorstep. Yes, those were the black and white days of the Fifties when my world was so safe and so small!

In our tenement there was not too much room for exploring. Our attic flat was reached up a final flight of curved stairs. Three doors led off of a small landing, one into a tiny living room with a large coal fire and gas oven on the far wall. A single gas mantle was the only lighting and there was a small skylight type window, which, if my father climbed on a stool, let him look up Park Street towards Justice Street and the Castlegate. The other two doors led to bedrooms, but I don't ever remember us using them; mum and dad slept in the living room, my sister and I in the smallest bedroom and the other big room was just a play area with nothing in it. I think a lack of furniture and the cost of keeping the whole flat warm were the main reasons for that.

It always amazed me that our sink was situated on that final sharp bend in the stairs about four steps down from the landing. My mother, father and sister had all become adept at standing, flamingo like, on one leg, on the stairs to wash their hands and faces. I was too small to reach the sink from the lower steps and in too much danger of falling down the stair if I tried it from the steps above, so my sister would be given the job of standing on the steps below me, helping me to keep my balance, whenever I needed a wash or a drink of water. Being just a wee bit messy or thirsty didn't seem too much of an inconvenience back then.

People other than my mother, father and sister soon became part of my world. A colourful band shared number 74 with us. Beldie and her bairns, who would become our first pals; Nan MacGregor and her two young sons who were both trawlermen. I remember the 'stand off of the stair rods,' when the boys had removed them all for firewood. My mother was adamant that, with two young kids, their social re-cycling would not progress beyond the bottom of our curved flight of steps. Jackie MacGregor was reputedly a bit of a tough guy and I think my father was none too keen on the prospect of a showdown. It never happened; Jackie was no match for my mother in full flight when she tackled him. A few choice words from her and a few muttered apologies from him were as far as it got. To the day we left the building that final curved flight of stairs was the only one with a full set of stair rods. I vaguely recall the old woman in the basement flat who kept about four greyhound dogs that were probably the reason we couldn't play down in the green, but the other neighbours are even greyer figures in my memory.

At three or four years of age any journey away from the cocoon of home is a great adventure and my horizons had the foreign lands of grandmothers to voyage to and explore. My mother's parents lived on Canal Place off Mounthooly in those days. We would visit there in the afternoons mostly, just mum and me. My father would be at work and my sister had left me to go to a strange new place called school. Mounthooly was a huge junction near the heart of the city, full of shops. We could walk there from home, along King Street and then Nelson Street. A rough earth road, which ran alongside the railway line from Kittybrewster to the harbour, led to my grandmother's house. There was always a train to see on the line, as they ferried all manner of goods to and from the docks.

A steep flight of wooden steps led up to my grandmother's front door, which opened into a small vestibule, which in turn accessed a large square living room. A roaring coal fire always seemed set, but the visiting kids were always keen to go beyond and into the 'L' shaped hall. This was a great place to play. My abiding memories of visits to my grandparents were crowds, card-schools and tea. Twelve children and their offspring meant they always had visitors and when the Thomsons got together they liked to play cards and drink tea. Queenie was the favourite card game and a pot of tea was always brewing on the stove.

My grandmother only had one lap and to me it always seemed that someone else had got there first. Perhaps I was just too shy and too small to be first there and be pampered. 'Spud' and 'Teenie' Thomson's children were Ruby, Molly, Ina, Mina, Phyllis, my mother Gladys, Doris, Billy, Stanley, Sydney, George and Albert. They had actually had fifteen children but three, Charlotte, Christina and Douglas, had sadly died during childhood. What an amazing couple, what a colourful family!

Nicknames were soon given to all that entered this busy social scene and I quickly came to be known as Noddy. My grandmother had a clock with a little Noddy figure that rocked to and fro with each passing second. My neck often ached from the effort of trying to follow his every move. Well into my teens most of mum's side of the family only ever called me by this name.

On one occasion we all visited on a Saturday and on the way, mum and dad had taken us into the local paper shop for some sweets. Whilst inside, I fell in love with a plastic guitar and Annie and I began doing our best impersonation of Bill Haley and the Comets in an attempt to convince them to buy it. Nothing doing. On the way home after tea there was panic—I was missing. They all looked for me everywhere, to no avail. Much to my mother's relief, I was eventually found quite close by leaning against the rear wheel of an old Corporation Bedford truck, strumming away to my heart's content on the plastic guitar. How the guitar or I got there no one knows and I honestly can't remember. Without another word we four headed off in the direction of home. Annie and I loved that guitar!

A faint remembrance of a visit to 66 Virginia Street lingers in my mind, but by now my Grannie Nicholson had moved to Drum's Lane, off the Upperkirkgate, in the city centre. Almost at the St Paul's Street end of the lane, a single flight of stairs led up to her tiny flat. We usually visited her of an evening or at the weekend. My dad's elder brother Percy would sometimes be there but more often than not would be away at sea or out with his pals.

She'd had seven children, Cissie, Laura, Gracie, George, Percy, John and my father Sidney. Gracie and Cissie were married and lived in England, whilst John was in the Merchant Navy and was soon to emigrate to Australia. Laura lived across in Sinclair Road in Torry with her husband Kit and my two cousins Betty and Sandra. Percy was the, mostly loveable, rogue of the family, but he was a great trial to Grannie Nicholson due to his heavy drinking. George's story was heart breaking; when he was only a babe-in-arms all eyes in the house had momentarily left him. In that split second he'd fallen from a table and tragically suffered a fatal injury. She was therefore often alone and Annie and I seemed to be the joy in her life. She cuddled us, sang to us, always had a penny for a sweet, and gave us that most precious gift that can be given to any child, time.

I had a nickname in her house too; she always called me 'Flower-pot,' and needless to say I was glad that only she, Mum, Dad, and Annie ever made any use of it. We seemed to listen to a lot of radio when we were there: Jimmy Clitheroe, Arthur Askey, Uncle Max, Family Favourites, Ted Ray, Vera Lynn, Jimmy Edwards and The Goons are some of the star names I recall from those times. I'm sure 'Gunsmoke' was the show my father always had to listen to whenever it was on.

Only one other trip stays with me from those days. Annie and I were scrubbed and dressed up one Sunday and Mum and Dad took us on a tram up Union Street and then another along George Street. We were to be taken to my father's grannie's house in Ann Street. As we walked from the tram stop to the house we were told to be very quiet and very still whilst we were in the house. We both were, and I can remember nothing other than a little old lady dressed in black. Later we were told she was ninety years old and, looking back now, she could have been Queen Victoria—and would indeed have well remembered that great Queen's reign.

There are great days in all our lives and my first lives with me as clearly now as it did that August morning in 1956. Only the mix of panic and excitement has dimmed but going to primary school for the very first time was a great day.

My mother, dressed in her Sunday best grey suit, walked me along Park Street, up Scotty's Brae and down Urquhart Road to the school gate. There was a crescendo of noise from the playground, which stilled instantly at the shrill blast of a whistle. As one all the children ran to form orderly lines and I think I glimpsed Annie smiling back at me as they all marched inside.

As I stood there with my mother, I was suddenly aware of a terrible screaming noise. A lady in a green suit was dragging a small redheaded boy, desperately clinging to any handhold he could find, towards the school gate.

"No, no, no," he screamed, " I don't want to go to school."

"Perhaps this isn't such a good idea after all," I thought, but suddenly my mother and I were through the blue front door of that imposing, castle-like granite building and in Miss McKinnon's office. A small grey-haired lady, she had a brief chat with my mum, then asked me some things and simply said, " Yes, Sidney will do for Mrs Allan's class."

As she showed my mother out and ushered me to the door of Mrs Allan's room I saw the lady in the green suit struggling to hold the still screaming redheaded boy on a chair in the corridor. Miss McKinnon knocked on the door and I slipped across the frontier of a new land. A sea of small faces seated in orderly rows of double desks eyed me curiously, all boys and girls I didn't know. The kindly face of Mrs Allan smiled at me and offered me a seat next to one of the boys. I sat down without hesitation and instantly became a member of the class.

A few minutes later, the still screaming redheaded boy was dragged, one leg and one arm at a time, into the classroom. He put up a wonderful fight and it took the lady in the green suit, Miss McKinnon and Mrs Allan together to get him through the door. The lady in the green suit somehow didn't seem to want to leave him now, but was eventually persuaded that he'd be alright and she could go. She left in tears and he stayed—still screaming.

That boy turned out to be Malcolm Watson. I still see him now and then to this day. We talk and laugh about those times but what would today's 'PC' brigade think of the fact that he then spent most of his first week at school standing in a corner facing the wall? One morning he came and sat down at the desk just in front of me. He too had crossed the border and entered that enchanted land of knowledge and learning.

I would spend the next two years in Mrs Allan's class. Boys like Bobby Burns, Robbie Clunas, Jim Davies, Jim Soutar, Graeme Yule and Davie Calder would become, in an ever turning circle, firstly best friend, worst enemy and then friend once more. Those strange creatures, girls; girls like Dorothy Norrie, Rosemary Allen, Sandra Rose and Linda Mutch, would also become friends, and in those childlike secret moments would also become a first love.

As I look back now I can see that, for me, it took seven years for the world to come up with a description of how starting primary school felt. From that first eventful morning, every day was like walking into Dr Who's Tardis for the very first time. There was always something new to discover and any piece of knowledge once understood is as great a thrill as a journey to the farthest part of the cosmos could possibly be.

To a five-year-old King Street Primary School was a gigantic place, a huge granite building surrounded on all sides by playgrounds. We could enter up two flights of stairs from Bodie Place, where we all became regular customers at the small sweet shop on the corner or go through the main entrance off King Street. For the brave and bold there was another way in but this meant running the gauntlet of passing the janitor's house; a green metal gate off Jackson Terrace led past Mr Garrow's house but he never did take kindly to any of the kids using that route.

The playgrounds were teeming with school life as kids ran, jumped, skipped and learned those 'other' school rules of what to do and when. 'Film

Stars,' 'King Ba,' 'Sappy Sojers,' 'Tick and Tack' and 'Kick the Cannie' were some of the first games I recall. The girls would always be playing with ropes and balls and their games always seemed to involve an accompanying song. They played one game called 'Beddies,' which involved chalking squares on the ground and kicking an empty polish tin or similar shaped piece of wood around them. I always felt that boys would be better at this game than girls, and away from the mocking eye of school pals, I took every opportunity to prove this to my sister Annie when we played together.

Inside the school was a maze of huge corridors; every wall was beige in colour and every piece of woodwork, every coat peg, every bench and every door was painted pale blue. Mrs Allan was a teacher and a mother figure and combined those roles so well I was always happy to be in her class and often daydreamed, that just like my mother, she would cuddle me and stroke my hair. From the moment we were given our first reading book about Mr and Mrs Brown and their two children, who I think were called Tom and Mary, there was no stopping us. We were like sponges as we soaked up all the knowledge that Mrs Allan could pass to us. The mysteries of reading, counting and spelling unravelled for us on a daily basis and we were always ready to absorb more. A short break to drink our perfectly shaped one third of a pint bottle of milk in the morning and we were off once more.

I remember so well us all singing in class and our delivery was in that age-old style of five and six year olds, the whole song sang on a single note. 'Jesus Loves Me' was the most often sang but my favourite was the 'Road Safety Song,' and the words stick with me to this day.

"We must have safety on the Queen's highway,
So stop look left, look right, then look left again.
Then off we go if the road is clear,
Safely home to mother 'cause there's nothing to fear.
Don't be in a hurry going to and from the school,
Kerb drill for you is the golden rule.
We must have safety on the Queen's highway,
So stop look left today!"

Our own efforts at pictures and stories covered the walls and the very best would find themselves proudly displayed for all to see in the corridor outside our room. Drawing was never a strong point of mine and my failings would haunt me four years later when, in primary five, the first ever Parent's Evenings were introduced. Our teacher then was Miss Hadden, a stern woman but a grand teacher. She had decided that for the occasion we would be very topical and draw a queue of people outside the pictures; cinema was still the great mass entertainment media and families flocked to see the latest movies. It had fallen to me to draw the Commissionaire, one of those gentlemen who in those days would dress in uniforms that would make even the most pompous 'Banana Republic' dictator look quite drab. In one of her softer moments Miss Hadden spared my blushes and my parents' embarrassment in one fell swoop. By neatly changing the legs of my grotesque creation into wheels and the head into a flashing light she successfully, on the night, passed him off to all the visiting mums and dads as an ice cream kiosk!

That would raise a laugh in the future but in March 1957 I scored 65 out of 70 in an unseen test given by Miss McKinnon. I was so proud of that first report card and my mum and dad were so pleased too. Not a bad effort for a five year old! Mrs Irene Allan must have seen another side to me and her comments at the foot of my report card mentioned my mischievous nature and a need to improve my behaviour.

Primary school times were to prove the halcyon days of my educational years and none were better than those two with Mrs Allan. The then Prime Minister, Harold MacMillan, would enrage the working classes in the summer of 1957 by telling the country, "You've never had it so good."

Had he at that moment meant those words just for me then, "He'd never have got it so right."

If school was an adventure then it was no less so at home. From where we lived it was only a few hundred yards down Constitution Street to Aberdeen's beach area and the golden sands, that to me seemed to stretch from one end of the world to the other. Mum and Dad would take us to play there on a Sunday, and as we got even bolder, Annie and I would sneak off to the swings there as often as we could—much to my mother's annoyance, and we both became quickly aware of the high temper she could have.

A family of Sikhs had moved in to a flat just across the road from us and my mother wove them into a scare story that I think was meant to stop us roaming around. It involved the men carrying daggers in their turbans, but it didn't deter us one little bit. Kids have no misguided preconceptions and we would go out of our way to talk to them; and of course they were happy to talk to and play with us.

At the time Aberdeen styled itself as Scotland's leading holiday resort and in the summertime during their 'Fair' holiday, the air would ring with Glaswegian accents along Constitution Street, where there were several guest houses. As we played and wandered back and forth to the beach we'd banter with them. It was all great fun. The 'No Vacancies' signs were always in the windows then.

Even as a child the hurt and fear of the world can't be shut out forever and it was now that I would meet them for the first time. My mother and father were so happy when they told us that we were soon to have a new brother or sister; Annie and I were so excited. I remember that one day Mum had to be taken to hospital and we went to Grannie Nicolson's for a night or two. My father came for us on his own, and he seemed to have been crying. He did cry as he told Grannie, Annie and me that we'd had a little sister, Gladys, who wouldn't be coming home but had gone to heaven instead. My mother had carried Gladys for the whole nine months only for her to be tragically stillborn.

We were told to be extra especially good when Mum came home and we tried our best. She seemed so sad and quiet. We didn't know how to help. If a child as young as I was then can feel grief then I recall that mine was not for the sister I would never know but for myself and the sister I would never have. At night in bed Annie and I would cry together about Gladys and could hear Mum and Dad do the same in the next room.

Time and tide wait for no man and we four too got back to normal things; work, play and just enjoying being a family again. Life was hard enough for my mother and father as they struggled to raise two children on his £7 a week wage, earned by five and a half days labour each week for John Ellis, who ran a market garden business at Cove. My father enjoyed the outdoor work and always spoke well of Mr Ellis, but it was ever a struggle for my mother to make ends meet. Our parents always spared my sister and I any hardship and it was only as we grew older that we saw what an effort they had made and what a good life they had given us.

Gladys had brought grief to my young life. My mum, my dad and Annie had helped me deal with it. Not long after that time I was to feel the first real fear of my life; I know there's a God because he sent an angel to look after me—my sister Annie.

Annie, Isobel Ann Robertson, as dark as I was fair, annoyingly then always several inches taller than me, long-suffering of my mother's favouritism towards me, always there when I needed her and who never ever gave me less than everything.

We were learning that not all was well with my mother's health; she'd a weak heart and was going to have to spend some time in hospital. My father would have to keep working—it was strictly no work, no pay in those days, and my sister and I were going to stay for a while at the Children's Shelter.

We were taken up to see the place on a Sunday by my mum and dad; I was heart-broken, terrified and inconsolable all at the same time. We'd only be there for two weeks at the most; it might as well have been two years to me. I've no bad tales to tell of the people there but no good ones either. I was only five years old and five-year-olds need the understanding of their own mums and dads; they simply need to be let off with things a lot of times.

A few years later I'd encounter a harsher regime at Linn Moor but, being a little older, was just about able to look after myself. Here, I was lost, sad and lonely; but Annie had other ideas. She never left my side, helped me through meal times and even saw me to bed, often with me crying, before going to her own dormitory. Think of all the little, simple, personal things that a five-year-old can't do. Annie did all of those things for me. She was only seven!

Life is a weird box of tricks and we have not remained close in adult life, but I never think of her without my throat tightening and a tear forming in the corner of my eye.

Mum was soon home, and so were we, and in no time life was wonderful again. There always seemed to be a laugh around the corner, none better than when Dad chased a dosser off of our landing early one morning. That guy must have been nifty because Dad could shift in those days. He was to learn that morning that he was quicker still in reverse as the only clothes he was wearing, his 'Long Johns,' started to fall down as he sprinted past Michie's the Chemist. The dosser made his escape and Dad beat a hasty retreat back to number seventy-four.

My mother loved a cup of 'Camp' coffee in those days. The label on the bottle was a picture of a piper standing at a table on which stood a bottle of 'Camp' coffee. The label on *that* bottle had a picture of a piper standing at a table and so on and so on. I could spend ages looking deep in to that label just to see how many pipers I could count. I was also fascinated by mirrors but could never turn round quickly enough to catch myself turning round, however sneaky I tried to be. I could keep everyone in stitches with my antics in front of a mirror.

My world then from 1951 to late 1958 had known grief, fear, wonder and expectation but most of all my world had known love, laughter and much happiness. The world outside of home, family and school had meant very little to me but it was a world of amazing events.

The great war leader Winston Churchill had returned to power in 1951 but resigned from politics four years later. Dwight D Eisenhower was then American President and Stalin had died. It would be years before the truth of his monstrous reign over Russia became known. The 'Father of the Nuclear Age,' Albert Einstein, had also died, leaving an uncertain world, unsure of the power of the technology at its disposal.

We were presented with the original cause for every couch potato who has ever lived, the TV remote control; and the parking meter made its bow on the streets of Britain.

Movies were still a huge part of people's lives and would soon become so for me. Some classics made their first appearance in those years; *The African Queen, High Noon, Singing In The Rain, Calamity Jane* and *White Christmas* to name but a few. Those marvellous Ealing comedies typified the essence of the age, a country surviving harsh times but a people who could still laugh at them.

Elvis Presley had cut his first demo at Sun Records and soared to stardom. Such was his impact that the name of his first movie was changed from *The Reno Brothers* to *Love Me Tender,* the title song.

At Shawfield in 1955 an Archie Glen spot-kick saw Aberdeen beat Clyde and become champions of the Scottish Football League for the first time. Magnificent Union Street was still cobbled and on a famous night in 1958 the Corporation burned the last of the trams at the Beach.

Another Middle East crisis, this time over the Suez Canal, had Dad talking of war and Mum feeling very scared. Most amazing of all the Russians launched *Sputnik 1* and the Space Age was well and truly born.

Forty years later I would learn from a neighbour, then in his seventies, that 74 Park Street and the smaller tenement it backed on to had been known as 'Big Hell and Little Hell.' They may well have been slum dwellings but such had been my life there that I will only ever recall that time as, 'Days of Heaven in Big Hell.'

Loving times in loving arms,
That sheltered me from harm.
If a sadness came my way,
I was sure it wouldn't stay.
Loving days and loving years,
My world emptied of all fears.
Done for me a son and brother,
By father, sister and my mother.

Electricity, The Rubber Shop and the Eleven Plus

Around the summer of 1958 I was about to enter a period of great change in my young life. My mother and father were constantly talking about moving house. It seemed that old seventy-four was past its sell-by date and was due for demolition. I think it was a couple of years after we left that it was finally consigned to history and to this day nothing has ever been built where it stood. The sunken drying green was filled in to street level and a few ornamental bushes and a bench, for any weary passer-by, mark the spot where all my early years of life were spent. Amazingly, many face-lifts down the road, 'Little Hell' stands to this day and behind its walls, life stories still twist and turn.

My father had finally bowed to economic pressures and left the employ of John Ellis. He was now making £10 a week working as a labourer for 'Brucies,' the builders in Miller Street. Aberdeen was just beginning the expansion programme which would carry on through the Sixties and see the huge development of areas like Summerhill, Mastrick and Hazlehead. There was overtime to be made in the building trade!

All my grandparents had moved home too; Grannie Nicolson to a wee flat in Jopps Lane and Granda and Grannie Thomson to a first floor flat on Links Street not far from the Hall Russell's shipyard. At school too moves were afoot; Mrs Allan had taken us to visit another class and Miss Okoberg was to be our new teacher when school restarted after the holidays.

Amid great excitement the day arrived for us to see the new home the council had offered us. Mum had collected the keys in the afternoon, Annie and I had rushed home from school and Dad had managed to get home a wee bit early, so off we all set. It wasn't a long trip and we wouldn't need to jump on one of the old green and cream number twenty-one buses that ran up and down Park Street in those days, bound for either the Golf Links or Broomhill. We were travelling no more than two hundred yards up the street to number 112.

A three-storey building, it stood at the junction of Lemon Street and Park Street, its drying green and outhouse surrounded by a wall almost as tall as my father. The ground floor flat had a doorway on the pavement and we entered through a gate in the wall, then climbed a turning, exterior, stone staircase. Fifteen steps to a small landing and then a turn of six steps to another led us to the outer entrance. Just inside the small lobby was an old brown wooden door, its paintwork flaking after years in the sun. It was into the lock of this door that my father pushed the key. Annie and I watched, sitting at the foot of an internal flight of stairs, which led to the flat above, as my father edged the door slightly ajar. He reached inside and we heard a sharp click—light streamed through the open door into the tiny lobby; this house had electricity!

We all walked inside; a small, almost square room greeted us. The wall on the left angled away as the room widened to its back wall. A sink, with only a cold water tap, sat below the window on the angled wall. The back wall had two doors leading to the bedrooms and a tiled fireplace that included an old black gas oven was mounted on the other wall.

My mother and father seemed well pleased and began discussing the possibilities of what could go where while my sister and I each ran and opened a bedroom door and a simultaneous sharp click was heard. I know today my own granddaughters would smile at the idea but until my father sharply reminded us to stop, my sister and I simply ran round those three small rooms switching the lights on and off. This house had electricity!

Outside, a large drying green lay behind a big outhouse building. This building contained the toilets, a washhouse and the cellars. The grass on the drying green was knee-high but the entire outhouse was being used; this was a better place than seventy-four and I could tell that my mum and dad were happy with what they had seen.

It was only a matter of days before the move had been made and a new life had started for all of us; Annie and I would not have the upset of changing schools. We'd make new friends and have new street corners to explore but happily for us two youngsters, much of our world would remain the same.

As the Fifties drew to a close we were blissfully unaware that a momentous explosion was about to hit the world. It would be known simply as 'The Sixties' and nobody's life would ever be the same again. We would all be affected socially, culturally, economically and domestically. On the 12th of April 1961 Yuri Gagarin would be come the first man in space and this event would be the symbolic touchpaper that sent a decade into orbit. The world was to be dragged from an era of black and white into an age of glorious technicolour.

The Fifties wouldn't pass with a whimper and there was a major bombshell for me when, in 1959, they closed The Casino! The glory years of the famous picture palaces of Aberdeen were drawing to a close. Television would soon be king and those fabulous family nights out at the pictures would vanish forever.

I remember them all so well. The Casino on Wales Street was nearest to our home and my favourite; it was magnificently styled like a Spanish villa, with a long sloping corridor leading from the ticket kiosk to the seating area. The Kingsway, The City, The Grand and The Regal were our other regular haunts. Union Street could boast The Capitol, The Playhouse, The Queens,

The Gaumont and The Majestic with its imposing staircase. We once travelled as far as The Astoria on Great Northern Road; I thought we were going on holiday! Torry had its own cinema and The Odeon, which Mum said was too posh, was just off Holburn Junction.

The cinema then was such a cheap form of family entertainment that we'd often go twice a week. Annie and I would get sweets and maybe a tub of ice cream as a special treat. Most cinemas would change the programme in midweek; there was always a main feature, a 'B' movie, the newsreels and the coming attractions for the next programme. You could snuggle up to Mum or Dad when you were getting tired or if you were scared; I often woke up at home just as father laid me down and wondered how I'd got there. The eerie intro to the Edgar Wallace thrillers always got me with the revolving bust turning in and out of the shadows; Mum and Dad would smile as I buried my face in my hands. People always applauded at the end of each film and many stood for the Queen when the national anthem was played at the end of the evening. Unforgettable times from a bygone age; we were spoiled for choice.

I recall one night we had gone to The Kingsway to see *The Incredible Shrinking Man;* that fight with the spider is still one of my scariest movie moments. As we headed home along Frederick Street it was a cold but absolutely clear night with a full moon. I clutched my father's hand and stared up into the myriad stars in the night sky and began to feel myself as small and insignificant as the hero I had just thrilled to.

Some years later we were gifted four complimentary tickets for the Aberdeen premiere of *My Fair Lady* at The Odeon. "This'll be a posh do," my mother had told us, "Best behaviour please."

We were impeccable but sadly she wasn't. In the famous horse racing scene, in best Eliza Doolittle fashion, she yelled out, "Come on Lester Piggot!"

Parents, you can't take them anywhere!

Annie and I were happy with the move down the street even though we had to share the wee bedroom for a couple of years, until I was shipped out to a 'Z' bed in the living room, which doubled as mum's ironing table during the day. We made many new friends; Jackie Christie became a lifelong pal and was best man at my wedding. Madcap Brian Muir, who was game for any stunt, could swim like a fish, was a fearless climber, could jump off a higher washhouse roof than any kid on the street and on Guy Fawkes' night could hold a lighted banger in his hand until his fingers caught fire. Brian saved his best stunt for the day he was showing his brand new bike to the whole neighbourhood. No hands, one foot on the saddle, both feet on the handlebars, Brian was magnificent. For the throng of admirers he kept his best trick until last, speeding from a distance to brake sharply in front of his enthralled audience. Sadly no one had taught Brian the front brake, rear brake system! The bike shot upwards from the rear and catapulted Brian through the air. Brian wasn't our hero for nothing and in gymnastic style landed so softly that he wouldn't have left a mark in a long jump sandpit. The bike however, being an inanimate object, showed no mercy, did a triple loop and crashed on the unsuspecting maestro. Aye, there's many a slip 'twixt cup and lip and Brian's pride was badly bruised that day—but he was a great pal.

Jackie's uncle lived up a cul-de-sac opposite our house, which was known locally as The Pennie. Jackie lived in Torry with his widowed mum Betty, but his Auntie Evie and Uncle John stayed in our street and they spent most weekends there. The great news for Jackie and me was that the Yorston family stayed next to The Pennie and their famous son Harry often came to visit. Harry Yorston, Dons' legend and Scottish international footballer, who had retired in his prime to become a fish market porter. All the adults said he did it for the security and he could earn more at the fish market. What would today's mercenary millionaire footballers think of that? Harry was a gentleman and would often come and have a kick-about with us kids and mesmerise us with his keepie-up skills.

Our immediate neighbours were Johnnie and Madgie Lonie who lived above us and had three boys; their flat was even smaller than ours was! Young John was in Annie's class at school, Graeme was a year younger than I was and Ian was the baby of their family. Bertie and Mrs Miller lived below us, their son Robert was also in Annie's class and their daughter Patsy was a few months younger than I. They and many others became our firm friends, occasional enemies and mostly just kids we had an awful lot of fun with. *Tiger Bay* remains to this day one of my favourite films—I know the streets and houses that Hayley Mills is seen in, I've played and lived in them.

Like Annie I was now old enough to be sent a message to the shops. Rennie the newsagent, Ernie Merchant the grocer and Mrs Barclay's sweet shop were near at hand and my trial runs. I even recall taking a three-penny piece and a slip of paper, for my mum, to the street bookie that would stand at the entrance to The Pennie. Everyone of my generation remembers their mother's Co-op number, the annual excitement and the queues on Loch Street at 'divi' time. My mother's number was 32654 and woe betide you if you came back from running a message to the Co-op without the wee check ticket, properly marked with that number and the amount that had been spent. All those tickets would be kept, counted and the 'divi' payment worked out to the penny well in advance of the official notice.

A Saturday morning trip to the shops with Mum was a great experience. We'd perhaps stop at Michie's Post Office counter and get a savings stamp each, usually a Princess Anne one, which was worth a shilling. The Prince Charles ones cost two shillings and Mum couldn't afford to buy us both one of them. Each page in the little stamp book had room for ten stamps and each book had ten pages. You could cash in a single complete page and I don't often recall Annie or me ever getting more than that one page filled.

Those trips to the shops were an assault on the senses. From watching sausages being made in the butcher's shop, the floor of which was always lightly covered in sawdust, to walking up on to Union Street and savouring the marvellous smells of Lipton's and the Home & Colonial. These shops would have a display in huge glass counters of all varieties of hams, cheeses and cooked meats. Staff had to climb tall ladders to reach the highest shelves, stocked full of tins, packets and bags of all the grocery needs a person could want. I would exhort my mother to buy her packet of tea at a particular shop as I'd be saving the latest set of cards given away free with a particular brand. Trains, boats, planes and by then space ships too would be the subjects. Carefully rescuing a card undamaged from the layers of wrapping was an achievement on its own and well rewarded—if you didn't already have the card inside.

My mother would always have to visit Marks & Spencers, big and little Woolies and Maxwell's in the market was never missed out. We'd often stay outside when she was in Markies and play around the base of the statue of Queen Victoria, which stood then on St Nicholas Street. Union Street was alive with people, buses and cars; we'd walk its length just to gawk at the sights. The rich smell of coffee as you passed Andrew Collie's and the almost sterile atmosphere of posh shops like Watt & Grant's. A street photographer would always seem to be snapping away and pressing a card in people's hands explaining how to get a copy, I've held dear, to this day, many treasured photos taken in this way.

George Street was a treasure-trove of stores from its St Nicholas Street junction as far as Hutcheon Street. The Equitable, Reid and Pearson's and Isaac Benzies are just a few to mention. No trip to George Street would pass without a visit to Bruce Miller's, where beautiful pianos, accordions, guitars and brass instruments would be on display. We'd browse the sheet music and Annie would dare me to play a note on one of the pianos. The highlight of the visit would be Mum asking to hear one of the latest hit records and we three would crowd into one of the small listening booths to hear the song. Then we'd follow our well-rehearsed routine of sneaking out, as Mum had neither the money to buy the record nor a record player at home to play it on.

No shopping expedition would end without an exploration of the Co-op Arcade on Loch Street. Mum would be in and out of all the shops on its split level, whilst Annie and I would run along the top landing, sit beside the polished Peterhead granite memorial or the fountain and climb the steep flight of stairs that led out onto the Gallowgate. I always liked to be around if mum bought anything from the clothing shop on the top level. I'd be spellbound, as the assistant would place the cash for the purchase in a brass-ended glass cylinder which would speed away along a tube and amazingly speed back seconds later with mum's change—and her Co-op check of course.

Not *just* a trip to the shops then, but a visual, audible and aroma filled rite of passage that all we youngsters shared in those days. If only I could now explain to my granddaughters when they laugh at me for not getting excited about shopping on the Internet.

Visiting our grandparents was still a major part of life. At Links Street the legendary afternoon card schools were still being played at the Thomson household and I was now of an age when occasionally I'd be dealt in. It was a hard school and the ribbing would be merciless from uncles Albert and George or Auntie Doris if the trace of a tear formed after my three pennies had been lost. A seat in front of the Noddy clock, which still ticked away on Grannie's mantelpiece, would be a child's escape. It all taught me a great lesson for the future—don't gamble!

Often at a weekend my grandparents or uncles and aunts with wives and husbands would visit our house. Usually there'd be a few carry-outs brought in and the evening would progress to a typical family singsong, with everyone, kids included, expected to do their party-piece. My uncle Albert was an excellent singer, Al Jolson was his speciality and a few beers would soon loosen the inhibitions of the rest. In no time there'd be a Perry Como, Connie Francis, Alma Cogan, Conway Twitty or Bobby Darin rendition ringing out around the house. Some great laughs, just the odd row when the drink was in and once or twice a knock on the door from a passing bobby telling us to keep the noise down. Now there's an endangered species of the modern world, the passing bobby! When I remember how small our house was, I never can work out how they all got in at the same time.

Visits to my Grannie Nicolson's were a highlight of the weekend and Annie and I would be up and off as early as we could on a Saturday morning. We had secret places to go on the way there, starting with a visit to either Mrs Barclay's or Tommy Neris' to spend our few pennies of pocket money. Treats like bags of brown sugar, toffee apples, lucky tatties, penny caramels, coo candy and lucky bags would soon have us skint.

You might really strike it lucky and find a silver three-penny piece inside a lucky tattie but usually you just chipped your teeth on a wee plastic horse. Mrs Barclay could have been our grannie but we would buy 'Smokin' Caney' in her shop. If memory serves me this was a cigar-like cinnamon stick, which was, sickly sweet to taste but could be set alight and smoked; the smell from it was awful! We'd smuggle some matches out of the house, light up and puff our way boldly down the street. Most adults would just laugh; smoking wasn't the social evil in those days that it is now.

One of our favourite stops on the way to Jopps Lane would be the Bissett's bookshop on Broad Street opposite the Marischal College. It was there that I first thumbed through the pages of a *Biggles* book. The treasures of the College museum were also open, the spine-chilling mummy in its sarcophagus, or the stuffed two-headed calf, always held our attention. Annie and I always had notebooks and would write endless facts and figures into them. The Art Gallery with its museum downstairs, a forerunner of today's wonderful Maritime Museum in the Shiprow, and the Central Library were also centres of our early self-education.

There was however one special place, one jewel in the crown, whose hallowed precincts had to be visited at all costs—The Rubber Shop!

On George Street, just beyond the Upperkirkgate, with its spell-binding glass frontage, this was heaven on earth. After an age of gazing at the toys in the window we would almost float inside and up the single flight of stairs that led to the toy department. Dolls' houses, train sets, spinning tops, skipping ropes, chemistry sets, nurses' outfits, cowboy sets, Meccano sets, teddy bears, scrapbooks, Snakes and Ladders, Ludo and Dinky toys, all the treasures of the world were there for the both of us. Brian Sherriff's, farther up George Street, or the Toy Bazaar on Correction Wynd, couldn't hold a candle to this place. It would be like comparing Aladdin's Cave to a box of Christmas crackers.

The Holy Grail that lay within the Rubber Shop for me, was a glass display cabinet holding all the Matchbox models of the famous cars, lorries and buses of the day. I never had the success of the young number taker in *The League of Gentlemen*, whose effort helped catch the crooks, but I would list endless registration numbers of all the great marques in a notebook, for what purpose I can't imagine.

There though, for one shilling and sixpence, you could have a beautiful miniature model of your favourite, neatly packaged in the trademark matchbox sized cardboard box. The big Fords, Consul, Zephyr and Zodiac, Austins, Vauxhalls and Hillmans. The stately Rover, quirky bubblecar, bulky Morris Oxford and flashy Triumph. The Ford Popular and Morris Minor were ones I loved and the Mini which burst on the scene in 1959. The lorries were spectacular too—Foden, Albion, AEC, Bedford, ERF, Seddon and Atkinson; all sadly now just stars in those 'years gone by' calendars. My absolute favourite was the Scammell Scarab with its three-wheeled cab; you'd often see them running mail out of Joint Station or goods out of the British Road Services depot on Guild Street.

When we were at my grandmothers on a Saturday, Mum would arrive late morning and Dad early afternoon after work. I could usually drop enough hints to encourage each of them to give me sixpence and then the race was on, back to the Rubber Shop, to get yet another special model. Oh the despair if I was beaten to it and got there to find an empty space in the immaculate display.

My grandmother had the knack of making any visit to see her seem like the most special thing that had ever happened to her and that ability made you feel special. One day we arrived at Jopps Lane, climbed the stairs and apart from Manxie the cat, found the place empty. Annie and I were both puzzled, checked the bedroom which was empty and sat down in the living room. I thought I saw the curtain, which hung across the entrance to her tiny galley kitchen, move but Manxie scratched the back of my hand and distracted me.

Suddenly a figure leapt from behind the curtain; Annie and I were terrified. The figure bellowed, "On guard, who dares enter the castle of Sir Lancelot?"

It was our uncle Percy!

Our terror fizzled to fits of furious laughter. He was dressed in his long johns, his jacket on back to front, and one of my grandmother's feathered hats on his head. A metal dustbin lid was his shield and a sweeping brush his sword. My grannie had popped out to the shops and told him to look out for the bairns who'd be arriving soon. How long had he hidden there to spring that surprise?

Percy was an enigma to us all, a hard man who lived a hard working, hard drinking, mostly solitary life. He was a great trial to my grandmother who'd often show him the door. He'd then spend time living at the lodging house, known as the Modeler, on East North Street. There he'd fall in with all the winos and tappers of the day; but she would always relent and take him back home. His drinking would eventually cause him to be suspended 'Sine Die' from Aberdeen's fishing fleet. His elder sister Cissie, who's husband, Roy Beamish, was skipper of a Hull trawler, would help Percy regain his self respect in his last years, helping him to get work with the Hull fishing fleet and kick the booze.

Percy John Ellnor died in his Fifties and was buried at sea off Hull. A man who'd fought for his country as a teenager in the African desert and whose life had sadly seemed to have little point. True that may be but he certainly made me and Annie jump out of our skins and then laugh until our sides were sore one Saturday morning a long time ago.

Miss Okoberg turned out to be just a teacher but I'm sure that was no reflection on her abilities, more an indication of how I'd grown up over the last two years. There was no longer a need in me for a mother at home *and* at school. On more than one occasion she had to summon my mother to school because my spectacles, which I'd worn since I was three, had yet again been found by Mr Garrow blocking the boy's toilet where I'd disposed of them. "Pink glasses Mum, those horrid National Health ones, how could you?"

Miss Okoberg added much to my education and at the end of my two years with her I was one of only two boys in the class to score VG in the seven-plus examination.

Apart from my last year at primary school when Jim 'Bomber' Gordon became headmaster, Mr Main was the boss. During all my time there I never had occasion to have any contact with him and remember him only as a grey suit and bald head that we hid from whenever they appeared in a corridor.

Miss Hadden took us across some wobbly rope bridges in our ascent of the mountain of knowledge, fractions, decimals, joined up writing, punctuation, multiplication and division. She was the first teacher to scare me a little and with her school became a far more serious occupation. Disciplinarian she most certainly was but even she couldn't legislate for the arrival in our class of Alan Reekie.

If ever a boy was aptly named it was Alan; he'd been 'promoted' to our class at the start of the year and was a really cheeky character, always smiling. Alan's party piece was to be able to fart at will and not only that, his ability was positively ventriloquist-like. Alan would deliver his short sharp shock but Miss Hadden, always dressed in a bright green overall, could never determine from whence the offending emission had originated. She'd wheel round from the blackboard, face bright red, screaming "Who made that noise!"

Facing her would be fourteen red-faced girls, twelve boys desperate to laugh and one cherubic innocent totally oblivious to her wrath, Alan himself. Her face would twist in rage until we all felt that she too was about to let go and we were all by then in danger of peeing ourselves with laughter.

"Not another sound!" she'd bellow as she wheeled away from us and Alan would synchronise a real ripsnorter with the scratch of her chalk on the blackboard.

The whole class would now be in hysterics and she'd no hope of ever discovering the culprit, as we were all laughing so hard, that by then most of us really had farted too! Alan's mother must have known something of his prowess for she never failed to turn him out at school in anything other than brown corduroy trousers!

Primary Six was to be the best year of my school life due entirely to one special man but it started with a real shock—Annie grew up on me! She was off to Frederick Street Secondary School and in many ways that marked the fork in the road where we both set out on our separate journeys through life.

The special man was Jim 'Bomber' Gordon, deputy headmaster and known to us strictly as Mr Gordon. Miss Hadden had built the strong foundations of our education but he would make us aware of what that education could mean to us in the outside world. A tall, straight-backed man he carried a high red colour and his lips were almost blue. His voice seemed to come from the soles of his shoes and he was always dressed like my father on a special Sunday.

He threatened the strap often but he never used it; his speciality was ear pulling. Woe betides the offending chatterbox or daydreamer, always boys, who incurred his attentions. You always knew the lads in Bomber's class, they wore their war wounds with pride in the playground; all had ears the size of African elephants. A teller of tales more than a teacher, he made us aware of why and how knowledge would help us through life. He once spent an afternoon telling us about Wales, its mining, industry, rugby and people. Not perhaps the most interesting topic for ten year olds but to this day I can still make a fair attempt at spelling Llanfairpwllgwyngwllgogerychwyrndrobwilllantsiliogogogoch; he was that sort of man. The name means something about a church in a hollow near a whirlpool and a red cave but I wasn't that good a student!

I played my first football trial under Mr Gordon at the Nelson Street playing fields that we shared with St Peter's Roman Catholic school. My dreams sank in the mud; the small matter of not having a pair of football boots perhaps didn't help. I never did make the school football team but did go on to captain the cricket team the next year—we were awful!

In adult life I kept in touch with Mr Gordon and learned he'd been a Lancaster pilot during the war, hence his nickname. I often met him for a pint and a blether after work on a Friday at the Rosemount Lounge; he always called me young Sidney and I always called him Mr Gordon. I admired the man so much and now want to clear my conscience of the time I lied to and cheated him.

It was announced at school that entries were invited for a national poetry competition. Keen to enter but with no poetic thoughts in mind I devised a masterplan that offered the easiest option. Annie was brilliant at stories and poems; a play she wrote called Girl From The Orphanage was done as the School Play at Frederick Street School during one of her years there. Easy peasy for me then, a few minutes one evening copying out one of her poems and hey presto! The next morning 'my poem' was on the pile of literary hopefuls on Bomber's desk.

The poem was soon forgotten about but it sticks in my mind that I'd broken a window at school and had hopefully not been spotted in the act by anyone. When Mr Gordon asked me to step out of class with him one morning my spirits sank and I was ready to admit a fair cop for the window. My confusion was total when his voice boomed, "Excellent work young Sidney."

Clutched in his hand was 'my poem' and an official looking letter from which he read, the poem was to be one of five selected from entries in the North East of Scotland to be submitted to the national finals. I sensed he might have harboured a lingering doubt as he asked me quietly if the poem was all my own work. Shifting between a fainting feeling and the need to burst into tears I somehow managed to answer that it was, he patted my head and we walked back into class together.

Thank goodness, for once Annie must have had an off day and I never heard another word about that poem. I could never have kept up the pretext but I did enjoy the brief admiration of my peers for being such a brilliant writer. I've often wondered if he'd discovered my duplicity, would he have resorted to the strap or would I just have ended up with ears bigger than Dumbo's.

The drive through our last year at primary school was geared towards the eleven-plus examination, which would determine our places at senior or junior secondary school. Mrs Leigh would hone our skills towards this final goal, but that year a terror would be unleashed on us all that had us believing the world was coming to an end. When it didn't, a tale of another international sportsman would be woven into my memory. This was the easiest year I ever had at school; the eleven-plus was all about puzzles, sequences, shapes and number problems. Mrs Leigh gave us endless test papers to do both in class and at home, I was good at them and they never seemed to take long to do, just the sort of work I loved.

The Cold War had been festering for almost two decades and the super powers, America and Russia, were involved in a game of brinkmanship that seemed certain to embroil the world in a nuclear holocaust. John F Kennedy had become American President in 1960 and the western world prayed he'd be the harbinger of lasting world peace. Nikita Khrushchev was the Russian leader, bogeyman of my childhood, and those two men and their nations were irrevocably set on a collision course. The juggernauts finally locked horns over the Cuban Missile Crisis.

As the drama unfolded before an astonished world, the Americans were adamant they would brook no Russian plan to construct missile bases in Cuba. They introduced a blockade and a tense stand-off ensued. We children all worried that the world would end and more terrifyingly we could sense that parents and teachers harboured the same fears.

The world didn't come to an end; the Russians backed down, we went on a class trip to Edinburgh Zoo and one Alastair Wood became our student teacher for a while. In 1962 this great marathon runner took fourth place in the European Championships in Belgrade and then, unluckily, had to retire from the Commonwealth Games race in Perth, Australia whilst suffering a bout of food poisoning. He was still our hero and had been on the telly! The whole class queued for his autograph at the end of his brief teaching spell with us.

King Street Primary School holds nothing but great memories for me of great teachers, great friends and great laughs. I had come through seven years of education in an almost unchanged class of thirteen boys and fourteen girls, surely a comment on the place of the family in society at that time, and such stability was wonderful for me as a child. One lesson, that I did learn for myself, that followed me through life, was that I wasn't a tough guy. In that class of twenty seven I'd worked out scientifically that I was the eleventh best fighter, but as three of the ten rated above me were girls, I'd have to discover other methods of fighting my corner as I grew up.

The eleven-plus results would follow during our summer holidays, I actually won a bursary to Robert Gordon's College but Mum and Dad didn't think they could afford to put me there, even with a little financial help. We decided on Aberdeen Academy and a new chapter would open in my life; I just didn't realise then that my best school days were already behind me.

These were glorious days in my life; I was much loved at home and the world was changing at break-neck speed as it hurtled into the space age. Yet the austere Fifties still clung on and it was easy at times to believe that all this progress was passing us by. Tick mannies and insurance collectors still called at the door for weekly payments and Annie and I would be sent to join the queues at the Auld Breeder on Harriet Street, where many like us were not too proud to accept the bargain prices offered on yesterday's bread, buns and cakes. The buses still had both a driver and conductor; the conductor weighted down by his ticket machine and black leather moneybag. One old penny could take a child to any destination across the city. Kids thrilled to the annual autumn Timmer Market fair on the Castlegate, where all manner of toys, goldfish, candyfloss and other delicacies would be on sale. An epidemic of cut lips would break out due entirely to the wounds inflicted by the glass pea-shooters that traders were amazingly allowed to sell to kids of all ages.

At play my pride and joy was a Tri-ang train set I'd been given one Xmas, the engine and carriages all done up in the beautiful LMR livery. Annie and I shared the general knowledge quiz game, the Magic Robot, all done, we were told, by magnets in his feet. We however never ceased to be amazed as he spun around and always ended up pointing to the correct answer to the question he'd been asked. Most wonderful and cheapest of all, the comics; for a few pennies we were transported to magical places and mythical times. Annie would read and re-read the Four Marys in the *Bunty*; I could hardly decide where to spend my money! The *Eagle, Victor, Hotspur, Hornet, Wizard* and *Rover* with such heroes as the tough of the track *Alf Tupper, The Amazing Wilson, Dan Dare, Limp Along Leslie, Braddock VC, Roy of the Rovers* and *Gorgeous Gus*. How many heroes could one young kid deal with?

The comics were closely rivalled by Saturday morning visits to the Regal Cinema on the Shiprow for the children's show. *Batman, Superman,* cartoons, cowboys, Indians and spacemen could all be found there. One of the highlights of the show was when the manager came on stage at half time holding a mirror, and reflected the projectionists' spotlight onto the faces of hundred of cheering kids. When he stopped the light would shine on the face of just one child, who would be guided by that light, to a place on the stage beside him. I used to pray that one day that light would shine on me, and one day it did. A bar of Toblerone chocolate and a colour photograph of Rhonda Fleming were my rewards for my brief moment in the spotlight.

I still remember the song all the kids would scream out; singing would hardly be the best description of the noise we would all make.

We are the boys and girls well known as minors of the ABC

And every Saturday we line up to see the films we like and shout aloud with glee.

We like to laugh and have a sing song just a happy crowd are we,

We're all pals together we're minors of the ABC.

At home the coal fire was the focal point of the house, and as young as Annie and I were, we could both set a fire. Making toast on a fork and gazing at the ever-changing faces and figures that danced across the flames and embers was almost hypnotic. Sadly the end product of that trance like state usually turned out to be the dreaded corned beef legs, a common affliction in those days.

One afternoon Annie and I had had an early tea and Mum had popped across to the shops. Dad's supper, a pot of home-made soup and a pan of custard, was simmering on the two-ring gas burner above the stove. He was working a little late and we thought to stoke up the fire to warm the house a little before he arrived. It didn't seem to take and as I'd seen my mum and dad do before I opened the chimney vent which usually caused the flames to leap high immediately. Perhaps I'd opened it a little too far or too violently but the usual fanning of the flames did not occur and I was horror-struck to see the soup and custard showered with soot from the vent which was directly above the gas rings.

I'd barely closed the vent when mother came back in and praised Annie, who was busy giving the soup and custard a stir, "Good lass that'll save them from sticking to the pot."

An hour later we watched spellbound as Dad arrived home, ate and thoroughly enjoyed the soup, custard and soot and took the trouble to compliment Mum on how nice it had all tasted!

Mum and Dad might sit of an evening and plan an imaginary holiday trip to Butlins. Perhaps in the futility of knowing that they'd never be able to afford it, both were certain that if the government hadn't spent all those millions on the Blue Streak missile then they could have given every family in the country a week there.

One sad memory of those times was the Saturday afternoon when death arrived on Park Street. A motorcyclist had somehow managed to collide with the lamppost outside Atholl Still's bookmaker shop at the Summerfield Terrace junction and had been catapulted against the shop wall. A crowd, including Annie and me, had gathered round the stricken man, who seemed lifeless apart for one leg that continually twitched. People said he was dead before the ambulance arrived; it was such a strange feeling to witness death for the first time in such a matter of fact way.

My Uncle Percy was the catalyst for the strangest thing I did in those years. Leaving the Empire Bar very much the worse for drink one Saturday he'd picked up and eaten several slices of spiced ham from a butcher's counter in the New Market. Apprehended and brought to book on the Monday his previous history of minor misdemeanours went against him and he was fined £10 with an alternative of fourteen days in Craiginches Prison. Paying the fine was not an option so off he went to 'do his time;' you'd hardly get much longer for robbing a bank these days! I went with my father to visit him and have never forgotten my sense of foreboding as I entered that place.

Ordinary lives are filled with ordinary moments but those years from 1958 to 1963 were so pivotal in my life. Such ordinary events become the bedrock of our lives, the foundation stones of life's memory storehouse and those lives would be all the less without having savoured the experience of living them.

Around 1958 two events took place in my young life, one remains movie-like in my memory, a blockbuster that I played a part in, and the other confuses me to this day as it still causes me to feel unjustified shame and deep anger in equal measure.

I will remember the blockbuster forever as The Battle of St Andrew Street, and it produced a punch-up to eclipse the fracas between Granger and Mills in *Waterloo Road*. Soon after her move to Jopps Lane my grannie had become involved in a war of words with a neighbour, which all came to a head one Saturday afternoon. Annie and I had been playing out the back, doing nothing in particular, when suddenly we were on the end of a tongue lashing from the neighbour and more scarily, her adult son.

My mother came out to take us back indoors and my grandmother exchanged a few 'pleasantries' with the pair. As usual father arrived at Jopps Lane after work and was soon updated on events, by my mother in one ear and my grannie in the other. It was late afternoon when, as usual, the four of us headed home. It was then that my father noticed the man standing at the grain store end of the lane. He was about the same age as my father and wore dark trousers and an army-style soldiers' blouse. As we walked towards St Andrew Street he hurled abuse at my father and drew ever nearer to us.

I had been holding my father's hand but he had ushered mother, Annie and me ahead. Suddenly the man launched himself at my father and they fell to the ground in a swirl of flailing arms and legs. In no time and from seemingly nowhere, a crowd of late afternoon shoppers had appeared from George Street and formed a circle around them. My view was through legs and between arms and I could see that father was trapped underneath the man, due as much to a long brown coat he was wearing as to any superiority of the other man. I was amazed too to see Annie beating seven bells out of the man's head with her wee brolly, "Leave my Da!" she demanded.

What followed was an almost dream-like sequence for me, a man next to me called out incessantly two words in turn, "Fight, police, fight, police!"

My father had managed in best Houdini style to extricate himself from the brown coat and Annie; satisfied it was now a fair fight, was cheering my father on. My mother and grandmother stood in tears nearby. The fight seemed long and fierce with both men giving as good as they got but suddenly the man tried to break off and escape through the tight circle of people. Harder said than done, and he was to suffer somewhat for his initial attack.

Bells were now ringing everywhere and soon the scene was full of police officers. They quickly broke through the crowd and had the two gladiators restrained in separate lobbies of houses in St Andrew Street. My father was enraged as he felt the injured party but had been quietened down by three officers. One either side of him held his arms and the third, who was talking quietly to my father, calming him down, had lit a cigarette and was giving my father the occasional drag on it. Standing just at the entrance to the doorway I then witnessed one of the most cowardly, unwarranted actions that I've ever seen. A fourth, very large, policeman swaggered into the lobby, glanced at my father and spat, "Is this the little bastard causing all the trouble?"

As he spoke he launched a vicious punch to my already restrained and passive father's stomach. Mistake! The red mist was back up immediately; somehow my father managed to wriggle free, returning the blow in kind. The very large policeman quick exited the lobby in somewhat less dignified fashion than he had entered it and was neatly side-stepped by me in the process. With a tense situation now needlessly inflamed again my father was fighting anything that moved, especially police uniforms. The whole event ended with my father disappearing into a Black Maria vainly protesting his innocence and off the entourage went to Lodge Walk.

It was a long worrying weekend for my mother and us but at court on the Monday my father was admonished on the grounds of provocation by the other man and as I knew by one very large policeman. My father spoke highly of his treatment by the police and I have worked for them for the last twenty years of my life. I count many as good friends and colleagues, but the incident taught me that every barrel can have a rotten apple in it, no matter how appealing the label.

St Andrew Street had designs on my memory cells that year, and my future confusion would revolve around an incident at a little fruit-shop on the street called Harrow's, and an older lad who lived nearby who was their 'Saturday Loon.' I had not been involved in a major crime since the Mounthooly Guitar Caper but took up a challenge from Annie. From the eye-popping display of fruit in boxes outside the shop I picked up and ate one single, solitary cherry, one summer Saturday morning. The Saturday Loon had spotted me but we ran off as he came raging out of the shop. For ages after and after he'd stopped working at the shop, he tormented me mercilessly. If he saw me in the street he would shout out, "Robertson's a thief and so is his father."

The hurt I felt for myself was nothing compared to the shame I felt when he mentioned my father's name and in my whole life I have never come so close to hating anyone as I did him. He ruined many otherwise happy days at my grandmother's, a high price to pay for a single cherry. I still do almost hate his memory, I never resumed my criminal career and I always erred on the soft side with my own children as I taught them right from wrong and made their punishments fit their crimes.

Growing up isn't a bed of roses and you need to understand and cope with both the love and the hurt to help you read the map of your life's journey. I was becoming aware that all was not well with my mum; physically she was often poorly but there was also at times a mental fragility about her too.

There were strange mood swings that would herald dark days. As much as they'd try to hide it from us kids, life was tough for Mum and Dad. These moods would usually culminate in them having a big argument and at the worst of times my mother would go beyond threats and leave home, and she, Annie and I would be on the road. These 'leavings' would usually result in a hitched lift on a lorry to Dundee, Perth or on one occasion Glasgow. Then a couple of nights in a Salvation Army hostel, followed by a tearful return home on a bus after my father had sent our fares to the local bobbies.

That one night in Glasgow my mother stood with us on a bridge over the River Clyde. We three stood and looked down into the pitch-black waters and she said that she wanted to jump and take us with her. I've never forgiven myself for immediately planning to run away as fast as I could. I was too young to help her, and she was just too ill to know how much she was hurting me. She never did hurt me deliberately and through my life for every single bad thing she did to me she did a million good. My mother would fight her personal demons most of her life and lose many battles, but in the end she seemed to be winning the war, before her untimely death. One memory is only a moment in time but a million of them shape you as a person; and I'm proud of what she has done for me.

The object of my desire stood gleaming in the second hand shop window opposite our old house at seventy-four. It had been there for weeks with its newly painted wine coloured frame and beige mudguards, it cost £5 and I ran from school to check it was still there every day. My campaign involved meeting my father every night on his way home from work. In those days I'd be fighting against the tide of men coming home from the shipyards or 'the batons' and just picking my father out was difficult enough. I'd be pushed onwards by the river of girls leaving Tinnie Robertson's; you could tell the time and how hungry you were by the amount of people in the street.

I'd engage my father in conversation about the bike and make sure we stopped to admire it in the window. Each night I'd try to venture farther to meet him which would allow me more time to extol its virtues. One Saturday morning my mother suggested we both walk out to meet him and on the way home they stopped and took me into the shop! I was oblivious to the fact that it was really just an old bone shaker with a lick of paint, weighed more than I did and was far too big for me. I had to have it and mum and dad struck a deal with the shopkeeper to buy it at £1 a week. What a long summer it became; but I knew the sold sign in the window meant it was mine. But I checked every day, just in case, to make sure it was still there.

How my father managed to push the bike home the day it was paid for with me sitting at an angle of forty-five degrees, I'll never know. Our downstairs neighbour, Bertie Miller, worked at John Fleming's, 'the batons' and promised to fit wooden blocks to the pedals so I could reach them. Once they were fitted my extremely wobbly cycling days began. My father would walk miles with me, holding the bike and me upright until one day along the

Beach Esplanade he ran past me and smiled, "You've got it now, you're on your own."

I could certainly cycle in a straight line and throw a wobbly curve round a corner but mounting and dismounting the monster would take me weeks to perfect. I'd go out to play of an evening and mount the bike by leaning it against a wall then push myself away on my precarious course, often finishing under the bike before the wheels had actually turned. Once I did get going my problem was getting off and when I was ready to dismount I'd circle Park Street, Lemon Place and Lemon Street and on each circuit shout up at our window for my dad. My cycling session would last as long as it took to attract his attention and he'd then come downstairs and play aircraft carrier to my returning fighter plane. The slower I went, the wobblier I became, so most landings were made in rough seas. He told me years later that he always heard me on the first shout but just wanted a few more minutes peace and quiet with my mum.

The bike almost broke my heart one Saturday morning. My father had deserted the 'riches' of the building trade and for slightly less money had gone back to work for Mr Ellis at Cove; he gave me permission to cycle there to meet him and we'd come home together as he had his own racer by then. I followed his directions to the letter, out past the prison and up and up and up Wellington Road towards Cove. When I got there my father and Mr Ellis and his brother were just finishing work for the day. I proudly told them I'd cycled all the way from Aberdeen, straight up Nigg Brae and past the prefabs without coming off once. Their smiles betrayed the fact that they didn't believe me, but I had told the truth and their doubting hurt so much I could have cried. For £5, that bike was one of the best gifts I ever received during my childhood; I wish I had £1 for every mile I covered in that two-wheeled tank.

This all perhaps sounds a little dangerous for a youngster, but back then there was almost no heavy traffic, as we know it today. The biggest dangers for cyclists were finding your wheels trapped in the old tram lines or them disappearing between the grills of a drain cover—in the latter instance the dismount became acrobatically compulsory. I was, however, banned from the National Cycling Proficiency test at school because of the wooden blocks on my pedals!

Technology was simply taking off in those years and there was no way it could possibly pass our family by for too much longer!

Until then radio had been the main source of entertainment at home. Sport was just beginning to play a major part in my life; my father and I religiously kept two scrap albums, one for football and one for boxing. I read and re-read them almost every evening. My last great memory of those radio days was being awoken by my father around 3am to listen to Floyd Patterson defend his World Heavyweight Championship against Sweden's Ingemar Johansson. Floyd would sensationally fall foul of 'Ingo's Bingo' in three rounds and lose his title but months later he became the first man in history to regain the heavyweight crown; Johansson would never scale the heights again but only ever lost twice in his entire career, both times to Patterson.

It was a major sporting event, the Rome Olympic Games, which would finally entice dad to bring television into our home. He and mum had spoken about it often and always decided that it would be too expensive, but the lure of a sporting extravaganza proved too strong. The majority of people rented sets in those days and so, for eight shillings a week from Clydesdale and £7 to have an aerial fitted, a twenty-one inch screen Ferguson television entered our lives—and they'd never be the same again.

I vividly remember running all the way home from school on the day it arrived, watching the test card for almost an hour, being somewhat disappointed by a ten minute cartoon from Czechoslovakia and then spellbound by an episode of *The Lone Ranger.* In no time at all the whole family was hooked. We kids thrilled to *Bronco Lane, Whirlybirds, Crackerjack* and oddities like *Noggin the Nog.* Herge's *Adventures of Tintin,* in ten-minute episodes, became my personal favourite and adults and kids alike loved *Pinky & Perky,* whose squeaky voices would bring versions of all the current pop hits to the screen. Mum and Dad always watched the *Tonight* programme, never missed *What's My Line?* and Mum had a crush on Dale Robertson the star of *Wells Fargo,* although I kept telling her it wasn't as good as *Laramie.*

Television would be an ever-changing medium and gritty dramas like *Z Cars* and *Coronation Street* would bring stories of ordinary people like us into the living room. In 1961 Grampian Television came to Aberdeen and the Pandora's Box of ITV programmes flooded our screens. *Ivanhoe, William Tell, Sir Francis Drake* and *Robin Hood* were classics for children and families thrilled to *Take Your Pick, Double Your Money* and *Opportunity Knocks.*

People who spoke with accents just like mine appeared on John Mearns' *Bothy Nichts* and Torry's favourite quine, June Imray, always made us laugh. Our continuity announcers were usually the posh sounding Douglas Kynoch or the man with the silly name, Jimmy Spankie. Andy Stewart on BBC's *White Heather Club* and Callum Kennedy on Grampian battled for the Scottish audience. Television was wonderful then and entertained us all with a sadly lost innocence.

The Rome Olympics had brought this magic to our lives and proved to be a spectacular event that brought heroes and heroines so close you could almost touch them. The world would also become aware of one man who would be remembered as one of the most special human beings of the century, Muhammad Ali, then known as Cassius Clay.

What did people think of Jim Davies and I as we raced to and from school with our bums wiggling in unison as we tried to emulate the style of our diminutive, walking champion, Don Thompson? Annie, who could swim almost as well as Brian Muir, was going to be the next Anita Lonsbrough and Britain had as always her glorious failures in the sprints, Peter Radford and Dorothy Hyman. Their stature was not diminished one whit by their respective bronze and silver medals; Dorothy had lost out on gold to one of the finest athletes of all time, Wilma Rudolph. Kids ran, jumped and threw in the playground and claimed as their own the names of all those Olympian gods. Top stars for me were the Antipodean Princes of middle distance running, Herb Elliott and Peter Snell and the fabulous American field athletes Ralph Boston and Al Oerter, whose amazing career would culminate with a fourth consecutive discus gold at the Mexico Olympics in 1968. Perhaps in magnificence above them all, was the incredible Abebe Bikila of Ethiopia, once, more romantically, known as Abyssinia. He astounded the world by entering the stadium to claim marathon gold and after crossing the finishing line performed a series of press-ups and stretching exercises—despite have just run twenty-six gruelling miles!

Like the television at closedown, the Fifties were fading to a tiny white spot on the world's screen and the modern world flooded all our lives with new wonders every day. Quaintly, Annie and I would still be sent with bags of old clothes or bits of metal to Ross's scrap yard on Constitution Street, where a man would make great show of weighing it all on a huge set of red scales. Not that we would have had any idea of its scrap value but he'd solemnly make us an offer of a shilling or two and we would always accept. We'd take this home to mother and always find her disappointed at the amount.

Then just to make sure the decade hadn't ended without incident, the Queen Mother almost killed me!

To be fair she didn't make the attempt personally, but she certainly was the catalyst. She'd come to Aberdeen to open the new dual carriageway leading from Justice Street to the Promenade. It was to be called the Beach Boulevard and we kids had been given the afternoon off school to witness the opening ceremony. I really wasn't too interested but was delighted to have the afternoon off to play.

I ended up bored on the washhouse roof and became intrigued by the crowds walking up Park Street; I decided to tag along. A huge crowd had gathered at the top of the street and I wriggled my way to the front, from the Hanover Street School side of the pristine new thoroughfare.

The pushing, jostling, flag-waving multitude now awaited the Royal procession and as her open-topped limousine swept along the virgin tarmac I was swept directly towards its front wheels by the forwards surge of the cheering host. A rush of terror swept over me; I seemed destined to be trampled underfoot or crushed beneath the wheels of the Royal carriage, but the dear lady kept her Royal cool, waved serenely, and the vehicle somehow swept by apace, leaving me gasping for breath, but miraculously uninjured, in her Royal wake.

I followed one other procession that year, but it was less hazardous; I was simply in awe of the man on stilts as the Bertram Mills Circus paraded the length of King Street before raising the big top at the Beach Links.

Our home entertainment seemed complete when dad bought a Decca record player; it could stack six records at a time although we only had two, *My Old Man's a Dustman* by Lonnie Donegan and *My Love is like a Red Red Rose* by Kenneth McKellar. That would soon change, for Mum loved music and actually started to buy records on our Saturday shopping trips. A single cost around four shillings but Woolies had their own label, Embassy Records, which did cover versions that sold for half a crown. *Red River Rock* was the best one I ever bought there.

It was just before we got our own record player that I became aware of how compelling a part of our lives music can be. A memory, a smile, a tear, they can all be triggered by the sound of one line of a long forgotten favourite. The late, great Jim Reeves was storming the charts with *He'll Have to Go* and Mum adored it. As soon as Annie and I got home from school we'd all set off to a wee café at the top of Commerce Street, where they had a jukebox!

There in the shadows of the old Castlehill Barracks we three would sit with our cups of tea. I'd often run across the road to gaze into the huge glass windows of Cocky Hunter's, who'd moved there from his more famous shop in Castle Terrace; all manner of stuff was on sale. I wouldn't see a shop like that again until Auntie Wainwright became a fixture on *Last of the Summer Wine*. Mum would play her tune three or four times at sixpence a shot and we'd enjoy too, all the music that other folk would play. Sometimes we'd still be there as Dad made his way home from work and he'd call in for us.

Those were years of change in music too and as we moved from the Fifties to the Sixties acts like Shirley Bassey, Emile Ford and Russ Conway were still vying with Elvis for the top spot. There was a new breed arriving, though, and Buddy Holly, Cliff Richard, the Everly Brothers and Eddie Cochran were the wind of change. When Johnny Kidd and the Pirates reached number one with *Shakin' All Over*, the world knew the change was here to stay.

In 1961 a terror descended on Aberdeen when an innocent six-year-old, June Cruickshank, was horribly murdered in the Woodside area. Parents talked of it in whispers and held their children close. The poor wee soul had just been running to the shop yards from her front door. The monster responsible would escape justice for two years until he committed a second hideous crime, almost on our doorstep. A seven-year-old, George Forbes, went missing from his Justice Street home and I remember police officers calling at our home one night on their door-to-door enquiries.

Acting on information they'd received from another child in the area, the police interviewed a man called James Oliphant, who confessed all, and took them to his Castlehill allotment where the body of tragic George was buried. This horrendous double murder was all the more difficult for us kids to comprehend; the allotments were a place where Annie and I had often played. These events placed a sense of fear and mistrust in me but sadly perhaps such feelings are needed, as a part of learning how to cope with all the strange things and people that life can throw at us in its darkest moods.

Fear may be a help to us in life but thankfully you can never remember how much hurt hurts until it happens and breaks your heart once more. In 1961 my Grannie Nicolson died and all our worlds seemed suddenly empty. She died in hospital at quarter to three in the morning and a clock she'd given my mum and dad as a present stopped at that exact time, never to work again. My father was devastated; he perhaps remembered a harsher, crueller world that she had brought him through, and the toll it must have taken on her. I remembered her simply as a soft, warm, loving person. I clung to Tubby the Teddy who'd been my special gift from her and for a spell he was once again my bedtime sleeping partner. I would not feel such hurt again until my mother's untimely death over twenty years later.

Life's roller coaster steams on at break-neck speed and in youth you are saturated with wonderful new experiences. On an April Saturday in 1961 my dad came home from work and told mum he was going to the match with his pal Charlie—and I was going with them! Top of the league Glasgow Rangers were the visitors to Pittodrie and from the moment Dad, Charlie and I joined the crowds walking towards the stadium, my heart pounded and my skin tingled.

We stood high on the south terracing at the Merkland Road End and between the gasometer and the advertising board behind us my dad pointed out all the people trying to catch a glimpse of the game for free from the aptly named Miser's Hilly. The papers the next day would say that 20,000 people watched the game; I thought everyone in the world was inside Pittodrie, the noise was deafening. Football was not offensively tribal in those days and we stood with and chatted to many friendly Rangers supporters. A crescendo of noise greeted the teams as they ran out onto the pitch. The perfect lush green surface, the brilliant contrast of the red and blue of the opposing teams; the whole scene was magical. There was a momentary silence as the referee signalled the kick-off, then I didn't hear myself speak again for the next ninety minutes.

Aberdeen—Harker, Cadenhead, Hogg, Baird, Kinnell, Fraser, Cummings, Brownlee, Little, Cooke, Mulhall. Rangers—Ritchie, Shearer, Caldow, Davis, Baillie, Stevenson, Scott, Brand, McLean, Penman, Wilson.

Rangers were top of the league with Kilmarnock in hot pursuit that season. Their international full-back Eric Caldow went off injured early on and in six scintillating minutes the Dons scored three goals, two from Bobby Cummings and one from the waif-like Billy Little. Caldow returned and yet another internationalist from this team of all-stars, Alex Scott, pulled one back. The wise old wags in the crowd were warning of a second-half onslaught from the league leaders. It didn't happen; George Kinnell, who, legend had it, used to enjoy a pint or two at the Pittodrie Bar before popping along to do his bit for the Reds, was magnificent in defence. When Cummings completed his hat-trick early in the second half the stadium went wild. Charlie threw his bonnet in the air in celebration; it seemed to stay in orbit for ages and although we never found out how it happened, it was in shreds when finally he recovered it into his grasp.

The Dons were now unstoppable. Brownlee added a fifth and the finest player I have ever seen in the flesh, Charlie Cooke, added a sixth. The final score, Aberdeen 6, Rangers 1, was unbelievable and I became, there and then, a Red for life. In 1968 Charlie played so well for Scotland in his only game against the Auld Enemy, a 1-1 draw at Hampden, that the famous Sunday Post sports writer, Jack Harkness, penned the headline, "Oh For Eleven Charlie Cookes." Charlie was always a football magician for me.

This match was one of a series of 'super firsts' I've had in my years as a Dons' fan. In 1963 I took Annie to her first and to my knowledge only football match, when the Dons beat Raith Rovers 10-0. My first away match was a Scottish cup-tie at Dundee in 1967, when my old Boys Brigade pal John Mitchell and I saw the Dons win 5-0. That same year I saw the Dons venture into Europe for the first time and emerge 10-0 victors over KR Reykjavik of Iceland. Perhaps the most memorable of all was when I took my seven-year-old son Paul to his first match in the, by then, all-seater stadium. The Dons scored a marvellous 3-2 victory over an SV Hamburg side that included the legendary Kaiser Franz Beckenbauer, that in spite of the famous Leighton-Kennedy gaff and a Strachan penalty miss.

As I was walking down Merkland Road I met a band o' strangers,

And they said to me have you come tae see the Dons beat the Glasgow Rangers.

In the summer of'62 Annie became a local pop-star at the Beach Bandstand when she won the daily heat of their talent contest with a great rendition of Brian Hyland's *Ginny Come Lately*. In the weekly final at the Pavilion theatre on the Promenade she was brilliant but mysteriously finished second to a pair of sisters from Glasgow who, dressed in matching blue dresses, chanted maniacally about *Roamin' in the Gloamin'*. Well it was the Glasgow Fair and none of the judges sounded as if they came fae Torry. In a bid to restore the family honour I teamed up with a pal called Bobby Walker the following week. Third place in our heat saw us into the final where sadly our version of Alma Cogan's *Sugartime* sank without trace; the Everly Brothers we were not. Our consolation prize for being able to deliver a three-minute song in fifty-seven seconds flat was a bar of Toberlone chocolate. This was the second time a brief moment of fame for me had coincided with a bar of this particular chocolate; I was now beginning to develop bad feelings towards the brand.

Such amazing times, huge queues outside cinemas still for classics like *Ben Hur, Psycho* and *Spartacus*; the compelling screen persona of Burt Lancaster as Elmer Gantry, an 'X' rated movie I'd not see for a few years. He could make you believe all things were possible and his evocative delivery of Canaan Land remains one of my favourite musical movie moments of all time.

True to life British dramas like *A Taste of Honey* reflected the mood of the times as did the apocryphal 'reds in the bed' thriller, *The Manchurian Candidate*. The world was hooked on the saucy celebrity of Burton and Taylor and shocked by the tragic yet possibly lurid death of an oh-so-sadly young Marilyn Monroe.

Craiginches Prison lost none of its air of menace, as Henry Burnett was the last man to hang in Scotland, for the Jackson Terrace murder. The Sixties began with a nation still able to ban the public from reading books like *Lady Chatterley's Lover;* but the doors of liberation, freedom and enlightenment were pushing themselves open everywhere. I would not presume to guess whether the speed of those changes turned out to be for better or worse, but the impact of those momentous times in my life have not diminished over the last forty years.

I was about to try and cross a barrier as I moved to secondary education and at the same time the most iconic man of the age, John Fitzgerald Kennedy, spoke in 1963 of the need to challenge barriers, when he addressed the world from the Berlin Wall, the Cold War's symbol of hate, ignorance and fear. It amused me later to discover that his 'Ich bin ein Berliner' speech had literally meant in German, 'I am a doughnut' but the entire Western World were in no doubt as to the true meaning of his message. In five month's time the world's most powerful man would be dead, slain by Lee Harvey Oswald. The circumstances of his death are debated and re-enacted to this day. History may not have been as kind to his memory as he may have deserved but he was unquestionably a great man of his time. Jackie Christie and I were playing football next to Dod Sim's garage in Lemon Place when we heard the news of his death on a transistor radio. We rushed into the body shop to impart this sensational news to the panel beater, and were chased out by him using the choicest of language, loosely translated to, "Go away you stupid kids!"

My friendship with Jackie Christie survives to this day; yet has been severely tested on two occasions and both times have been when we fell in love with the same woman. When Ursula Andress stepped out of the sea, in that bikini, in that famous scene from *Dr No* we were both hooked. You're eleven years old, what a name for your first fantasy woman, Honey Rider! A series of bubble gum cards came out for the movie and you had to swap ten ordinary cards for one of Ursula. Jake ended up with eleven to my eight and in the logic of youth had proved his greater love, I wanted to strangle him!

I could not leave this part of my life without adding my own clarification to a modern historical mystery. On Sunday the 6th of January 1963 the Beach Ballroom in Aberdeen must have been a very busy place. I've lost count over the years of the number of people of my age and those with somewhat more tenuous links to the early Sixties who claim to have seen The Beatles at the Beach. I was eleven and certainly was not there, they did not play as The Quarrymen and they were not booed off the stage. *Love Me Do* had charted in October the previous year and brought The Fab Four into the public eye; this was the last gig of a *short Scottish Tour. In February Please Please Me failed to oust Frank Ifield's Wayward Wind* from the top spot, then in May, *From Me To You* hit number one and the rest as they say is history.

From infant child to boy I grew
And felt not care nor fear.
The warmth of love was all I knew
There was no danger near.
Then tapped a stranger at my door
And when I did reply.
Came in and stayed for evermore
The hurt that makes you cry.

Ad Altiora Tendo

On the 28th of August 1963, no-one in the whole world had a greater dream than Martin Luther King. In front of the Lincoln Memorial in Washington DC the American Civil Rights leader addressed a crowd of over 200,000 people and a waiting, listening world. President Kennedy was one of those who heard him tell of his dream and for all those who heard, its truthfulness, poignancy, power and simplicity will never diminish. It never has for me.

"I still have a dream. It is a dream chiefly rooted in the American dream. I have a dream that one day this nation will rise up and live out the true meaning of its creed. 'We hold these truths to be self-evident, that all men are created equal.'"

His delivery of those words was spellbinding. Images from that day are etched in my mind and I never cease to be compelled by the sincerity of the man and the justice of his cause. If only a tiny particle of his dream could brush off on all of us, what a wonderful place the world could be.

Martin Luther King was one of the great men, if not the greatest, of my lifetime and it is with immense pride that I treasure a personal memory of the man and those times.

Like millions, the fight for civil rights in America moved Annie and me. Annie wrote a lovely poem on the subject and a schoolteacher encouraged her to send it to Mr King. Weeks later our family was awe-struck when a personally signed reply arrived from him, thanking Annie for her support and sympathy and letting her know her poem might be used in campaign literature. His signature in bold black ink was almost copperplate in style and we would sit for ages reading the letter again and again and staring in admiration at the stamp of that great man. Tragically both letter and poem have been lost and I pray that one day Annie will find them in one of the shoeboxes of old papers that we all hoard in attics. A measure of the man for me was that I never once felt any envy of Annie for having penned the poem or for having received the letter. I'm so proud to have held that letter in my hand and till my dying day will treasure the thought that it allowed me, in its way, to touch one of history's greatest pages.

At almost the same moment, Sidney and Gladys Robertson had a dream and they placed it in me. Mum and Dad were aiming high but in me I always felt they were firing the wrong bullet. It's so hard to explain that to grown-ups when you're just a kid. I felt Annie was the talented one but the more chauvinistic attitudes of those days meant the opportunity to make good was thrust on me. If I'd had half of Annie's guts I might have made it but I struggled almost from day one.

When the morning arrived to make that first trip to Aberdeen Academy Mum and Dad delivered the pep talks about the future and I tried to conceal my cares and fears. I walked there with David Calder; only he, Terence Graham and I would be going there from primary school. My mother had struggled to put my uniform together over the school holidays; I sensed the expense of it all had been much more than she'd expected. In green blazer, grey trousers, grey shirt and grey jumper I'm sure I looked the part. Dad had taught me how to tie a Double Windsor knot in my green and navy school tie, and whatever else I failed to achieve at Aberdeen Academy, I never sported a tie that resembled a cowboy's lasso. The last thing Bomber Gordon taught me at primary school was the meaning of my new school motto and it shone from the badge on the breast pocket of my new blazer.

We reported on that first day to our form teacher, Mr Bewick, who would also turn out to be my English teacher that first year. We quickly learned of the four school houses, my own, St Nicholas, Belmont, Greyfriars and Gilcomstoun. Houses, teachers wearing black gowns and mortar boards, this really was the stuff of *Goodbye Mr Chips*. Time-tables and class periods became important factors of life, none more so than morning assembly taken usually by the Rector Mr Goldie or occasionally in his absence by his deputy Mr Scott.

The school was huge and finding one's way about was the biggest problem, with little help on offer from any source. I at once found myself more in awe of the place than inspired by it. In my first two years there I would be taught English, Arithmetic, Geometry, Algebra, History, Geography, Chemistry, Physics, Biology, French, German, Music, Art, Woodwork and Physical Education. The entire spectrum of classical education was there to be grasped at but it would slip through my fingers and no-one ever made me understand what a serious business school was and what miraculous, life-changing qualities all those subjects held.

In hindsight I crossed the Rubicon with Aberdeen Academy on my fourth day there when the last thing I thought would fail me did; my abiding passion, something I was really good at, sport! On our first Thursday we had PE with Mr Rae and like all the boys I was eager to get into the gym. As we formed in a semi-circle around him he beckoned me forward, asked my name and then enquired, "And what do you think you are, Robertson?"

I didn't know the answer but he soon told me, " You are improperly dressed!"

It dawned on me immediately, I was in my primary school kit of black shorts and black shoes and everyone else was in all white. "You will never appear in my gym improperly dressed again," he bellowed.

For the next two years I never did and although I was hurt and embar-

38

rassed then, I know now that he was the teacher and he let me down. He should have known that improperly dressed I might have been but what I really was, was a frightened twelve year old.

At the end of the period we were all given a list by him; it was all the things we needed for our sports kit. I gave it to my mum when I got home but it wasn't until after tea that she and dad sat down to talk with me. "We just can't afford all this stuff," said dad.

I didn't know what to think or say but I suspect if I'd guessed the solution they'd come up with I'd have pleaded to join Annie at Frederick Street. Senior Secondary school was such a great thing for them and they would make any sacrifice to keep me there, to give me a future, just like any loving parents. A few days later my mother gave me a medical note from our family doctor to take to school. I read the typical doctor's scrawl before I handed it to Mr Bewick and made out that it asked for me to be excused from PE and games because I was too frail for such activities.

Sport is for me an essential part of growing up, perhaps even more so for boys than girls, it is a character builder and friendship maker. For two years I was denied that opportunity and was isolated at a crucial time from my peers. I was as fit as a butcher's dog but would never kick a rugby ball at school or run in a cross-country race. The business still saddens me to this day and I wrongly blamed Mr Rae for my woes. It was nothing to do with him at all, but he could have taken me to one side, put an arm on my shoulder and simply asked what the problem was.

It has never entered my mind to blame my parents in any way for my sporting exile. They had performed miracles in achieving what they had in life and on this occasion were well and truly stuck between a financial rock and an economic hard place. Their own dreams of what I might accomplish may have spurred them to keep me at Aberdeen Academy at all costs but never knowingly to cause me any sadness.

Who needs sport? My banishment from the playing fields of The Chanory caused no end of trouble at school; they had to find somewhere to put me on Friday afternoons. To my absolute delight I found myself farmed out to the art class of the lovely Miss Frewin, who was later to marry the well-known artist Eric Auld. Two sixth-year girls took a shine to me and I became their regular model when they were sketching, fully clothed of course! Ursula was going to have to look to her laurels to keep her place as my number one girl.

So school became, for me, almost a compulsory non-event. I think it came too soon for me and I was never ready for the opportunities that were on offer to me there. Knowledge is an Arthurian castle of myth and legend, a weave of work and play, a puzzle of trial and error but its strong ramparts are built by those who can educate and those who endeavour to be educated. I had too quickly turned my back on all this and finished an anonymous first year at Aberdeen Academy with an average of 56%. At this stage my knack of fiddling through with the minimum of effort was still standing me in good stead.

School might not have been all I had hoped for but the world was a wondrous and wonderful place right then. Just towards the end of the year a sharp-tempered old man with long silver hair hit our television screens. He travelled in time and space in an old telephone box called The Tardis, which metamorphosised into a time machine for any unsuspecting soul who passed through its door. A quaint parody of the Sixties I thought, clinging still to the past but looking ever more to an amazing future. When Dr Who was pitted against his arch-enemies the Daleks, a cult show was born that would travel through time into the television screens of the next century.

In real life names like Ronnie Biggs and Buster Edwards became part of criminal folklore for their part in the Great Train Robbery. The tragic death of the train driver some time after the event, the prison escapes of the crooks and Biggs' famous exile in Brazil, all added to the legend of this crime. The words one million pounds still made people catch their breath back then; newspapers give away bigger prizes for collecting tokens these days.

Titillation and scandal swept the pages of the press, Mum and Dad would stop in mid sentence if I entered the room and because of the silence I'd know they were talking about the Profumo affair. Didn't they know I could read, and didn't just stop at the sports pages when I glanced through Dad's weekly copy of *Tit Bits?*

The *Titfield Thunderbolt* has always been one of my favourite movies and perhaps that is borne out of the spirit its characters displayed. The spirit of a by gone age which oh so politely and mischievously railed against bureaucracy. The Beeching Report and the man who implemented it, Ernest Marples, were the bad guys then but they won and changed a way of life as the nation's rail services were decimated for all time.

Annie was fourteen years old now, and in many ways I was becoming a bit of a nuisance for her. Music, boys and fashion, I'm not sure in which order, were now her main priorities. She never quite shut the door on me but often needed a reminder from Mum and Dad to leave it a little ajar. A couple of years later I'd have helped her slam it closed, I must have been the bane of her life in those days. She was a teenager of the early Sixties and I was a pesky kid!

Truthfully both our worlds' were in orbit, our music was beginning to rule the airwaves and kids were never on the streets without their transistor radios. At night the crackling sound of *Radio Luxembourg* would be searched out on the dial of our trusty Ferranti at home, dad had introduced me to the wonders of that channel. *Radio Caroline* was the most famous of the pirate stations but we had our own *Radio Scotland*, not the modern BBC version, which did a fabulous Sunday afternoon chart show. How could anyone blame us, The Beatles, The Rolling Stones, Dusty Springfield, Cilla Black, Lulu, The Searchers, Freddie and the Dreamers, Gerry and the Pacemakers, The Bachelors, Cliff, The Shadows, Billy J Kramer and the Dakotas, The

Dave Clark Five, The Merseybeats, The Four Pennies and The Animals; our choice of favourites was endless. Disc jockeys like David Jacobs, Pete Murray, Alan Freeman and Jimmy Saville made sure we never missed a number one or a new release.

Football was my sporting passion and Jackie and I spent our every spare waking moment talking about and playing football, mindful to always have a radio handy playing the latest hits. My football life had begun with kickabouts with Dad and Annie, and progressed through school playground games. Those involved almost everyone in the playground chasing a tennis ball around like greyhounds after a hare and it would have been almost impossible for an onlooker to determine if there were actually two sides and in which direction either was playing.

Britain finally scaled the European heights in 1963 when Tottenham Hotspur won the Cup Winners Cup, thrashing Athletico Madrid 5-1 in the final. I had vague memories of my father's shock at the Munich Air Disaster which took the lives of so many fine young Manchester United players, and television had brought the wonder of Real Madrid's 7-3 win over Eintracht Frankfurt into our living room. In 1960 I had been just too young to appreciate the brilliance being displayed before me but I was old enough to burn with humiliation after Scotland's 9-3 thrashing by the English at Wembley. Kids all dreamed of being Law, Greaves, Charlton or Pele but I only ever wanted to be Charlie Cooke.

Tea cards, Ursula in bubble gum cards and now football in many mediums had set me off on a hobby that became a lifelong passion, card collecting. My prize possessions were postcard-sized photographs of all the great teams of past and present, issued in sets of twelve or sixteen cards in the Victor and other comics. I'd be camped outside Mrs Rennie's papershop an hour before the wholesaler arrived on delivery day just to make sure I didn't miss out on that particular week's treasures.

I devised a game involving the team photos, dice and playing cards then played out all my own league and cup-tie competitions. Each score was faithfully recorded and a league table produced every week, which my father had to convince me, was the most important sporting news he'd read all week. He never let me down and always did just that. I'd spend hours with all the world's great players, in all the world's great stadiums and mum would carefully set the table for supper around my intricate lay-out when she sensed a crucial match was in progress. Football was my passion!

The Sixties were beginning to trouble the establishment and it was brought home to us locally when the *Evening Express* ran a series called, *The New Morality*. It questioned the 'anything goes' attitudes and worried over sexual misbehaviour among the young. The mini-skirt was frowned upon by many but worn by the right girl was a delight for lads like Jackie and me, although we'd no idea at all of what sexual misbehaviour might be. It was still a world of 'look don't touch' and I'd make my way through the permissive Sixties doing an awful lot of looking and precious little touching.

In this world of change it was amusing that if 'Ernie' picked your numbers on the premium bonds, a £5000 win could still be a life-changing event. Dad was working at the 'batons' now and he and Mum would often spend an evening planning what to do if they won first prize. To the best of my knowledge they never owned a premium bond in their lives!

On the day I became a teenager I started my second year at the Academy. I believed that meant I would return to school as a grown-up but in the long summer holidays of 1964 there was still a childhood dream for three boys to fulfil; there was a raft to be built.

On West North Street from the Seamount Steps to Mounthooly there were many old derelict buildings and Brian Muir, Jim Ritchie and I had discovered that one of them had been a joiner's yard. We hatched a plan to remove enough wood to build ourselves a raft; sea-going of course, and the launch would be off Aberdeen beach.

The procurement of materials proved to be more of a problem than we'd expected but Brian's fabled mountaineering skills worked in our favour. We three would edge our way across the creaking roof and drop down through the old skylight, on the very first occasion without working out how we'd get back out. Brian standing on me, standing on Jim, who was balanced on an old tea chest finally did the trick, we could have escaped from Colditz.

The place was a gold mine for us, a treasure-trove of pieces of wood of all shapes and sizes. We carefully selected only the best. As a loading bay the tea chest and human pyramid method let us down, too dangerous even for we three musketeers but our D'Artagnan was at hand. Annie was added to the squad and would lie on the roof and grab the planks of wood as Brian passed them up; our production line was a smooth operation! It took us a week to remove all he wood we needed and the raft was constructed in our backie and stored in the washhouse.

On launch day we four, each supporting a corner, marched from Park Street to the beach; this was *Swallows and Amazons* stuff! Annie played the Queen Mother and remained aloof and dry on the beach; all that was missing was a bottle of champagne for her to properly mark the moment of the maiden voyage.

I sensed all was not well when Brian, Jim and I were chest deep in the sea and realised we seemed to be keeping our creation afloat rather than launching it. Brian obviously held no such misgivings; in typical fashion he left the water like a young dolphin and landed square atop the now wallowing craft. His miraculous conversion from dolphin to stone was instantaneous and both he and the SS Flounder disappeared silently beneath the gentle swell. Annie's hysterical laughter rang from the beach and once the human fish surfaced, he gasped in masterful understatement, "It's sunk!"

With a ready made salvage crew on hand it wasn't long before the stricken vessel was wrestled back to the shore, where Annie laughed even harder as

42

we stood there in silence scratching our heads. Luckily a modern-day Isambard Kingdom Brunel, cleverly disguised as an old man walking his dog, was able to impart the technical explanation for our failure, "Ye'll nae sail far in that loons, ye've made it oot o' chipboard!"

I suspect that at that moment Annie peed herself!

The raft was quickly abandoned and was last seen in semi-submersible mode heading in the general direction of Norway. The Labour Party was also trying to correct a miserable failure right then; they called it 'thirteen years of Tory misrule.' Khrushchev, the bogeyman, had fallen from power in Russia and Mao Tse-Tung's China was now, frighteningly, a nuclear power. The free world always needs a bogeyman to keep things, or is it us, in order. Ho Chi Minh was unknown to me but the flame of war would engulf his North Vietnam in a conflagration with America that would be a dread for the world for the next decade.

In 1964 Aberdeen had to face an alarm of its own when it was struck by a typhoid epidemic. Our medical health officer, Dr MacQueen, would make comforting announcements in the press that things were under control and then another poor soul would fall foul of the ailment. A tin of corned beef at a William Low's supermarket in Union Street was confirmed as the source but corned beef and tatties were my favourite and we didn't shop there so we didn't change our diet. All the victims were housed in quarantine at the City Hospital and there was a silver lining to the story—schools were closed for the duration of the epidemic. The panic passed but to this day I never go to the loo without washing my hands!

Jock Kynoch lived across the road from us and during the school holidays his teenage kids Eric and his two sisters spent most days at his house. We all became great pals and more or less had the run of the place when Jock was at work. The record player was never off and we must have worn out *Rhythm of the Rain, PS I Love You* and *Ferry Cross the Mersey*. The girls were lovely, but real-life girls your own age were very, very scary then and I must have been terrified because to my eternal shame I can't recall their names.

I suppose Annie's life and mine were beginning to drift apart; she'd leave secondary school and go on to the old Commercial College on Commerce Street for a year and become a very competent shorthand-typist. One event however was still to unfold that would typify her spirit and leave me asking questions of myself and I still don't like the answers I come up with.

A gang of us local kids had gathered at the bottom end of Lemon Street, doing nothing in particular. A few lads who didn't regularly play with us joined us; one of them was Joey Gill, who had a bit of a reputation as a tough guy. How it started I don't remember but Annie slapped his face and he slapped her back. I just knew this was something she simply wouldn't stand for. We all watched sheepishly as the physically ill matched pair traded blows. The more obvious Joey's superiority became the more obvious became Annie's refusal to give in. Neither pain nor punishment was a deterrent to her and Joey eventually became a victim of his own embarrassment. He walked off bemused and she stood defiant in the spot were the fight had started.

Could or should I have stepped in and taken some of the blows? The only answer I ever came up with was yes. Annie was unfazed by it all and never mentioned the incident to me ever again. In this life there are tough guys and tough guys, I was neither and Annie was without question the latter!

Jake and I were back at the James Bond movies again; special effect of the year was Goldfinger's in-flight exit. I thought the best movie of the year was The Day of the Triffids and I was surprised mother hadn't fallen foul of them when hanging out the washing; our unkempt back green was alive with them.

We were growing out of the old Wednesday Club at the North Church on Queen Street and had joined the Boy's Brigade. Attendance at Sunday School seemed a small price to pay for the chance to play football for the 5th Company at Hazlehead on Saturday afternoon or table tennis at Crimon Place in midweek. Those changing rooms at Hazlehead were desperate then and remain unchanged to this day, my son Paul can testify to that, but it was the only place to be at 3pm on a Saturday. What I didn't appreciate then was that the Brigade gave me the opportunity to meet and to learn from such wonderful people as the company captain Frank Diack, Ian Hogg and his dad, Frank Kelly and so many others. Jackie and I must have driven them all to despair.

We also met a man that year who would be a great influence on us for quite some time, Billy Sherriffs. Billy had taken over Ernie Merchant's grocer shop and in no time we had appointed ourselves as his official message boys. This was hugely influenced by the fact that Billy ran a football team, Unions XI, and was as nuts about football as we were. He didn't treat us like kids and spoke to us in a new way about things that my dad didn't. Billy was a learning curve!

By means of begging, persistence and sheer cheek Jackie and I had wangled our way in as ballboys at Pittodrie. Those were the days when Tommy Pearson was manager and Davie Shaw was his trainer. More importantly Ken McKenzie was the senior ballboy and drew up the rota for matches. There was no pay involved but we ran out with pride in the faded blue tracksuits for our allocated games. We turned up at the stadium before kick-off to watch all the players arrive. They relaxed before the match with a game of snooker and under Pearson's stewardship many were perhaps better snooker players than they were football players. Highlight of the day would be running the gauntlet of flailing towels in the players' dressing room as we plunged into the team bath. By the time we got there it would contain more mud than water but we didn't care. Ken and I are workmates to this day and I still go out of my way to keep in his good books.

The 'celebrity status' of ballboy was a juggling act between a desire to watch the Reds every week and the thrill of playing for the 5th Company at Hazlehead. Life has taught me I'm a player at heart and not a watcher, Jackie and I both made the same choice and left Pittodrie behind for the thrills, spills and happy memories of Boy's Brigade football. Aberdeen lost the Summer Cup Final to Hibs that year and Charlie Cooke would soon be off to Dundee; Pittodrie would never be the same again, until Fergie!

Little pockets of nervous looking kids stood around the playground, the new faces just up from primary school. Here was I, now a teenager and a sophisticated second year pupil. In truth I held no high hopes of school and was already just going through the motions and making plans to leave at the end of the fourth year. School did however become infinitely more interesting on that first day of year two when I met my new German teacher, Miss Russell, wow! Classroom space, then as now, was at a premium and the dining hall was shown on our timetable as the classroom for our German period. The hall was also a main thoroughfare and for almost ten minutes a procession of lost souls wandered back and forth as we waited aimlessly for direction. A tall dark-haired young woman, struggling to hold on to a briefcase and an armful of papers, stumbled into the hall and in a voice filled with panic, pleaded, "Is this second year German?"

A chorus answered in the affirmative but I stayed silent and simply stared at her, she was gorgeous! Tall, slim and smiling, she wore a green blouse and brown skirt hidden beneath her black gown, which happily failed to hide her shapeliness. Miss R, German had always been my favourite subject! I traded off my surplus Ursula cards that weekend but she was down to two for one by then anyway.

To my shame I became part of a group of bullies that year and how shocking that the bullying was directed against one of the masters, Mr Kildare. He was a young maths teacher in his first year at school, determined I'm certain to impart all his knowledge to eager youth. How sad for him that he ended up with a rabble like our class. His own good manners and mildness were his undoing and as only children can we took every opportunity to push the envelope as far as possible. Maths classes were times of absolute mayhem and his suffering at our hands was our loss in terms of knowledge gained. How sad that it all ended for him with a line of boys waiting to be belted. That it took almost the whole year for him to resort to those tactics spoke volumes for him as a man. He did not remain long at Aberdeen Academy and became, I believe, a maths master at Robert Gordon's where he cultivated a reputation as a stern disciplinarian. That had not been his ambition in teaching but we had forced the decision upon him.

I was caught out in year two and finished with a mark for the year of 46%. Learning was hard work and my natural brightness couldn't cover my laziness and disinterest. At the end of that year we had to make subject choices for the next two years which would lead to our 'O' level examinations and

I, as always, chose the easy stuff. Why, oh why, were kids of thirteen being asked to make choices that would affect the rest of their lives? My choices would end up making me a great Trivial Pursuits player, a good letter writer and a prime candidate for one crap job after another. Oh well, at least German was good fun!

Gerry and the Pacemakers had been singing about walking through a storm and their hit tune, *You'll Never Walk Alone,* would go on to become the most famous football anthem of all time. It seemed the world was walking into a storm as American military involvement escalated in Vietnam. I had been born into a world still reeling from the ravages of war and thought, in those days, of family tales of war and suffering. These tales were of my grandfather and my Uncle Percy, they had not been related to me by them personally but re-told by other family members in that old tradition of storytelling that keeps our memories alive. I have no reason to doubt that these events actually did take place.

In the Great War my grandfather had been shot in the leg during one of those countless, meaningless attempts to advance from one sodden trench position to another. As the abortive forward push turned to headlong retreat my grandfather lay stricken and cried for help. The great fear was the kiss of death from a German bayonet as they counter-attacked. His saviour arrived in the shape of a huge Glaswegian man whose voice boomed out through the inferno, "It's okay Jock, I'll help you."

In one swift movement he'd hoisted my grandfather over his shoulder and re-joined the breakneck retreat. Unceremoniously dumped in the comparative safety of his own trenches, my grandfather had neither time to thank the man, nor would he ever see him again or know what fate his saviour may have suffered in that maelstrom of horror.

Almost thirty years later a teenage Percy Ellnor stood in line waiting his chance to enter a safe shelter in the North African desert during a German air raid. An equally young man just behind him broke from the queue in panic and threw himself through the door of a nearby building. As the door opened he was simultaneously engulfed in a huge explosion, the sappers had not yet checked that building for booby traps and no safety flag flew in front of it.

On another occasion he was helping to process some Italian prisoners and one, a young man of perhaps seventeen years of age, was clutching to his breast a photograph of what appeared to be his mother and sister. His pleas to keep the photograph were ignored by a war-weary sergeant who stepped forward, snatched the photograph from his hand, tore it into tiny pieces and snarled, "Italian bastard!" as he threw them to the desert floor.

Who knows what experiences had driven him to that action, and why at that moment in their world of pain it had affected my uncle so deeply? Percy stepped forward and punched the sergeant full in the face. He leapt immediately to his feet, pulled out his pistol and with the weapon pointed directly at my uncle's head spat out the words, "I'll fucking shoot you for that Ellnor!"

"Go on then, shoot me." was Percy's soft, detached reply.

There in a foreign field those two men, comrades in arms, stood for interminable moments on the edge of life or death. Thankfully one's rage subsided and the other's resignation lifted and the incident became just another of those dark moments that the very best of men are driven to in war. Yet here we were twenty years later, a world still living in the shadow of war. Those tales are my only experience of conflict and I sensed then that war would always breed heroes, victims and savage hearts in equal number, by the million.

I never think of secondary school with the fondness that I feel I should. Most of that I put down to my own inadequacies but in 1965, school was certainly taking a turn for the better. All this was due to a paper round, Japanese golf clubs, a wee man with a pocketful of sweeties and oh, of course, German lessons!

Teenagers live their lives in three segments, school, home life and private time with pals. It's a schizophrenic existence with each of the three characters being played in turn. Getting the rotation right can be a problem and a source of trouble as I was to discover to my cost and pain.

I'd got myself a paper-round at a shop on Crown Street which was quite a way from home but handy for after school. I delivered the *Evening Express* after school, *Green Finals* on Saturday evenings and did an early morning round for the Sunday papers. Fifteen shillings a week plus tips, I was a wage earner!

With more than a little help from mum I bought myself all the sports kit I needed and looked forward to PE and games days with relish. One of my early encounters at PE is a favourite memory of mine from school days. Ian Spence, who had played rugby against the All Blacks, was our teacher, a bull of a man and referee of a fateful game of 'heading longball.'

As long as each deft flick of the head sent the football out of the semi-circle and evaded fielders you could run and score. I was doing well until the wrong teenage character put in an appearance. My low flick clearly carried over the line but Mr Spence thought otherwise, "Out!" he cried.

"Shit!" I disputed.

"See me after the period." said he.

Out of the game and sent to the changing room was bad enough but fifteen minutes to contemplate my fate was a nightmare. I trudged in trepidation to his office door and tapped ever so quietly on it. My spirits sank completely as his voice beckoned me in.

"Yes?" he asked with a somewhat confused look on his face.

"You wanted to see me, sir." I squeaked.

The blank expression on his face raised my hopes, he'd forgotten! Well maybe he had, but at his request I related the details of the earlier incident, expletive omitted, and a flash of remembrance crossed his face. Two of the belt was to be my punishment but at length, after much opening and closing of desk drawers, he bemoaned the fact that he couldn't find his belt. I could have helped him; it was in the top left hand drawer of his desk. It was the first drawer he'd opened in his search!

What followed was a masterpiece of Hitchcockian suspense and, I began to suspect, a well-rehearsed little cameo. I followed him first to Mr Ritchie's Geography class, where he explained his plight only to be told that Mr Ritchie had also mislaid his instrument of correction. On the first floor Mr Bewick had left his in his briefcase in the staffroom but winked as he gave the news!

My knees were trembling as I trudged behind him up the final flight of stairs to the science labs. Mr Dalziel the Physics master had a belt to hand and on the top floor landing I took my punishment with the air heavy with the smell of a rat! He didn't belt as hard as I thought a future Barbarians prop forward would but by then I'd well and truly been taught and appreciated the lesson; I'm sure he took it easy on me. I never mixed up my three teenagers again!

Charlie Chalmers was a character in my neighbourhood and a man all the kids tried to curry favour with. Charlie had been an old fashioned street bookie and when betting shops were legalised, had opened his own shop in Cummings Park. He was a busy man and each year would choose one of the local kids as his message boy or girl. Annie and Brian had both had their year and I was delighted when I got my chance to be Charlie's runner. The 'job' involved just being there at whatever time Charlie arrived home in his black Morris Minor, MRG598. He'd hand over some cash, tell you what he required, then it was a dash to the shops to obtain all his needs.

Charlie was a benefactor to many people on our street but some perhaps saw him as a soft touch and played on his generosity. Some weeks he'd give me two shillings every night just for popping across the road for a loaf of bread and a pint of milk! With my paper round, helping out at Billy's shop and running for Charlie I was doing quite nicely thank you. Indeed I was in a position to make my mark in the rich man's game of golf.

Television had made dad and I fans of many sports. Football and boxing were still tops then but I had already developed what would become a life-long love of tennis both as a player and a fan. What better time to discover a sport, Laver, Emmerson, Santana and those British stalwarts Sangster and Wilson? Such great female players as Mortimer, Trueman, King, Court and Bueno. Then almost as important as the players the velvet, all-knowing tones of Dan Maskell the doyen par excellence of all tennis commentators. The mighty Yorkshire county side dominated cricket and another Olympic extravaganza had come and gone in Tokyo with its highlight the fairytale gold medal of Ann Packer in the 800 metres.

Jackie and I had discovered golf at the nine-hole pitch and putt course at the Links. British golf was in something of a decline then and the world thrilled to the Big Three battles of Jack Nicklaus, Arnold Palmer and Gary Player. Nicklaus would be the only person that century to come remotely close to rivalling Muhammad Ali in the sporting arena but both as a man and a sporting man, time would tell that he had been blessed with true greatness.

My bid to join the big three started on Queens Street at Mackay's Army Surplus stores. Cheap Japanese golf clubs were appearing on the market and with my new found wealth I was able to buy a driver, a five iron, a putter and a pencil bag for the princely sum of £5. With this rare array of equipment I set off to conquer Aberdeen's finest fairways at The Links, Hazlehead and Balnagask. I never managed to work out how to use the driver but undeterred toured those courses using in effect only two clubs! I'd added a few £1 clubs from the pro's shop at Hazlehead by the time me, and Denis Golder and two other pals from school had set up a regular Sunday foursome at Hazlehead. I played golf regularly and badly for fourteen years and only ever play these days at my son's football team outings. I own a much bigger bag but can still use just three or four clubs properly, which always leaves plenty room for my beer.

Interests were branching out and Jackie and I often visited the new Lads' Club premises at Mounthooly. Many nights were spent at the Shiprow Tavern in Constitution Street playing snooker and table tennis. This was not only a place for kids but also a haven for men who were perhaps down on their luck. It had moved from its original premises on the Shiprow but the welcoming canteen was always filled with blokes who could make a cup of tea last from 6pm until 10pm when it closed. They could chat together and watch the telly and the wonderful Mr Coutts and his army of lady helpers never failed to make everyone feel welcome. We could play half an hour of snooker for a tanner and an old three-penny piece would secure a table tennis table there for an hour. Our first gambling was done there as we'd risk a bet against all comers at snooker, the risk never being more than one shilling a game.

As good as these places were I always favoured St Katherine's on West North Street. I learned the basics of my other great sporting love there; badminton looked a sissy game but boy was it hard to play. Nothing I've ever done in sport is harder than an evenly matched singles at badminton. Jackie never stretched to more than five feet five inches fully grown but he was always a goalie. An acrobatic shot stopper and fearless to a fault. In full sized goals the lob was always his Achilles Heel but at St Kay's he found his true stage. Between the sticks of the small gymnasium goals he was almost unbeatable and mainly thanks to him we rarely lost at five-a-sides.

St Kay's wasn't just about sport, there was a coffee bar with a jukebox and on a Tuesday the Strollers had their practice night. They were the first local group I had heard live and the first time I walked into one of their sessions in the big hall upstairs they were playing *In The Midnight Hour* by Wilson

Pickett, golden days! A pal of ours, Bobby McSkimmons, had invented a sort of cross-step jive dance and a group of us had perfected the steps and were ready to unleash our routine on an unsuspecting world. During one of the Strollers practice nights Bobby waited for the moment and the music. This new terpsichorean wonder soon had a clapping, appreciative crowd surrounding us and as Bobby's foot flicks got faster and faster the clapping grew louder and louder. Suddenly his right shoe shot through the air narrowly missing the throng of admirers and poor Bobby's black sock was exposed to all and sundry as having not quite enough material round its holes. Quick exit stage left!

The world still wasn't overly sophisticated and of a Wednesday evening I'd often join crowds outside the *Evening Express* offices on Broad Street to await news of the score if Aberdeen were away from home in an important game. The *Evening* was still our main source of local and sports news and like most men I'd developed that strange habit of reading in the toilet. At 112 Park Street that was often a quite Spartan exercise. An outside loo in mid-winter is a cold, cold place but the paper would come in handy to keep you dry when rain poured through the broken skylight window.

That year my sound finances allowed me to buy my first camera, a Kodak 127, which I still have to this day. I paid one pound, four shillings and eleven pence for it at Michie's the chemist. It produced eight postcard size photographs from a spool of film and went on to record many family events over the years. Mum, Dad, Annie and I all fell out over it the first time we used it on a day out at the Westburn Park. We all wanted to be photographers and not models, what a day that was!

After her year at college Annie was off to into the big world and her newly acquired skills had won her a job at John Bell's, the antique dealer, who had a huge shop at the bottom of Bridge Street. She now had a few quid to spend and was enjoying life to the full but always seemed to be looking for a wee bit more excitement and adventure. At least her wee brother didn't tag along all the time now as I'd done when we saw stars like the Rolling Stones, Dusty Springfield and the Searchers at the Capitol. I did see them but can't claim to have heard them, the noise was deafening as soon as they appeared and Annie could scream with the best of them.

Music was a wonderful part of life. *Concrete and Clay* was my top song around that time but we had a family friend who had a song that seemed his and his alone. Billy Paterson was the man and *Tears* was the song. Billy was a gentle man, didn't swear and in his angry or exasperated moments would deliver his own sanitised version of the f-word...fif! His index finger and thumb would simultaneously stroke his chin and he'd peer at the object of his disfavour or shock. So it was that we all simply new Billy as Fif and it suited him to a tee.

In medieval times Fif would have been a travelling minstrel but unlike the troubadour of Robin Hood's band, Allin-a-dale, he didn't carry a harp, he lugged a reel to reel Grundig tape recorder. Fif and my dad were boyhood pals; he was generous to a fault and oh, how he liked to sing. He'd arrive unannounced of an evening but was always welcome. His reel to reel was an extension of the family singsong, and weekday or weekend, Fif didn't need a dram to loosen his vocal chords. In truth we were all keen to put our party piece on tape and hear the result.

Once all the machinery had been set up Fif would take centre stage and launch into his unique versions of Ken Dodd's classic. He could hold a note longer than anyone I've ever heard could and as he launched into the opening words Annie and I would stand either side of him. His eyes closed tight, his face reddened and the word T..e..a..r..s would gradually emit from his mouth. Our positioning was based on the theory that as his eyes closed ever tighter his eyeballs were being forced outward towards his ears and at any moment would erupt like plugs from a tattie gun. When it seemed impossible for him to hold the note any longer there would be a rush of expelled air from his mouth, his eyes would open with a start and the song would flow on. Fif's eyeballs never did pebbledash our living room walls. He was a lovely man who brought a lot of fun and joy into our lives and I learned from him never to take myself too seriously.

Phil Spector was perfecting his wall of sound and Bill Medley and Bobby Hatfield in the guise of the Righteous Brothers epitomised some of the best of that style of music. Bobby's voice was made for *Unchained Melody* and I don't know about walls but him and Fif as a duo could have brought your house down. I shudder to thing what havoc they could have wreaked if Scott Walker had joined them to form a trio. Hatfield and Walker are undoubtedly two of the greatest singers I've ever heard and Billy Paterson was undoubtedly the most enthusiastic.

Going to the pictures wasn't a first choice night out any more, but *Those Magnificent Men In Their Flying Machines* was worth two visits if only to laugh at the antics of Gert Frobe and Jimmy Stewart was at his emotive best in the superb western *Shenandoah*. Britain was stunned into silence when our great war leader Winston Churchill died and I did exactly what was intended with my day off school, watched his funeral. In lighter vein the Beatles were awarded MBE's but fighting between India and Pakistan over Kashmir gave Prime Minister Harold Wilson cause to reflect that this was the worst threat of all to world peace. Is peace the cherished dream and war the harsh reality of man?

School had become less of a bind, outside influences had helped me make it a better place for myself and I felt more a part of things. I was playing for the school seconds at hockey, had hit a match winning twenty-eight not out for St Nicholas against Greyfriars in an inter-house cricket match and was about to impress a former foe, Mr Rae.

Richard Yule, who famously went on to play 270 times for Scotland, usually won the school table tennis championships. I drew him in round one and took fifteen or sixteen points off him in both games as I lost 2-0 on sets. Mr Rae was sufficiently impressed to abandon the usual practice of choosing the four semi-finalists to represent the school in the inter school tournament. He ordered a play-off involving the two semi-final losers and me. I made the team but lost again to Richard in the inter school singles semis then paired with Henry Lints to lose once more to Richard and his partner in the doubles final. Henry did a wonderful pencil sketch of me that year which is still a prized possession.

I'd also become good friends with a lad from Torry, Ian Barrie, and it was he who asked me along to a trials match for Walker Road under-15's football team. A wonderful wee man called Frankie Waugh ran the team; he always had an encouraging word for everyone and a pocketful of sweets to offer as a prize or consolation as required. We trained in midweek at Walker Road school and played on a Saturday at Tullos. I enjoyed my short spell with them but the lure of playing with pals like Jake and John Mitchell soon had me back at my Boy's Brigade football.

So there I was happy at home and at school, although boredom was never too far away with the exception of German lessons of course and I would carry an average mark of 56% into my 'O' levels year. Before I could start it however an event would occur that would haunt we Scots till the end of time, England would win the World Cup of football!

On the 30th of July 1966 I watched the World Cup Final with my father and two young American Mormon missionaries. Those two young men had visited our house on several occasions and Annie and I had even gone for a look around their church on North Anderson Drive, more out of curiosity than commitment if truth were told. I still went to church then, on a Sunday morning with the Boy's Brigade, but not since my early childhood and the regular home visits of Father White of St Clements-on-the-quay had religion seemed an important part of my life.

There were two attempts at conversion going on that day. They hoped to lead us into the Mormon faith and we were apostles bringing the beautiful game to the New World. Those nice young men seemed confused with the finer points of the game and even more baffled by the pro-German atmosphere in our house. When Haller put West Germany ahead they were bemused at our celebrations and then dumbfounded at our gloom when Hurst quickly equalised.

"Didn't we all fight these guys in the war?" questioned one.

"Yes we did and whupped their ass," clarified my dad "but that was war and this is football!"

They never understood it nor comprehended the euphoria that Weber's last gasp equaliser brought. Extra time would end with Kenneth Wolstenholme's classic 'They think it's all over...well it is now!' line but the Scots, Irish and Welsh all knew it had only just begun.

We never became Mormons and I'd guess they never watched a soccer match again. The Scots, English, Irish and Welsh have continued their sporting battles and together, when the need has arisen, continue to attempt to put the world in its place. It's a funny old game!

The other piece of football history made that year came two months before that final courtesy of a cancelled Boy's Brigade match at Hazlehead. With our game off Jackie and I had jumped on a bus and headed for Aulton to watch Billy's Unions XI play Rob Roy in a league match. Billy was like a caged tiger when we arrived, pacing to and fro at the entrance of the dilapidated changing rooms. We gathered that only ten of his players had showed up for the crucial encounter. I didn't think he was talking to me when I heard him say to get stripped but jumped when he shouted the command again and told me there were only five minutes left until kick-off.

I was playing! Fourteen years old and about to make my debut in the old District League for players up to twenty seven years of age, I hope that might still be some sort of record. My dreams of glory evaporated in a starry daze ten minutes into the game. Their left back, big Mike Watt, sent me, the ball and the watching Billy into orbit and onto the adjacent pitch with an agricultural challenge of thunderous impact. We did go on to win the game 2-0, one of the goals a header from a corner taken by yours truly. I played the last eighty minutes in a blur of dizziness and was at the end of the game, absolutely clear on what separated the men from the boys. It would be a couple of seasons before I played more regularly for Billy and I was happy to remain with the kids for a while yet.

I look back on my footballing days and I knew even then that I'd never scale the heights as a player. The tiny clip in the Green Final about my youthful debut only confirmed my fears, in print Sidney Robertson didn't even look like a footballer's name and you'd never be able to use it in a terracing song. In all the years I played I only ever saw the ball and my shoe laces, the only time my head was ever up was when I captained the Boy's Brigade team and managed to win the toss at kick-off. Mike would hit me a few more times over the years, he was six foot tall, built like the side of a house and I never once saw him coming! I loved football.

Carnaby Street was the centre of the fashion world but fashion didn't seem to travel well and by the time it reached the grey north-east it had diluted into a strange mix. Jackie and I would think we were the bee's knees in our hipster trousers, floral shirts and those amazing checked jackets, which looked like deerstalker hats with arms.

A new disco opened in Aberdeen at an old church on Rose Street. It was to be for members only and called The Place and being a year younger than Jake I lied about my age to join. Harry Dowson the tailor on George Street wasn't London fashion but he was cheap. For our first appearance at The Place I bought a chocolate brown suit for £6 and a pair of brown suede shoes for £3. Annie said that mum watched until I was out of sight and then cried her eyes out the first night I left home to go there. Knowing Mum it would have been the lime green socks that had driven her to tears.

We Scots needed an alternative to 1966 and all that. Made that year but not seen in cinemas until the next summer it was a Scot, Lulu, who sang *To Sir With Love* in the superb film of the same name. A virtuoso performance from Sidney Poitier and marvellous support from a wonderful group of young actors caught the spirit of the time to perfection. There was still room for schmaltz though and even I can't keep it a secret forever, yes I saw the *Sound of Music* and yes I thoroughly enjoyed it.

This was a time when the world was looking forward to an amazing future but still struggling to escape from a desperate past. The impact of a television play, *Cathy Come Home*, was far reaching and fuelled all sections of society with a desire to solve the problems of the abject poverty, homelessness and despair that could and did still exist in our nation. A tragedy of immense sadness burned itself deep into our minds when the Aberfan disaster occurred. In moments of indescribable horror over one hundred people, mostly children, died when their school was engulfed in a sea of mud and earth as a slagheap collapsed upon them. The country wept and that tiny Welsh community was left with every heart broken.

The world turns and for me a great place to be that summer was still the bandstand at the beach. They'd play all the top tunes over their loudspeaker system and with Manfred Mann, the Spencer Davis Group, the Walker Brothers and Chris Farlowe all storming the charts there was plenty great stuff to hear. They decided to run a seven-a-side football tournament that summer and Jake and I got roped into a team organised by Chucksey Benzie.

Organised isn't a word that would spring to mind when thinking of Chucksey, who was tough but mad in that delightful way that some tough guys are. He may well have gone on to become John Cleese, then again he might be out there doing Grace Jones impersonations. You didn't argue with Chucksey and when he told us he would play in goal himself Jackie immediately discovered a talent as a left back. For two days in brilliant sunshine we battled our way through five matches to reach the final. Chucksey had been superb in goal, aided no doubt by his pre-match threats to single handedly beat up all our opposition if they dared score. In the final he actually saved a penalty just by staring at the spot-kick taker, and we went on to win, thankfully, I mused for their goalscorer, 3-1. A few weeks earlier the magnificent Bobby Moore had held aloft the Jules Rimet Trophy. At risk of life and limb I disobeyed Chucksey's command to do a lap of honour holding aloft yet another bloody bar of Toblerone!

Then it was time for serious days and hard work, back to school for 'O' Level year. There was a disastrous start for me; Miss Russell had proved that her heart was as beautiful as the rest of her by heading off to a remote part of northern Canada to teach Eskimo children. I never did quite understand what benefit there would be for them in learning German or what use it would be to them in hunting seals but then I should have known she was bound to be much more than just a pretty face and German teacher. Never seeing her again was going to be a hard pill to swallow.

Thankfully there is a God and he kindly fixed my broken heart by sending me an angel in a fur bikini, Raquel Welch! From the moment she walked on screen in *One Million Years BC* I was smitten. Christie fancied her too and I could foresee problems. He was about to start work as an apprentice brass finisher at Hall Russell's and if she came out on bubble gum cards, with his spending power, I wouldn't stand a chance. Luckily he took a shine to a wee girl in a blue overall in the baker's shop where he bought his morning rolls on his way to work, the coast was clear Raquel was all mine. Twenty seven years later Tim Robin's character in *The Shawshank Redemption* concealed his tunnel entrance behind a life-size poster of the lovely Raquel. If I'd been in prison with that poster for company, digging tunnels would have been the last thing on my mind!

I'm proud to remember that I did, at least once, find myself academically inspired by a master at Aberdeen Academy and it came as a huge surprise to me. Our last two periods on a Friday were study time where an English teacher, Mr Robertson, supervised us. It was too late in the week for studying and I'm sure too late in the week for him to teach. As a noise reduction exercise he began to read to us from a book called *Cider With Rosie* by Laurie Lee, memories of a childhood spent growing up in the Cotswolds. His wonderful interpretation of that marvellously descriptive text was addictive; the next reading couldn't come soon enough. I took inspiration and tried to write something descriptive and thoughtful of my own; I wrote a poem and called it *Leaves of Autumn*.

Filtering through the air, staying only long enough to catch the wind once more.
Tanned a golden brown, displaying all the splendour of a glorious summer now sadly lost.
Diving up and down, propelled by chance of nature along a mysterious unknown course.
Resting in a valley, surveying all the beauty slowing fading in the birth of Winter.
Leaping over rivers, searching far and near for prolonged life and strength.
Sadly in a ditch, an ending unfit for beauty with no mind yet suggestive in its time.

My scribblings were like chaff before the wind but I thank Mr Robertson for imbuing me with a love of language and words and think of him every time I open the page of a dictionary to make friends with yet another stranger.

Things went well during the first half of 'O' Level year and in the estimates

I averaged 61%, German was the only subject I failed but given my focus in that subject over the previous two years that didn't altogether come as a surprise to me! Dark old friends paid me a visit and played on my frailties that year and I see through their disguise now and know they were laziness, ignorance, lack of character and betrayal.

Mum hadn't been well and had to spend a fair bit of time in hospital in early 1967. Dad as always was up at the crack of dawn and off to work with Annie not far behind him. It was just too easy for me to turn over and go back to sleep. A day off became a week and a week became a month. The attraction of hanging around Billy's shop, helping out behind the counter and listening to his tall tales beat school hands down. I chose to ignore the harm I was doing to my schooling and my future and closed out the thoughts of how I was letting my parents down. They had sacrificed so much to give me a golden opportunity and I repaid them by settling for a few late mornings in bed and learning how to use a meat-slicing machine in a back street corner shop.

Being last out and first home had made my deception all the easier and it was lucky for me that the postman did two deliveries in those days. One lunchtime, in the second delivery, a letter arrived addressed to my father and the official markings on the envelope clearly showed it was from school. There was little guesswork required to know what was in that letter. To my eternal shame I opened the letter and was filled with panic as I read the contents which were asking my father to explain his failure to have me attend school and requested his written reply on the matter and confirmation of when I would return.

My father's failure! Those words leapt out at me, swamped me with guilt and reduced me to tears. My parents had never failed me and had brought me near to adulthood in what was often a world of pain for them but was always a world of love, joy and plenty for me. Their one failure was to have dreamt that I might have amounted to something. My disgrace was compounded by the fact that I'd need to live behind a lie to save my own skin but at least that lie made sure that no blame for my shortcomings would attach to my father.

In total confusion I showed the letter to Billy and between us we hatched the plot to wriggle me off the hook. He wrote the letter of explanation and signed as my father, I returned to school the next day and spent half an hour with my form teacher. The letter spoke of my mum's poor health, the strain that was placing on our family and the particular upset it had caused me, hence my prolonged absence.

This recipe of a lie woven within the truth calmed the stormy waters at school; I was back on the strength and, until this moment, was never exposed to my father as a failure. At least I had the courage to talk to him that very evening and explain that I felt I'd be best to leave school after I sat my 'O' Levels and find a job. He knew me better than I thought and simply said,

"I think finding a job could be the making of you son."

By mid April 1967 I'd sat my six 'O' Levels, English, Mathematics, Arithmetic, History, Geography and German. The next day I took a letter from dad and stood nervously outside the Rector's office. I touched lightly on the door and the firm voice of Alexander Goldie, J.P., M.A., B.Sc., Ed.B., bade me enter. He remained seated and held out his hand as I requested to show him my dad's letter. It was a simple request that I be allowed to leave school a little early to seek employment.

He spent no more than ten seconds reading it, held out his hand and said, "Good luck."

I accepted his hand in mine and replied, "Thank you."

I had been at school for almost eleven years and here I was on the last moment of the last day talking for the first time to a headmaster. Good luck with what and thank you for what? There was not a hint of sadness in my heart as I turned, left his office, quietly closed the door and walked out of the main school entrance onto Schoolhill. I got out of secondary school exactly what I had put into it...nothing! At least I'll apologise to my dad for that in this world and I will say sorry and hug my mum in the next. I also owe an apology to those who were yet to join my journey through life, I know now, I could have done so much better.

Life's a joy when you are young
There's never woe nor worry.
Days of fun as you grow up
Going nowhere in a hurry.
If only I had but thought
To please not me but another.
I could have shared those dreams with
My father and my mother.

A job, a Pint, a Girl and a Heartbreak

Hello working world! My first trip into it was no epic voyage of discovery but a morning walk in the rain to the Youth Careers Office in St Paul's Street. Mr Ross Henderson was the man I had to see and in those days we had an expectation of work, a belief that we were entitled to it. I strolled there, curious as to what I would be offered but with no fear that there would be nothing for me.

A brief interview established I could spell and count to ten using both hands and I was despatched with a green card to see Mr Peter Barclay at the firm of Flockhart & Grant, Chartered Accountants of 1, Bon Accord Square, Aberdeen. The place was as quiet as a reference library and as dark and dull as I remembered the corridors of St Clements-on-the-quay had been. The buttons on my new Harris Tweed jacket looked like little footballs and I twisted them round and round as I awaited my interview. It was more a case of 'you're here, we'll take you' than an interview and I was to become the firm's office boy for the princely sum of £20 per month.

On the first of May 1967, still fifteen years of age, I dressed in the trousers of my brown suit, pulled on my brown suede shoes and donned my herring-bone patterned Harris Tweed jacket to set off to work for the first time in my life. Sandie Shaw was top of the charts with *Puppet on a String* and little did I know, that was exactly how I'd feel about working life almost forty years later.

My job was mostly to deliver mail around the city centre; it was obviously cheaper to employ me instead of buying stamps. I also ran errands for all the other staff, spoke in whispers when I entered the partners' rooms and operated a franking machine, which regularly chewed letters to bits in seconds. Once a month I was sent with a little locked leather satchel to the National Commercial Bank of Scotland, at the top end of Union Street, with a note to hand over to the cashier. The satchel was always taken from me and returned still locked but by then it had mysteriously become extremely heavy. Little did I know I was collecting all the cash for staff salaries and little did they know I once left the heavy version in a shop after I popped in to buy a sweet! Thankfully it was still lying there when I retraced my steps and thankfully I never drew the attention of any crooks as I toured Union Street with my little satchel.

I only stayed there for four months and my resignation seemed to shock the senior partner, J P Grant, also a well-known local golfer. He couldn't believe I'd consider leaving the world of accountancy for a dull job in the Civil Service! My best memory of the firm was playing for them in a football match against Davidson's Paper Mills at their Mugiemoss pitch. I scored a cracking headed goal to win us the game 2-1 and was a celebrity at work the next morning, but only until it was time to take orders of eats for the morning tea-break.

Football was high profile in town right then, Aberdeen had reached the 1967 Scottish Cup Final against Jock Stein's all conquering Celtic side but lost 2-0 on the day. The Celts would soon step into history when Simpson, Craig, Gemmell, Murdoch, McNeil, Clark, Johnstone, Wallace, Chalmers, Auld and Lennox clinched immortality and the European Cup with a 2-1 win over Inter Milan. The whole side assembled from players born within a few miles of Parkhead, it just couldn't happen today.

As a Dons fan I was down, but a footballing Bannockburn was just around the corner and we Scots loved it and revere the moment to this day. A little fancied Scotland side took on the World Champions at Wembley and goals from Law, Lennox and McCalliog, allied to a mesmeric, mischievous performance from 'Slim' Jim Baxter saw the Scots triumph 3-2. The thought always remains that the wily old fox Alf Ramsey had purposely played the full World Cup winning eleven with one exception; Jimmy Greaves had replaced Roger Hunt. We'd never have the satisfaction of being able to claim that we'd beaten his greatest side. Rangers fans, far from being satisfied were still having nightmares over their Scottish Cup exit to Berwick Rangers earlier that year, surely still the greatest giant killing act of them all.

Annie won her own war that year and had to join the Army to do it! Her free spirit had been a cause of trouble between her and Mum and Dad for several years. The more she grew up the more they tried to hold on to their wee girl. In the end they just had to admit that she had some world shaking to do and when she told them of her plan to join up they put up surprisingly little resistance. Annie's time in the Army would be brief but would bring changes and a joy to all our lives that none of us could have foreseen. She wouldn't have been my sister if it didn't bring its share of fireworks too!

Twenty quid a month wasn't a lot but at least the taxman wasn't interested in my new-found wealth; my take home pay was almost £18. My mum took £8 of that for my keep and £4 went to the Provident to pay for all the new clothes I'd bought. That left me £6 a month to enjoy the wonders of the Sixties but St Kay's was a cheap place to socialise and a packet of ten cigarettes cost less than two shillings. I hadn't quite yet discovered booze but would soon find out that a pint cost just less than half a crown. A fish supper cost the same as the fags so imagine it, a night out with smokes, six pints and a fish supper on the way home for less than a quid!

This was the year of free love and flower power with Scott McKenzie's number one hit reminding us all to wear a flower in our hair if we went to San Francisco. Jake did the next best thing and bought himself a floral kaftan; sadly he looked more like one of Fu Manchu's henchmen than a man about to find free love in Aberdeen on a chilly autumn evening.

Dad surprised me by taking a liking to a pop tune that year and it was one that I'm not sure anyone knows the meaning of to this day, *A Whiter Shade of Pale by Procol Harum.* Was this the same man who had banned Annie and me from watching the Beatles on telly when they appeared at the London Palladium?

A strange blot was appearing on the Aberdeen skyline as the formless skeleton of St Nicholas House began to rise out of the rubble of old Broad Street. Creative architecture certainly seemed to be passing the Sixties by and so many of the decaying, soul-less high rise blocks of the present time date from that era.

War is never afraid to push its ugly face to the forefront and the somewhat benignly named Six Day War between the Arabs and Israelis lit a torch of terror and conflict that has burned its way on into the twenty first century. One man made a stand against war; Muhammed Ali refused the draft to fight in Vietnam. He paid for that by losing the best years of his boxing career. Many of those who went to Vietnam paid with their lives but the world came to admire Ali as a man of principle. His legend was only just beginning and his sporting prowess and personal courage would scale inspirational heights for us all.

At home, the Labour government devalued the pound, but on £20 a month I couldn't realistically be devalued any more and can't say I ever felt the need to tighten my belt. Jackie and I could have a night out at the cinema for just a few shillings and dancing at St Kays was still free on practice nights and only two shillings if we went to see the Strollers in their full rigs on a Saturday.

My 'O' level results arrived in the post that summer and I surprised myself by passing five out of six. There was no shock that I failed German but I felt it was time for another visit to Mr Henderson, if only to see if he could offer me something more challenging than being able to remember how many pies and sausage rolls to get from Gordon's Bakery in Dee Street every morning. Accountants certainly could polish off their grub but it wasn't the life for me.

Ross Henderson was a well-known bowler and would go on to represent Scotland at the sport. I myself would take up the sport in the Eighties and he and I would become good friends and sporting rivals. As ever in those times there seemed to be work available for the young and an interview was arranged for me at the Ministry of Transport at Greyfriars House on the Gallowgate. I got the post and my wages soared to £7 a week. In spite of his surprise JP accepted my resignation and for the last two weeks in August I taught my replacement in the skills of pie purchasing, torn letter repair and leather satchel safety. Then I was off to become a Civil Servant.

The struggle for civil rights and racial equality was never far from the hearts and minds of millions in the late Sixties. A film like *In the Heat of the Night* could encapsulate the struggle for us all in powerful images. How strange then for two events, which would once more fan its flames, to occur in the same month, April of 1968.

Martin Luther King had championed the cause in America and his dreams had kept the torch of hope burning bright for us that man could rise above all the problems and make a better world. His tragically untimely assassination in Memphis left many major American cities reeling from the violence of race riots. We were sharply reminded that this wasn't a problem confined to the other side of the Atlantic when Enoch Powell made his infamous 'Rivers of Blood' speech at Birmingham. Here was mankind, racing towards the conquest of space, yet still with so many problems to be solved on our own planet.

A world of change and no little trouble was about to hit the Robertson family. Annie's brief spell in the Army was to end when she became pregnant. The father was a serving soldier and already married. The Sixties hadn't yet changed the world enough to shelter her from the perceived stigma that society still attached to being an unmarried mother. After the initial pyrotechnic display, Mum and Dad were excellent and stood solidly behind Annie. There were no easy options in those days, and it as often as not fell to the girl with, god willing, the help of her family to prepare for the unborn youngster's future.

From where I stood the father was no loss to Annie or the child soon to be. As far as I am aware he showed no further interest in either of them and would put Annie through the humiliation of a court case which ended in him being required to pay £2 a week for his child. He never once in the years that followed made any increase to that paltry sum; I trust he didn't ever think of himself as the father. Neither £2 a week nor £2 million make you a father, time makes you a father. Time to heal a hurt, time to wipe away a tear, time to catch a smile, time to see a first faltering step and time to be there just in case.

Annie's beautiful baby daughter, Paula, was born on September the 21st at Fonthill Nursing Home. Much wanted and much loved, she would bring great change to all our lives just as her expected arrival had already done. There was no way that old 112 would be able to accommodate the returning Annie and a new baby, so the push was on to find our growing family a new home. A new development of houses was springing up in Torry; they later came to be known as the 'hen houses,' and it was there the council offered us a new place. A three bedroom terraced house at 139 Girdleness Road to be precise. The kitchen and living room were upstairs, three bedrooms downstairs and how can I ever forget it? The upstairs housed a treasure of modern living; there was a bathroom!

At sixteen years of age and having lived all my life to date in the same street, I was moving to Torry. Not only was I moving but I'd be able to have a bath inside my own home! This was going to save me a bit of money; I'd no longer have to pay a shilling to scrub up at the Hanover Street School showers on a Friday night. It was a ritual a pal of mine, Syd Davidson, and I followed every week. Like me, I think Syd was still waiting for that special something to happen of a weekend but as sure as eggs are eggs we were both going to be spotless clean when it did. Syd was working as a tyre fitter in those days and they should have charged him double for his shower!

Syd, Ronnie Kavanagh, Jim Davies from primary school days and Derek Wright were, along with Jackie, the best pals of my late teenage years. We shared a love of football, our taste in music, a liking for Morecambe and Wise and an ignorance of girls and alcohol. Sadly it was the later ignorance that Syd and I clarified one hot spring holiday Monday afternoon. A football session at the beach had left us all with a raging thirst and our usual watering hole was the Inversneckie Café for a bottle of coke and an ice cream. One dare led to another and Syd and I were the ones who eventually took up the challenge to go into the bar next door for a 'real' drink. Two bottles of McEwan's export later, seventeen-year-old Syd and sixteen-year-old me emerged as the heroes of the hour. An intermittent fog was about to descend on my life, a fog that wouldn't lift for the next three years but strangely it would only come late on a Friday night and occasionally when I'd won a few quid on the horses.

Sixties music was sensational and now we were out and about savouring the local music scene. I developed a love of all live music in those days. The Beach, the Palace and the Palais were our regular weekend night-spots and we could have a few drinks at 'music pubs' like the Holburn Disco, the Swan Disco, the Ferryhill Tavern, the Anchorage, the Elite, the Blue Lamp, the Carlton, the Silver Slipper or the Copper Beach. Most of the social clubs in town would have a good band on too but in those days you really did need to be a member or be signed in by someone who was.

Like all big cities in the late Sixties Aberdeen was spoiled for choice and there were great singers and musicians everywhere. The Strollers had whetted my appetite and soon I'd thrill to the sounds of Sony Pearce and the Facells, Ally Dawson, Tommy Dene, Frankie Robb, Rhubarb, Twilight Zone, Stan Fraser, Tucker Donald and the big bands at the Palace and the Palais. The bands always had a super girl singer on the stage. Head and shoulders above them all for me was Bobby Vincent who was the singer for a band called the Throb. Bobby also played harmonica and was a cross between Paul Jones and Mick Jagger, a brilliant singer. The Throb covered a lot of Drifters stuff, which I loved, and when Bobby sang *Some Kind of Wonderful* you were never in any doubt that it would be. I did see some big names around then too, Alan Price was excellent live, Dave Dee, Dozy, Beaky, Mick and Titch were much better than I'd expected and the Troggs brought the house down at the Douglas.

As a group we did most of our 'pub drinking' at the Pittodrie Bar and the Scotia. I had my first drink with my dad one Friday lunchtime in the Scotia and as a sixteen-year-old was warned by the staff there for taking a wee lassie into the pub. The wee lassie was my sister Annie, home on her last leave from the Army and nursing a half pint of Guinness; which she'd been told would be good for her and the baby. Changed days all round!

I entered the Civil Service the same month Paula entered the world and I doubt if it would have taken her too long to learn the job either. My main task was to write out licence discs for lorries, all done with special ink and scratch nib pens, and to attach licence applications to operators' files. This was at least just a tad more difficult than writing out the morning pies list. I enjoyed the M.O.T though and one of the reasons was a fellow called Bob Holmes, a mysterious character and a big gambler.

My gambling ran to the extent of a two bob double at Doug Herd's on Upperkirkgate and I had to win on a Monday to prolong my betting spree for the week. Bob was always in there and as often as not in a huddle at the counter with the manager. He never seemed to bet in anything other than folding money. Occasionally he'd give me a tip and the ones I risked a few bob on lost and the ones I ignored always won!

One afternoon Bob asked me to leave the office at three in the afternoon, gave me £50, the name of a horse and strict instructions to place the bet at Herd's seconds before the off in the 3.15 race. I'd never had fifty quid in my pocket before and when the horse won at 6-1 I actually looked around for my little leather satchel as the manager counted out the winnings. Bob gave me a fiver for my trouble and said he might have a few more bets I could place for him. It turned out Bob had been warned off of most of the betting shops in the city centre and needed an anonymous runner. Incognito! I bought myself a fedora hat and started smoking cigarillos especially for running Bob's bets but gave up on the moustache when one of the girls at work tried to rub the ink mark off my top lip. I ran a few more big bets for him but with more winners than losers I didn't get many more fivers. Bob soon moved to another department and I went back to two bob doubles on a Monday, for which even I realised there was no need for a fedora.

In three years at Greyfriars House I'd have a lot of fun, make good friends in lads like Ian Davidson and Frankie Robb, who worked there whilst torn between the nine to five and becoming a full time musician. Luckily for Frankie and us he chose his music. Ian introduced me to his own circle of friends, a great bunch of lads who mostly worked at the Donald's meat factory at Portlethen. We all enjoyed a beer together and played snooker at the Exchange, Burroughs & Watts and Burtons. I was the table tennis champion of the group at the basement tables at Burroughs & Watts. I was able to rely on the skills I'd honed at the Boys Brigade and being the smallest; I was the only one who was never in any danger of splitting his head on the low roof. By 1970 I would be totally confused as to where I was going in the Civil Service and what they could offer me, so one day I simply resigned just to see where life would take me next.

1968 had been an Olympic year and in keeping with the times I remember those Mexico games mostly for the Black Power protests of the American sprinters; there were memorable sporting moments too. Who could ever forget Bob Beamon's amazing long jump leap and David Hemery's gold for Britain in world record time over the 400 metres hurdles?

A genius returned to Wimbledon at the beginning of the era of open tennis; Rod Laver had been a Grand Slam champion in 1962, returned to win the All England championship and would repeat his Grand Slam feat the following year. How great might his record have been had his career not spanned the transitional years between amateur and professional tennis? Speaking of genius, no one had a better view of it than Glamorgan cricketer Malcolm Nash did at Swansea. No doubt he could have seen it far enough as Gary Sobers smashed him, in one over, for six consecutive sixes, an unforgettable moment of sporting magic.

Such great genius often comes at high personal cost to the soul in which its fires burn and the wayward genius of George Best shone bright that year as his dazzling skills inspired Matt Busby's Manchester United to follow Celtic as champions of Europe. The quest for European glory, pursued by Busby from the tragic air disaster of Munich to that Wembley final ten years later, was one of the most poignant and heroic tales of sporting history. Best would sadly waste his towering talent and his career at the pinnacle of the game would, in effect, be over by his late twenties.

I've a wonderful sporting memory of the great Carnoustie golf course that summer. With a workmate, John Stewart, I walked the famous links marvelling at the world's finest golfers. The South African, Gary Player, fought them all off to become champion. Gary was as tough a competitor as they come and on one occasion, when asked by a scribe about his good fortune in holing so many bunker shots, simply replied, "Yes and the more I practise the luckier I get!"

Since radio days and then his classic television series, with episodes like *The Blood Donor* and *The Radio Ham,* Tony Hancock had always been a favourite of Dad's and mine. Another genius troubled by the human frailties that haunt us all, his ill-starred suicide in Sydney saddened us both and stunned the world of entertainment. Genius is a slender thread of gold that most of us will never wrap around our finger but why, for those who do, must the price often come at such a high cost?

The North Vietnamese launched their Tet Offensive and the American nation seemed ever more compelled to question where their involvement in the war could possibly lead. The My Lai Massacre further served to swell the flood of anti-war opinion and although it would be 1973 before the end finally came, 1968 was possibly the year that signalled the beginning of the end of American commitment to the war.

Stanley Kubrick's *2001: A Space Odyssey*, adapted from an Arthur C Clark story, *The Sentinel*, had been astonishing film goers for a year but an unbelievable wonder of space was about to come directly into our living rooms and eclipse it completely. The televising of the moon landing on the 20ᵗʰ July 1969 held us all in awe. Neil Armstrong's historic speech encapsulated everything that was incredulously unfolding before our eyes, "That's one small step for a man, one giant leap for mankind."

Along with Buzz Aldrin and Michael Collins he had fulfilled the promise of the late President Kennedy, that America would land a man on the moon before the end of the decade. This unbelievable technological achievement had happened just over a year after I first lived in a house where I could use an inside toilet or take a bath. Progress certainly doesn't move in all fields at the same pace! One of the great television presenters of those moon landings was the astronomer Patrick Moore and it always amused me that he brought to television commentary what Bobby Walker and I had brought to singing, pure speed!

Mankind has made precious few giant leaps throughout history when it comes to ending war and conflict; the late Sixties would prove no different. In attempts to disentangle what now seems the unsolvable problem, armed British soldiers were on the streets of Northern Ireland, with pain and sorrow for all, the only certain outcome. A civil war of horrors had erupted in Nigeria as the people of Biafra strove for independence and in a brief unequal struggle the images of starving children sparked appeals for aid from the rest of the world. This was also the year that Yassir Arafat became head of the Palestine Liberation Organisation. We were it seemed, as ever, a world in conflict.

At home we saw a nation in economic decline, deeply troubled by industrial unrest. At work I was making little progress and at eighteen years old could no longer hope to serve an apprenticeship or learn a skilled trade. I often wished I'd served my time as a painter and decorator. My dad had me helping him at home when I was fourteen and it's something I've always enjoyed doing—and the results showed I had a knack for it.

A bit of unrest was about to enter my private life, when for the first and only time I was banned from a pub. All the worse that it was my local, the Pittodrie Bar. We were all there celebrating my eighteenth birthday and the head barman, John Abel, enquired as he cleared away the sea of empty glasses what the big party was for. I think it was Syd Davidson who innocently mentioned my eighteenth but none of us thought much of it.

John was an ex-soldier who ran a tight ship; the pub was always spotless and he and the staff immaculate in their grey jackets and white aprons. He quietly laid down his tray of glasses looked straight at me and said, "Out!"

"Why?" I protested, "I've done nothing!"

"You've been drinking underage in my pub for more than a year." he said firmly, "Now out!"

With the celebrations brought abruptly to an end I slunk off home. Four weeks later I slunk back into the bar on a Saturday afternoon just before a

Dons game. I was hoping John might not see me in the pre-match crush. He did and walking past me quietly asked, "Will the Dons win today Sid?"

I managed to stutter out a reply in the affirmative and he carried on clearing tables, the ban was off.

Another ban hit me that year and it was musical, a ban by my father on Fleetwood Mac! I'd bought one of their albums and was happily blasting it out on our radiogram when he arrived home from work. *Oh Well* was the track playing and it obviously wasn't to his liking. A few choice words and expletives later and they were off the turntable, banned from being played altogether and thus consigned to the musical history of 139 Girdleness Road.

Dad was forty years old that year; his sense of humour had never left him, Fleetwood Mac excepted, and he was enjoying being a granddad. Paula's arrival in our lives had been a calming influence and Mum, Dad and Annie had declared a truce. We had another addition to the family that year, a wee cross corgi mongrel we called Rogie. He was to be Paula's pal as she grew up but things didn't quite work out that way. We had him for over a year; he was great fun, loved walks to the Bay of Nigg and would swim forever in the rock pools there. He was a great friend to me for the time we had him.

We had a family party for my dad's fortieth, my grannie and granddad, Uncle Albert and his wife Sheila, Auntie Doris and husband Billy were all there. One thing I've always loved were the singsongs we had at family gatherings, sadly not enough of them over the years. Albert was in top form as Al Jolson and I had chipped in with remarkably allegro tributes to Dean Martin and Johnny Cash.

In the spirit of the evening my dad decided to demonstrate his party piece, his famed handstand, just to prove to us all that age hadn't diminished his acrobatic prowess. Dad's handspring landed him safely against the kitchen door but as he pushed himself to full extension the door began to fall open, followed directly by my now overbalancing father. The kitchen table, several plates of sandwiches and numerous bottles of beer mercifully broke his fall. The only danger now was to avoid being crushed in the rush of bodies heading to the loo for a laughter break.

As the end of the decade approached the Sixties had left a changed world behind. Freedom of the individual existed or was paid lip service to as never before and National Service had disappeared. The ugly spectre of Apartheid hung over South Africa and the super powers of America and Russia had the world split into the separate camps of the Cold War, which gave us the impression we were rushing headlong to Armageddon.

Two shocking incidents stunned the world and showed the growing capability of the media to bring all the horrors of our darker sides directly into our homes. The murder of the actress Sharon Tate and three others at her home by Charles Manson and his followers, vividly reminded us of the depths of depravity which man can plumb. The death of Mary Jo Kopechne at Chappaquiddick Island and the inaction of Senator Edward Kennedy, proved that human imperfection lives within the rich and famous as easily as it does in ordinary men.

I recall the talk of free love and permissiveness from the Sixties and must admit it had passed me by. A movie called *Bob & Carol & Ted & Alice* made light of it all and although funny and risqué at the time, it's a tame advert for those self-professed wild times when seen today. A night a the dog stadium at the Bridge of Dee could be pretty wild for a gang of young lads but the stadium closed that year and we all had to look around for new deserving causes to donate our hard earned cash to.

Led by the Beatles a new generation of musicians had transformed the music world and that era of change culminated with half a million people at the Woodstock Rock Music Festival. My own music tastes had diversified to rock, pop, country, soul and I still loved the crooners. I loved my music to be easy on the ear and I wanted to hear the words, songs for me should always tell a story. The Beatles were my favourites but I still played Jerry Lee Lewis and could happily listen to the velvet tones of Brook Benton for hours. Eddie Cochran had blasted me into the Sixties with *Three Steps to Heaven* but Frank Sinatra brought me in for a beautifully smooth landing with My Way. How strange then that a decade of magical music should close out with two almost joke-like numbers, *Sugar Sugar* by the Archies and *Two Little Boys* by Rolf Harris.

I remembered as a child sitting by the radio as my mother did her ironing. I'd be sitting comfortably waiting for *Listen With Mother* and she'd be waiting to hear the latest episode of *Mrs Dale's Diary.* I'd long since grown out of the habit but Mum had stuck with Mrs Dale as the show was transformed into *The Dales* and she was so sad when the BBC decided to drop it. "Yes Mum," I told her, "The Times They are a Changing."

It would have been more than I could have wished for to have known what 1970 held in store for me. Yet before my own 'Love Story' hit the screens a marvellous summer of sport would unfold, home life would be turned upside down and a near disaster would turn into perhaps the greatest moment of the American space programme.

It was nearly three years since I had crossed the threshold of Greyfriars House and I still felt as if I was at school. Section leaders had replaced teachers and I was on the carpet again. I was now in the Enforcement Section and checked registration numbers with local authorities to verify operators of vehicles that might have been seen operating outwith their licence conditions. I thought it would be fun to know who operated the vehicle with the plate SID 139.

I duly despatched an enquiry form to a local authority in Northern Ireland. The reply never came and one morning I was summoned to the office of Mr Edwards, the senior examiner. My hopes of a promotion were immediately dashed as the enquiry form was thrown at me. I'm sure if this retired police officer had possessed them I'd have been handcuffed, "What the hell's this?"

he barked.

It really was nothing at all, a youthful prank, an innocent lark but a diligent colleague in the Province had gone to great pains to write personally to Mr Edwards and explain it would be twenty years before this number was released. This happy soul also recommended severe censure for the perpetrator of this breach of privilege. Censured I was, but I felt the only breach of privilege I'd ever indulged in was when it was my turn to draw the line in the morning signing in book. Many sleepy heads, including the boss, had been grateful that I always left it until 8.45am before drawing the dreaded red line and thus saved them the embarrassment of having to explain their lateness.

Just as well they didn't know about Denis Lefevre and I writing to Radio Peking and carrying Mao's little red book in our pockets. Not that we ever understood what the hell he was talking about, it was just a youthful fad. If the bosses had known I'm sure it would have been a case for MI5. My career highlight so far had been the day I had a pint too many in a lunchtime session at the Blue Lamp and returned to fall asleep in the gents toilet. I awoke just in time to escape with the cleaners before I was locked in for the night and I took this as a fateful warning, it was time to leave before I got stuck in a rut.

That summer I did just that, I resigned and with no particular plans or job in mind waited to see what turn my life would take next. I was beginning to understand that the fault lay in myself as far as my non-achievement at work was concerned. However a turn was coming in my life and it would have nothing to do with work. I would soon set off on a course that to this day has filled my life with more love, joy and happiness than any one man deserves. I still pinch myself to make sure it's all really happened and shed a tear when I think how blessed I've been.

Cup-tie McKay, Jack Nicklaus, Ian McCafferty or Pele? Sporting heroes were everywhere that year and two of them are the only athletes I would ever talk of, in terms of sporting greatness, in the same breath as Muhammad Ali but in 1970 Ian McCafferty was the man for me.

The Commonwealth Games were held in Edinburgh and having battled through a sea of personal woes and worries, McCafferty had been chosen to represent Scotland in the 5000 metres. The legendary Kenyan Kip Keino was favourite for gold and the Scot with the Brummie accent, Ian Stewart, was our hope for a medal. I can still see Stewart surge past Keino in the home straight and suddenly for a moment McCafferty was on his shoulder, he might win! It was not to be, he crossed the line half a stride behind Stewart but pipped Keino for the silver. I've never been able to forget the smile on his face as he crossed the line. Not a smile of satisfaction, not the half smile of disappointment but the smile of a man who had looked inside himself and for thirteen minutes and twenty three point four sublime seconds had unravelled all the confusion that dwelt within him. I wish he had won gold that day and that smile has always convinced me he knew he could have.

Brazil, World Football Champions 1970! Jairzinho, Tostao, Gerson, Rivelino, Carlos Alberto and the incomparable Pele, need one say more? The finest football team I've ever seen, inspired by the finest player. The Dons found an inspiration that year too but not in the form of a footballing genius. A journeyman professional who had arrived on a free transfer from Dundee, Derek 'Cup-tie' McKay, would become their talisman. His goals saw Aberdeen through against Falkirk and then Kilmarnock to meet Celtic in the Scottish Cup Final. The Celts once again met the Dons as European Cup finalists but hadn't reckoned on 'Cup-tie'. A flu bug had paved the way for his fairytale appearance in the cup run and there was no way the Hoops would bug him in the final. His two late goals, added to a Joe Harper penalty, finally saw the Dons lift the trophy 3-1 and 'Cup-tie' write his name forever in the Pittodrie hall of fame.

Tony Jacklin had led British golf into a new era the previous year by winning the Open and that summer added the US Open but all golfers of all ages will need to stake their claim for greatness against the deeds of one man, Jack Nicklaus. He fittingly won the Open at the home of golf that year but our hearts went out to Doug Saunders who allowed Jack back into the title race by agonisingly missing 'that' short put on the very last green. St Andrews was a superb stage for Nicklaus to remove his sweater at the last hole of the play-off and drive through the eighteenth green, his closing birdie was enough to end Saunders brave challenge. Jack Nicklaus was a man whose sporting mastery was matched and complemented by his sportsmanship.

Paula's arrival had been a wonderful gift to us all. Mum and Dad had possibly taken too much of a parental role, and Annie and Mum together under the same roof was always a volatile combination. Paula was much loved and like all babies gave the greatest love in return, unconditional. Since Xmas Annie had started going out with an old schoolmate, Robert Robb, and everyone seemed well content but things were soon to change.

Physically Robert and Annie were ill-matched, he well over six feet and she barely scraping in at five but mentally they had that same 'devil-may-care' attitude to the world, and who's to say they were wrong. The announcement that they planned to marry on the 6th of June that year wasn't heralded with joy in all quarters. Their plans to live with Bob's mum and dad until they got a place of their own seemed to fill my parents with a fear that they would 'lose' Paula. I was happy for them but sensed that Bob and I weren't on the same wavelength and guessed we'd always be relatives rather than pals.

The wedding day came and went, Annie, Bob and Paula moved on with their lives and suddenly Mum and Dad didn't want the big house at Girdleness Road any more. Poor Rogie was the first casualty; he'd not fit into their plans for a flat. Thankfully he went off to a place in the country and was as happy as Larry; I missed him and felt a bit lonely for other reasons too. Apart from Jake, all my mates were still on the other side of town and I never thought of Torry as home.

We were all thrilling to the disaster movie *Airport* when a real life disaster kept us on the edge of our seats. The latest American lunar mission, Apollo 13, encountered problems en-route to the moon and we were glued to our televisions as the tense drama unfolded. The enforced radio silences as they looped the moon and then prepared for re-entry only heightened concern for the crews' safety. Their ultimate safe landing was a fantastic achievement for NASA.

So then, disasters real and fictitious were the order of the day but I was on the brink of a moment, which would banish disaster from my life. Love was about to blossom for me. Love brings joy, some tears and the occasional heartache but since I met Vera Ann Fraser on the 18th of September 1970 my life has travelled on a disaster free upwards curve. That's with the exception of the odd moments when my 'daft little idiot' other self has escaped from the bottle, or should that be escaped with the help of the bottle and tried to sing the whole world a song and tell everyone how much he loves them.

I wasn't expecting a momentous weekend; I was well and truly skint! My career move from the MOT had landed me at John Cook & Son Ltd., Shipping Agents, at the bottom of Marischal Street. I was training as a shipping clerk, interesting enough, but £10 a week gross hardly put me in the international playboy class. One good point was that my boss, a gentleman called Eric Todd, knew his stuff, didn't want to keep it a secret and was easy to get along with. I actually felt I was learning something at last.

"It's nae problem Sid, I've a good wage this week wi my bonus and over-time. I'll stand you a few pints, we'll go down to the Nordic Lounge, get tickets for the Palace and hae a great night oot!"

That was Jackie Christie's offer to me that night. I owe him for it still and in a way for all the happiness and love that entered my life that night.

Jake and I bounced into the Palace, our spirits buoyed by a few pints. A new era was about to start for me but we'd caught the end of an old era at the Volunteer Arms on Queen Street, which was due to close its doors for the last time the next day. It was making way for road improvements and the building of the new police headquarters. Another pint at the Grill and a couple at the Nordic had got us in the mood. He was flush but we weren't keen to pay the prices they charged inside the Palace so one bottle of beer in the upstairs bar was our lot then it was downstairs to the dancing!

Neither of us had been setting the heather on fire in the love stakes. Jackie was still heart-broken after discovering that his wee girl at the baker's shop was giving a little more than free pies to a final year apprentice engineer. Two nights out with a girl from Garthdee who loved Elvis hardly labelled me as a future lothario but I'd had some success at the Boys Brigade! I once took the Beadle's daughter's best pal home on a Friday night after football. Now how many guys can claim to have trapped at the Boys Brigade? I put the fact that she ran inside as soon as we approached her house down to me wearing my Brigade hat all the way there. Yes, the old upsides down flowerpot style one with the company number on it! I must have looked like an inverted aspidistra preparing to suck her to death. Come in number five, your time is up!

We wandered down to the dance hall and joined the traditional march of young men. We all trudged around the dance floor, hands in pockets, watching the girls doing the traditional shuffle dance around their handbags. You always knew if Spider and the Torry Mob were in, they would walk around the dance floor in the opposite direction from everyone else and there'd always be a couple of idiots who rose to the bait and proved that young men carry bigger metaphorical handbags than the girls real ones.

Failure had not diminished our optimism and Jackie and I had devised a new approach to asking girls up to dance. We started with the best looking and worked our way down; better to be refused by a princess than an ugly sister. This method only proved that the girls had us firmly in the frog category. Our record was thirty-seven straight refusals at the Beach Ballroom one Friday night. The placed was packed that night and we knew it would take a while to reach our own level. Mind you the pleasure of a dance with a princess now and then more than made up for all the knockbacks.

I saw a princess that night. She had long brown hair, was wearing a red mini dress and had a smile so bright that I thought the house lights had been switched back on. The band were having a break; not many people danced at the interval. Desmond Dekker and the Aces boomed out over the sound system, *You Can Get It If You Really Want.* I did. I asked, she danced, I asked again, she stayed, the world changed.

When I asked to see her home I wasn't sure what she'd say but fate took a hand. She'd no money in her handbag and needed sixpence to get her coat from the cloakroom. No problem, I had sixpence—or at least Jackie had! How could she refuse my gallant offer to redeem her coat and escort her home to Girdlestone Place in Torry? We walked hand in hand down South College Street, across the Chain Brig, up over the Mound and down to her house.

She lived in the top floor flat at 6e and as we stood downstairs in the lobby one stolen kiss hadn't quite proved the key to her heart. How could I persuade her to see me again? Fate again took a hand but my recollections are dim. My back was to the tenement door when Vera's mum stormed into the building. She'd been out at the Railway Club with Vera's dad. I would learn in the years to come that she could be a bit of a bull in a china shop but when the door struck the back of my head the lights went out.

Kismet doesn't lend a hand too often in this life and when it does you must take advantage. I was not averse to playing the sympathy card and through the fog I remember Vera agreeing to see me on the Sunday afternoon. Strangely enough my biggest hug that night was from her mum, who was so sorry she'd almost knocked me out. Little did she know I'd been completely knocked out two hours earlier. Yes the night I met my future wife I had stars in my eyes!

I was a little late for our Sunday meeting but just in time to see that long brown hair set off down Mansfield Road. I ran for all I was worth, touched her shoulder and as she turned and smiled I'm sure I saw a tear in the corner of her eye. Dressed in red trousers and a red and white poncho she was lovelier than I remembered, we walked and talked for ages and best of all we laughed a lot. That special something we all long for happened for us that afternoon. Within a week Vera and I would tell one another we were in love!

We were still both kids and impetuous, headstrong, often just plain daft, in a hurry and in love. Life seems to go at one hundred miles an hour when you're in love and in spite of parents and friends telling us there was plenty time we wanted to be together as often as possible. We became officially engaged on Christmas Day and our party a few days earlier took place at the old Railway Club in Albyn Place. Vera's dad Stan was a train driver and he and her mum Lilian arranged everything. Grannie Thomson was there but my granddad was very ill and couldn't make it. I took Vera on stage towards the end of the night and serenaded her with my best version of *They Try To Tell Us We're Too Young*! There's no doubt now that we were and how we held together through the anger, heartache and pain that was soon to follow only shows how much in love we were. I took hope from the title of my favourite Canned Heat number, *Let's Work Together*. To the amazement of many all those years ago we did but for many years it was an uphill struggle.

Rolls round the dance floor, long hair in a mess.
Is stirred by the girl in the red mini dress.
Suggestive the name of the record they play.
Hands held home together, can see her next day.
Comes dressed in a poncho with long hair so fine.
They whisper and cuddle with no sense of time.
In these fleeting moments his love sprang to life.
Knew then that he'd always want her as his wife.

Moving into 1971, I was happier than I'd ever been in my life. I loved my mum and dad and had immediately formed a great relationship with Stan, Lil and Vera's sister Lilian. Vera and I were happy as long as we were together, so where did all the anger and pain come from? As a parent now myself I can understand the fears and as, I hope, a better man now than I was then I can see where my own shortcomings contributed.

The musical year had started with Clive Dunn and a choir of kids telling us why and how much everyone loves their granddad. A sad coincidence saw my own grandfather die that year, his legacy of so many children and grandchildren would keep his memory alive in this world for many years to come. Vera and I had a favourite tune that year, *Hey Girl Don't Bother Me* by The Tams but I'd have been mightily disappointed if she didn't for many years to come.

We were dreaming dreams and making plans to live them. Looking back through the mists we had nothing but love knows no obstacles and always believes the pumpkin will turn into a gilded carriage. Vera made £9 a week working for Finnie's the jeweller in George Street, which, added to my £10, didn't let us plan too many fancy dreams. We started to plan and save for the future and decided that I'd need to find a job that paid more—easier said than done perhaps. Those plans seemed to annoy my mum and dad; perhaps they were still struggling to come to terms with the distance that marriage for Annie had put between them and Paula. Vera was all I wanted though and the harder they found that to understand, the more difficult life became.

Danny Stroud was Managing Director of Cook's and on one of my first days there he sent me out to get him a fry of fish and pressed a £1 note into my hand. He didn't say where I should get it, so I wandered over the old Regent Bridge and walked into the first fish house I came to on Regent Road. The workers all ignored me until one lad stepped forward and glowered at me, "Aye?" he mumbled questioningly.

"I've been sent to get a fry for Mr Stroud, the Managing Director of John Cook & Sons." I clarified.

He shrugged his shoulders, whispered something to a colleague and they came to the conclusion that Mr Stroud must be a friend of their own boss. I did nothing to dissuade them from this reasoning. Having established Danny's importance they proceeded to roll up two of the biggest parcels of fish I'd ever seen, one of white fish and one of smoked haddocks. Time to play the sympathy card again I mused. In my best poor little office boy voice I asked pleadingly if I might have a wee fry for myself, for which of course I'd be willing to pay. A much less bountiful parcel was wrapped and handed to me and my offer to pay was refused—they couldn't charge a friend of their boss!

Danny was with Ramsay Pirie, a fellow director, when I returned to the office. I slipped the small parcel into my desk drawer and then tapped on his door. "Well done Sidney, there's enough fish for us both here Ramsay." he boomed.

I was waved aside as I put my hand in my pocket to return his pound. "Keep the change Sidney, there can't be much out of a pound for all that." he concluded.

I did nothing to dissuade him from this reasoning and for the brief spell I worked for Danny this handy little bonus came my way every week. But it was neither a lucrative enough or reliable enough emolument to deflect us from our design that I would need to secure a better job.

Here were two kids planning to build a future when one of the cornerstones of my youth was laid to waste, they demolished the Casino in Wales Street that year. Oh the happy memories I had of nights there with Mum,

Dad and Annie. A penny for each one of them would have solved our cash crisis in the blink of an eye.

Vera liked the movies too and we went often, she loved to snuggle up during a horror movie so I became the biggest horror movie fan in town. Stanley Kubrick's *A Clockwork Orange* was released but in all the years of bans and controversy that followed I've only ever seen the first twenty minutes, which I thought were rubbish. So I guess I'll never know what all the fuss was about. I could watch again and again Richard Attenborough's faultlessly chilling portrayal of the murderer John Christie in *10 Rillington Place*. I still shiver when I consider the fate of John Hurt's fatally naïve Timothy Evans.

Naivety can cause so much heartache and Vera and I fell headlong into its clutches in February when we discovered she was expecting our baby in November. We'd made confused, muddled attempts to have Vera go on the pill after, as two innocents, we'd first made love together. We both, perhaps thoughtlessly, welcomed the prospect of parenthood but the admission to our families and the expected fallout from it filled us with terror. I broke the news to my parents who seemed quite calm; its different for the boy's family I'm sure. Vera chose to tell her mum on her own and although the sparks of recrimination flew, the same feelings of protection that my own mother had shown for Annie shone through from Lil too. Telling Vera's dad was going to be the hard bit, and Lil decided we four would go to the Golden Tee and break the news to him over a drink.

Stanley Fraser was a hard working, hard drinking railway engine driver and very much the king of his own castle. He'd a wicked sense of humour, always gave you the impression he was a tough guy and proved it to me on several occasions. Most of all he had a fierce sense of pride in his family and although I'd planned how to tell him, I was trembling as I walked back to the table with the tray of drinks. In typical fashion Lil charged straight in, as I laid the drinks on the table I reeled as I heard her blurt out, "We might as well tell you now dad, Vera's pregnant!"

The crashing blow to my jaw never arrived and Stan proved in that moment he was a far better man than I'd given him credit for. I loved her but she was still his beautiful little girl and the news had probably just broken his heart. He looked straight into my eyes, told me to sit down, took a sip of his whisky and quietly asked, "What are you planning to do?"

What we were planning to do was get married on the 1st of May. Vera and I could stay with my mum and dad until we sorted ourselves out. We didn't have another drink; it wasn't a celebration. I walked with them back to Girdlestone Place but didn't go in. They obviously needed to talk and somehow I felt there would be no place for me in their discussion.

Just after the turn of the year Mum and Dad had exchanged houses with a young couple with a wee bairn and so along with them I'd moved to a second floor flat at 135 Victoria Road. Of an evening Vera and I might pop down to the old Seaview Lounge in Sinclair Road, strictly soft drinks for her. The views over the harbour from the lounge were superb until oil arrived and all you could see were storage tanks. On two occasions I came home and visited the loo and watched spellbound as a tiny mouse scurried around the bathroom floor before disappearing somewhere behind the sink. Mum and dad scoffed when I told them and blamed a snifter too many at the Seaview for my hallucinations. The interloper was exposed in dramatic style one evening when Vera and I had stayed in to watch the telly. Mum had gone into the kitchen to make a pot of tea whilst dad and I had been left in stitches by the *Two Ronnies*. Vera's piercing screams from the bathroom could have come straight from the torture chamber in the *Pit and the Pendulum* and her ashen white face as she escaped into the living room made her a dead ringer for Morticia from the *Addams Family*.

"A moose! A moose! A moose! There's a moose in the toilet!" she shrieked wide-eyed.

I knew that! The hole was traced, successfully blocked and we never saw the wee fella again. I do recall being awakened in the middle of the night some weeks later by manic cries of fear from somewhere within the building. Dad was all for a torch and frying pan investigation but as I rolled over to resume my slumbers I allayed his fears in a drowsy slur, "Go back to sleep dad, it'll just be the moose."

Vera didn't often phone me at work and I could tell by her voice that something was wrong. She'd felt ill first thing and her mum had told her to stay in bed as she was having a bad bout of morning sickness. Now she said she felt very sore and had sharp pains in her tummy. I told Eric I'd need to go home and caught a cab from work to Girdlestone. Vera was in tears when I got there; she'd been bleeding a little and was so upset. We really didn't know what to do but I'd asked the cab to hold on and we got him to take us down to my mum's. She'd gone out shopping!

One of the things we'd done as we prepared for the wedding was to change Vera to the same doctor as me. Vera was still hurting and I was both useless and scared at the same time. I phoned the surgery from the shop downstairs and explained what was happening. To their and his credit Dr Simpson was at the house within the hour. How different times were then; I actually left the room as he lay Vera on the living room couch to examine her. Neither his face nor his matter of fact voice betrayed the sorrowful news he was about to deliver. The words, when they arrived, were a bombshell, "I fear you may be miscarrying, I'll need to get you to hospital."

He popped out to a phone to make arrangements and I sat and held Vera's hand. She cried in sorrow and pain and I cried because I had told her I loved her and now couldn't take any of this hurt away from her.

Only one month after becoming pregnant, Vera did miscarry, and after two distressing days in hospital I took her home in a taxi. We drove over Anderson Drive and I held her in my arms all the way home but we never spoke a word. In the days that followed there would be lots of words, mostly from parents and it all seemed to point to the fact that we were now somehow 'off the hook,' we could make new plans and we didn't need to get married. They may well have been right and their advice was certainly coming from the heart but I couldn't agree. I had adored Vera from the first moment I saw her, and for me there was no turning back now; troubled waters lay ahead on life's ocean. I just wish someone then had put an arm around our shoulders and tried to mend broken hearts.

Life often sends you to bed with a tear in your eye and wakes you up with a smile on your face next morning. We were trying to get back to normal and a good laugh was certainly overdue. Lil was a cook at Tullos Primary School and when the mood took her, she'd do a lot of baking at home. I was spending every evening at Vera's and overstaying my welcome into the wee small hours most nights.

On such an occasion I was sent home bearing gifts for my mum and dad, a bag of Lil's home bakes. It was a cold March night and a trip to the smallest room seemed advisable before I set off into the stormy darkness. Lil obviously wanted to get off to bed and rapped impatiently on the door three times, telling me to hurry up. What no-one knew was that I had well and truly snagged John Thomas in the zip of my trousers and was performing heroics in muffling my screams as I tried to extricate my little friend from that veritable bear-trap.

Mission accomplished I tucked the bloodied wee man back in, manfully said goodnight to the ladies and limped off into the bitter gloom clutching my bag of bakes. Enter PC Plod! Halfway down Mansfield Road the intriguing site of a man walking like a pregnant penguin, wearing a Balaclava...it was Stan's; Lil had insisted I wear it because it was so cold...and carrying a bag of swag had alerted the local crime busters.

"Excuse me sir, where are you going?" asked the constable, rolling down the window as the patrol car pulled alongside me.

"Home." I grimaced.

"A little late isn't it?" he enquired.

"For me or you?" I moaned.

"Do you always wear that Balaclava?" he quizzed.

"Only when it's cold." I gasped.

"What's in the bag?" he challenged.

"Baking for my mum from my girlfriend's mum." I groaned "Would you like a cake?"

"No thank you sir, get off home now." He said contentedly.

The, until now, silent driver chose this moment to display his obvious intention of pursuing a career in the CID, "One more thing sir, why are you walking like that?" he pondered.

By now I was almost bent double in pain and feared my expletive peppered explanation and the offer to drop my kegs and show them the disfigured Parson's Nose would land me in hot water but the window silently rolled back up and Fancy Smith and Bert Lynch stole silently off into the night.

There was pressure from all sides as our wedding day approached. My mum and dad had joined the 'don't get married lobby' and the more they all pushed, the more I dug my heels in. Vera was piggy in the middle and perhaps I pushed too hard and never gave her the chance to make her own choice for the future. Did I really leave her with only; it's them or me? The whole business got so difficult that I moved out and went to stay with my sister Annie.

Annie and Bob had quickly added to their family and the arrival of another lovely daughter, Annette, the image of her mother, had saw them move on to a place of their own, a flat at 2d Manor Walk. They had three bedrooms and no objection to taking me on as a lodger. It would take the heat out of things for me and the number thirteen bus ran door to door from Vera's to Annie's, so I ended up really just sleeping there.

What a pair, they were always skint, always waiting up for a fag when I came home at night, and never scared to put two fingers up to the world. Consequences are the glue that holds things together, as long as we all fear them. Annie and Bob didn't give a shit about consequences and lived life their own way. I couldn't do it but in a strange way I often admired them for their cheek. They were never cheekier than when I came home to get ready for a Friday night out with Vera just two weeks after I moved in.

"Where have you put all my gear Annie?" I asked.

"Oh I'm sorry," she apologised "there was a wee problem!"

That wee problem turned out to be a tick mannie who wouldn't take no for an answer. Annie's solution to get the money he demanded quickly was to pawn all my stuff, pay the bill and oh aye, buy a carryout with what was left! The consequences for me never entered her head. The annoying thing was I just couldn't get annoyed about it. We sat and laughed, when Bob came home from work he fell off his chair laughing, life with them was like that. Vera even came to Annie's that night and the four of us polished off the carryout and laughed till we cried. It cost me most of next week's wages to redeem my gear and I never got the cash back from them.

A new job for me was still our main priority; even I knew that as things stood we could only hope to build a house of straw on pillars of sand. I had everything crossed as I walked into a bed and breakfast establishment on Osbourne Place one cold rainy night. Those days saw the beginning of Aberdeen's oil boom and I had responded to an advert in the *Evening Express* for a Shipping Manager with an International Freight Forwarding Company soon to open in Aberdeen.

"Hi, I'm Dave Oakes." A guy not much older than myself beckoned me into a room so dark, I could barely see him when he closed the door.

I answered a few questions for him, filled in a few import and export customs forms in the half-light and then he told me of Rankin Kuhn Freight Ltd., a wholly owned subsidiary of BP. His almost immediate offer of the job and his enquiry as to my expected salary stunned me so much that he must have mistaken my silence for a bargaining technique. I had still not replied when he quietly added, "If £1200 a year sounds okay to you we've got a deal."

This guy was having me on, that was £23 a week, my silence continued. Finally I barely managed to shake his hand and clinch the deal. He wanted me to start work the week before I got married; what a present, wait till I told Vera!

Rankin Kuhn Freight Ltd would employ me until 1978 when I finally had to escape from the 'must do' culture of the oil boom. Sleeping with pagers and fawning over Americans with strange names like Leeroy Klingelsmith was not for me and I simply walked away from it all. Perhaps just in time as the firm perished not long after that, sold off into oblivion by BP after, it was rumoured, some naughty scandals at head office.

There was cash to be made there and those years allowed me to work all the hours God sent and provide a good life for Vera and the kids. I also discovered that I was more of an unsupervised office boy than a Shipping Manager and that Dave would have gone to £1500 a year that first night, if I'd been able to speak. Dear Eric Todd had been one of the other candidates who were unlucky that night but he must have taught me well. They certainly expanded during their years in Aberdeen and guys like Londoner Mike Isbell and an old hockey team-mate from school, Bill Lints, would arrive and drive forward that expansion. A troubling episode, of telling a young lad called John Burr that he was out of a job, proved to me I didn't have the killer instinct required for management and I'm so happy I've been made that way.

Vera and I have been married now for over thirty four years and I know that she and I have had many days to remember in that time. If I could choose to change one day, it would be the 1st of May 1971. She deserved so much more than I could give and settled just for me.

Things hadn't changed with the families but we had decided to go ahead with the wedding. My new job had given us hope for the future; we were even talking about renting a flat! In the meantime Mum and Dad had said we could have my old room at theirs but Vera's mum and dad had said if the wedding went ahead they wouldn't be there. In the end it all turned into a sad shambles, but our young hearts never stopped believing that in the end it would all work out well for us.

We married at the Church of Scotland on Victoria Road with Vera's sister Lilian as her bridesmaid and Jackie as my best man. When the Reverend Swinburne began the ceremony my dad was standing at Vera's side to give her away. Stan and Lil had relented and turned up but too late and stood at the back. I always pray that what Vera and I made of our life together made up to them in some way for that moment. My mother didn't come at all and that's a hurt I've lived with and still can't understand to this day.

Vera was beautiful in her matching navy and gold dress and coat set. The coat's high white collar set off her lovely face but oh my, those were hard moments for her. All she had done was fall in love with me and all that our parents and I had done was make this the hardest day of her life. She smiled at me as we took our vows but her heart was Crying in the Chapel.

Once upon a time doesn't always start as it should,
The search may be in vain for a fairy that's good.
If ever a princess stood lost and alone,
It was there in the springtime of seventy-one.

But a princess is special whatever the time,
She made this confused day the finest of mine.
If she longed for the silk and the satin and chic,
From her lovely bright face no sadness did peek.

Could I ever be richer or find words to say,
In my heart how I felt for her on that day.
Could I ever be worthy of love such as this,
So strong and yet pleased with a hug and a kiss.

No pictures for memories in future she'll find,
But the sight of her then is burned in my mind.
If I tried every moment till this world's last day,
What her love gave me then I can never repay.

I have forever admired Lilian for standing by her sister that day. She and Jackie joined us for a meal at the Yangtze River Chinese restaurant on Bridge Street and then we two kids quietly made our way home as man and wife. Vera fell asleep in my arms and as the streetlights filtered through the curtains I glimpsed the ten-pound note I had laid on our bedside table. It was all we had in the world and I cried tears of shame that I'd made such a botch-up of things. I vowed then that we'd turn that £10 into a good life for us and, when they came along, our children, a life we would all be proud of. It was the beginning of a wonderful journey that was never easy but always happy.

When love motivates your thoughts and actions, things don't always turn out as you'd hoped. I like to think that's where we all were back then and in time Vera and I would rebuild bridges with our parents. One thing however was lost forever for us both; that final flicker of child-like innocence was extinguished and we lived our daily lives with a more cynical view of everything and everyone!

So much had happened in such a short time that 1971 almost became a year where everyday events passed me by completely. Four years after devaluation came decimalisation, and boy did that push up the cost of living! My mother turned forty and my new job meant getting a phone installed for the first time. Rankin Kuhn were paying the bills for all usage and Mum was more impressed than anyone. She saw it as some sort of status symbol. What would she have made of the Internet? Our first number was 24089 and the Aberdeen code then was 0224. That phone became a real pain as it meant I couldn't ever get away from work. They didn't unplug in those days and for some reason Mum couldn't tell a lie on the phone—"Yes he's here, I'll just get him for you!"

Internment arrived in Northern Ireland as violence escalated on all fronts. The Provisionals intensified their campaign and people like me could only look on in disbelief as pain and suffering rained down on all sectors of the troubled Province. Many years later I would have the opportunity to visit Belfast and during my stay there, found the people to be amongst the friendliest I had ever spent time with. I had no need to know the political beliefs or religious persuasion of the grand folk I met.

It had taken Aberdeen over twenty years to bring the Scottish Cup back to the city but as a huge fire ripped through the main stand it needed the heroic actions of local firemen to prevent Pittodrie becoming the final resting place of the famous trophy. Eddie Turnbull shocked the fans by heading off to manage Hibs but Arsenal's double winning season in England was the football story of the year.

Muhammad Ali who had known only victory in the ring encountered defeat for the first time at the hands of Joe Frazier. Like all great sportsmen he proved he could treat those two impostors just the same. His story was only just beginning and is even a great man not more of a man when he loses that aura of invincibility with good grace? When I think of great athletes and try to place them in order of merit I imagine a race along Union Street starting from the Castlegate. Muhammad Ali has just passed Rose Street heading for the finishing line at Holburn Junction, Jack Nicklaus is just beyond the Music Hall and the rest of the runners are huddled together as they approach Union Terrace.

Lee Trevino waved his golf clubs like a magician's wand to win the US Open, the Open and the Canadian Open all in the space of a few months. We all took the Birkdale runner-up to our hearts; a hat-doffing gentleman from the Far East affectionately called 'Mr Lu'. At Muirfield a year later Trevino would win the Open again and break Jacklin's heart in the process, I don't think Tony was ever the same player again.

Scotland had a world champion in motor racing legend Jackie Stewart, but for me it was our Celtic neighbours, the Welsh, who provided the years' sporting highlights. In a golden age for Welsh Rugby Union they claimed the

Grand Slam that year. The sublime skills and artistry of Barry 'King' John, Gareth Edwards and J P R Williams, to name but a few, are a never to be forgotten memory of sporting wizardry.

Television could still sharply remind us of the despair and hardship that was the lot of so many in our society. An often far too brilliantly realistic performance by Patricia Hayes brought *Edna the Inebriate Woman* to the small screen. Heartstrings were tugged and torn as the homeless alcoholic struggled to cling to her identity with her drink-fuelled cry "I am not the vagrant." I'd seen so many like her and had simply forgotten that they were people just like me.

On a cold winter night Vera and I went with my mum and dad to the Playhouse Cinema. I was a happily married man now and no longer had room in my life for another woman. I had stayed faithful to the lovely Raquel from her dinosaur days, through her *Fantastic Voyage*, agreed she was the *Biggest Bundle of Them All*, never quite understood *Fathom*, joined her cowboy bands in *Bandolero* and *100 Rifles*, then envied Frank Sinatra as she got him hot under the collar in *The Lady in Cement. Hannie Caulder* was our swansong and I didn't even mind queuing for an ice cream for Vera as Raquel launched into one of her big scenes. Yes there was only one girl in my life now!

Grown up days come quickly,
Life's full of twists and turns.
The tears that choke so thickly,
The smile so bright it burns.
If love is ever given
Grasp it with both hands.
Love makes life worth living,
Embrace its golden strands.

Immortality and a bus ride to Mastrick.

Music is the drum that often beats out the rhythm of our lives and a single song may be the trigger for a flood of memories, both happy and sad. How fitting that, in the summer of 1972, Johnny Nash was high in the charts with *I Can See Clearly Now.* That was exactly how I felt about life right then, Vera and I were planning our future and dreaming dreams to last a lifetime.

Will this be a long adventure?
Will it stand the test of time?
Will she love me for a moment?
Will she love me for all time?
Two young children now together.
Two young children on their own.
Two young children building rainbows.
Two young children with no home.

I had settled into my new job, the money was good and Vera and I were wondering if we could rent a flat of our own. Living with my mum and dad was fine but you always felt in the way. The old story of two women in the same kitchen being a recipe for disaster was proving to hold more than a ring of truth. My mum wasn't the easiest to get along with and it made things very difficult for Vera.

If we could but see the future, would we balance out the cost,
Of the heartache known too early, or of love and laughing lost.
So confused appears the tender heart of this young wife of mine,
One day safe with her own family, next day left alone with mine.
Should I have been aware and helped her more in this hard time,
Could I have seen each heartache and drawn a quicker line?
If I failed her in these early days I can only say,
Her face every morning made each day a better day.
But it was never all gloom in that first year we had,
A thousand happy times for each one ever sad.
From one home to another we travelled man and wife,
Looking forward to our own home and soon the gift of life.

A piece of wonderful news had carried us into the New Year, Vera was expecting our baby in mid-June and we prayed that all would be well this time. It changed our plans about a flat though. Vera wouldn't be working with a baby to look after, so our finances would be stretched. There was no way we'd all squeeze into mum and dad's, so we put our name on the council waiting list and prayed for a healthy baby and a home to love it in.

The news was all we wanted, what we hoped we'd hear,
But thoughts were fraught with worry and not a little fear.
Once before the talk of babies had brightened up our lives,
And with no warning disappointment had wounded like a knife.
These were the careful days, a slowly passing time,
Time to wait and watch and worry that it all would turn out fine.

We had a few problems to solve but all were really just a swathe of life's rich tapestry and the solving of them a learning curve in our married life. Around us a sea of troubles seemed to have swamped the world. A million people were unemployed and industrial strife left none but the candlemakers happy as we suffered a series of power cuts.

A plague of terrorism had struck worldwide and none stunned us more than the atrocity committed by Black September guerrillas at the Munich Olympics. Eleven Israeli athletes were killed, nine of them during an elaborate rescue operation within the Olympic village.

Northern Ireland was nearing anarchy in the aftermath of the Bloody Sunday incident in the Bogside district of Derry. Bitter lines would be drawn after British paratroops opened fire on demonstrators, leaving thirteen people dead or dying. Cover-ups, allegations and counter-allegations of blame would merely fan the flames of the Troubles. Over thirty years later they have caused over 3000 deaths.

I could put all bad thoughts out of my mind with a glance at Vera. In these her sparkling days there was a glow and loveliness about her you could almost touch. She and the dawn of motherhood went well together. If love needs an anchor, she was for me a strong line holding firm in deep, deep waters. It was a time of uncertainty that tugged us through all the emotions of little panics and false alarms and in the end our tiny miracle was going to need a helping hand.

A blue Vespa scooter caused more than just a little panic and alarm for me and my dad one Sunday afternoon. It seems funny now but oh how foolish then! Dad had made a tilt at the oil boom, working in Vetco's pipeyard, but a little too much cash to spend had proved more of a curse than a blessing. With more than a little encouragement from Mum he'd found himself a job as a groundsman at the City Hospital in Urquhart Road. He would indeed settle there and I'm certain the family atmosphere of the place helped him over the difficult times that lay ahead when he lost my mum.

His pride and joy was a blue Vespa scooter that he used for getting to and from work. On the Sunday in question we'd gone out for a spin to Cove and I'd plagued him for a chance to take control. Eventually he relented and my five minute crash course on throttle use, gear change and braking saw us set off home down the old coast road towards the Bay of Nigg. It all seemed simple enough, as we approached the bay I was opening her up like a veteran but the term crash course was about to prove somewhat prophetic.

The old road simultaneously sweeps right and drops sharply as it reaches the bay and my father's shrill cry of, "Slow down!" was lost on the wind as we rounded the bend.

My lack of experience at the helm was compounded by the fact that dad had now placed a vice-like bear hug around my waist and continued to cry, " Stop! Stop! Stop!" in an increasingly falsetto voice.

As we left the road I spread my legs wide apart in an attempt to maintain balance and emitted a series of farts as we bounced along a boulder-strewn ditch which ran parallel to the road. Vespa scooters are just not designed for moto-cross terrain but on we hurtled. Disaster now seemed inevitable and I closed my eyes as a huge boulder loomed ahead. My unconscious decision to maintain our high speed and the boulder's smooth, sloping surface proved to be our salvation. We rose eagle-like from the stone, soared through the air and performed a perfect landing back on the tarmac road surface!

"Stop, for fuck's sake stop!" I heard from behind and remembered that dad was still holding on for dear life behind. In my state of shock I could only laugh at how silly it sounds to swear in a high-pitched voice.

" I will if you let me go dad, I can't move my arms." was my stifled, re-lieved reply.

We never went out together on that scooter again, I've never been on any type of motorcycle since and within months dad was using the bus to get to and from work again.

That was certainly more excitement than they were generating at Pit-todrie right then. Jimmy Bonthrone had led us to the 'dizzy heights' of a Drybrough Cup win over Celtic but firstly Martin Buchan and then King Joey were allowed to head south, it was hard to see where the Dons were heading. Rangers finally broke their European trophy duck and at the third time of asking in a Cup Winners Cup Final they clinched the cup by beating Moscow Dynamo 3-2. Yet another flawed sporting genius stepped on the world stage that year when Alex 'Hurricane' Higgins became world snooker champion.

Flawed thinking may, in hindsight, have carried the day in parliament as the House of Commons voted to give the Heath Government the powers to negotiate Britain's entry into Europe. Decades of disagreement seem to have followed and the only sure achievement seems to have been that we've thrown millions of the taxpayer's good money after bad. The EEC appears to have become a ravenous, bottomless money pit and for more than thirty years we've continued to feeds its insatiable appetite.

Vera didn't seem to be in a hurry to bring the new member of our family into this world. Her mid-June date came and went and so did the next fort-night! I would receive the key to the door that year but the key to mother-hood for Vera would need a helping hand to turn it. My favourite movie that year was *Deliverance* and the coincidental title made me smile in the months ahead.

Sunday the 2nd of July was to be the day. Vera and I made our way to the Queen's Cross Maternity Home just before 6pm and the staff were going to help her make the final push. The first push was the one that I thought Vera needed the biggest help with! Vera wanted me to be with her at the birth and so our vigil began. By midnight absolutely nothing had happened, Vera was comfy in bed and baby was still as comfy where he or she had been for the last nine and a half months! By almost 2am the nurses offered me a snooze in their basement rest room and I did manage to grab a couple of hours on the wee couch.

Vera started her contractions mid-morning but seemed more likely to pro-duce a record for going through cylinders of 'Gas-in-air,' which helped ease the pain, than a baby. The time, when it came, was special, amazing and in the end a little funny. In the attic floor delivery room I held Vera's hand, mopped her brow and quietly added to the encouragement that all the staff were giving. Ever so slowly a perfect, beautiful, bright orange baby girl en-tered this world at 1206 on Monday 3rd July 1972, weighing in at 8lbs 1 3/4ozs. Vera held her briefly and so did I, we both marvelled at how perfect she was and how clean the whole of her beautiful little orange body was. The midwife explained that she was so clean because she'd come into the world so slowly and the orange was a mild case of jaundice, quite common in newborn babies.

I kissed Vera, thanked all the staff at least twice and turned to gaze again at my beautiful daughter as she lay in the tiny cot they had placed her in. I was totally bemused when I heard a nurse say, "Just one more push Mrs Robertson!"

The thought of twins raced through my mind as I turned to be at Vera's side once more but how naïve could I be. It was the placenta and that mo-ment said much about both Vera and I back then. Here we were, mother and father, but still with so much to learn. A team of brave men had returned that very weekend from the barren outcrop of Rockall after fitting a navigational beacon. Our newly born daughter had just lit up a beacon of love that would burn bright for the rest of our lives.

We called her Leanne, movies and me, I had loved the name of a character in a Bobby Darin western, *Gunfight at Abilene* and more important Vera had liked it too. The name was lovely and we'd changed the spelling to make it a little more unusual. It wasn't a common name back then but all these years on it is very popular. Leanne had been born in the same room as I had almost twenty-one years earlier. What a wonderful coincidence! Oh the feeling of ecstasy, the sheer joy of it, no-one could have possibly done this before. Yet everybody knows just how special this everyday occurrence is, Leanne you wee cracker...thank you Vera!

In all of the time, eighteen hours or more,
Not once did my darling complain.
Of course I panicked once and ran out the door,
Crying, "Please fill the gas cylinder again."
As my thoughts raced round and round in my mind,
There was no way I could ever express.
To say how I felt no words could I find,
But I knew this was our love's success.
And I picture it still with senses amazed,
Such a perfect young girl with a bright orange face.
And there as on wife and daughter I gazed,
I knew that my world had been showered with grace.

I finally managed to get to a phone and let everyone know, they all seemed as happy as I did. One thing does stick in my mind and makes me think how times have changed. Mike Isbell had arrived from London to look after Rankin Kuhn's expansion and was now my boss. We'd moved from my tiny office in Canal Road to the perceived hub of the oil industry, the Aberdeen Service Company base in Regent Road. As I gave Mike my happy news I couldn't believe that he tore me off a strip for not coming back to work that day. I was back at work the next morning. From immortality to normality in less than twenty-four hours, bosses would never get away with that today!

So began our parental learning days, feeding, nappy changing, winding, bottle warming and lots and lots of kissing. Vera and I took turns on the night shift feeds and as often as not mum and dad would appear just to have a wee look too. *The Black and White Minstrels* and *Saturday Variety* were vying for the Saturday night telly audience on Leanne's first weekend at home but there was only one attraction for us and we were glued to her full time!

Leanne was all we thought of for a long while, grannies and granddads spoiled her to bits, Lilian was especially taken with her and saw her as often as she could. Annie and Bob were happy for us and by the end of the year they would add another bonnie lass, Corrie, to their own family. We'd been staying with my mum and dad for over a year and the strain of us all in the wee flat was beginning to tell. We couldn't afford our own flat now; the oil boom was pushing the price of rented accommodation out of reach. We were hopeful of a council flat because we now had Leanne but as yet we'd had no offer. Vera's mum and dad stepped into the breach and offered for us to stay with them until we got a council house, in hindsight it was the best solution for us all and probably saved any of us falling out again. So it was off to

Girdlestone Place for the three of us.

Stan and Lil were good to us when we were there and to be fair to my mum and dad they probably just needed and deserved a little of their own space back. I was a godsend to Stan and Lilian; Lil's cooking was notorious for its inconsistency. One meal would turn out cordon bleu and the next would be like eating a two-day old Aitken's rowie. Lil and I got on well together and they knew I wouldn't do anything to upset her. The dodgy meals always appeared when she'd had a dram or two and I'd dutifully polish mine off. Those two rogues would shovel all there's onto my plate as soon as her back was turned.

"Eat up Sid, a'body else is finished," she'd shout. I would and she'd fill my plate again! I piled on the pounds in our brief spell at Girdlestone but I never hurt her feelings.

The letter that marked the beginning of real family life for the three of us arrived in the post one cold November morning. I took the day off to head to St Nicholas House and there we were offered a flat at 5, Deveron Road in Mastrick. I rushed home to tell Vera and arrived just as Stan and Lil were coming home from their early shifts. It was a freezing cold day and we convinced Vera to stay at home with Leanne. We three then set off on the long bus journey to Mastrick. As the 22 bus climbed Mid Stocket Road a heavy shower of snow started to fall and this suddenly didn't seem the most welcoming spot in town.

The flat was a middle floor two bed-roomed one in a six-apartment block. The stairs were clean and tidy, the flat inside seemed nice enough, so I let Stan, Lil and necessity convince me that this was the place for my family to set up home. Vera and I got up to see it together a couple of evening's later; at £18 a month for the rent it was affordable, she was happy, it would be ours...Vera, Leanne and me.

We had planned for this day and moved in little more than a week later. A pal of mine, Mike Elrick, worked for M&D Furnishings on King Street and had stored a few bits and pieces there for us. He also re-upholstered my mum and dad's old three-piece suite for a tenner and got us a good deal at the shop on some bedroom furniture. We bought a beautiful old walnut-boarded double bed from a lady who advertised in the Evening Express. She wanted £10 but took pity on a young married couple and let us have it for £8. We pushed the boat out and got Ewen & Co to lay new vinyl in the bathroom and carpets in the living room, hall and bedrooms, the tiles already in the kitchen seemed okay. We were so impressed with Ewen's that we've rarely bought furniture or floor coverings from any other firm from that day to this.

You need a wee help now and then and at work we'd been passing a fair bit of work to a local removal firm, mainly moving American oil executives in and out of the country. They'd stored all our other gear for me free of charge and I must admit when they delivered it to Deveron Road we appeared to have added a few mystery possessions to our worldly goods, most welcome!

So that was us, weeks away from Christmas 1972 and settled in the home where we'd spend the next ten years of our life together. It felt like we were a real family at last, Vera with her daughter and her own things around her and me with a castle to build, reasons to make the daily grind worthwhile.

New Year was a fine time to meet up with the neighbours and nervous as we were, we joined in the traditional round of visiting all the flats in turn. We'd sisters, Dorothy and Sheila, above and below us, Jessie and Raymond were on the opposite landing, Susan and her elderly mum on the ground floor and Mr and Mrs Sharp on the opposite side at the top.

We were the youngest couple but we found them to be a nice bunch. The building was spotless and all the tenants took their turn to make sure it stayed like that. I'm convinced however that they all colluded in a plot and conned me into accepting that looking after the huge side garden was my responsibility. In time gardening would become a pleasure to me and a neat garden a matter of pride, so perhaps they did me a favour after all.

The flats were not well insulated for either sound or cold, there was no central heating and it was possible on a cold winter morning to make a snowball from the ice that formed on the inside of any of the windows. Vera was especially horrified when she discovered this, perhaps because she made the discovery when I slid a snowball inside her nightie as she slept one winter February morning.

Leanne was a joy for us then; she amazed us in her baby-walker by being able to travel around the house at high speeds but only in a backward direction. We considered fitting wing mirrors but she seemed to have eyes in the back of her head. It was almost the end of that year before she took her first steps but her self devised propulsion system prior to that was a wonder to behold. Seated squarely on her bum she'd frantically paddle her legs from side to side; forward motion amazingly ensued. She could go anywhere but she tore more holes in pants and nappies than our second hand twin tub washing machine.

Our flat at 5, Deveron Road was a great place to start our family life but it wasn't a home for life. Sooner than I thought I'd be spending more time away from it than I wanted to as work took me to Dundee during the week and for just over a year I became a weekend husband and father.

1973 had opened with Britain becoming members of the EEC and Edward Heath may have seen this as Britain's step into a brave new world, but it certainly didn't catch my imagination. I was more impressed by the magnificent music and superb portrayal of the innocence of the early Sixties in the wonderful movie *American Graffiti*. The film soundtrack is still one of my favourite music collections and talk of being in or out of Europe is still as boring thirty years on.

Rankin Kuhn were expanding beyond Aberdeen and had won the contract to look after the freight forwarding at a new pipeyard to be opened in Dundee by Brown & Root UK Limited. Mike talked me into taking the job of looking after our office; it was a one-man operation but would quickly grow he told me, the prospects would be great. So that Spring I began the weekly commute between Aberdeen and Dundee, 6 am train down on a Monday morning and the 5.30 pm home on a Friday night. There was no more cash for me but I was all expenses paid during the week and was a permanent resident at the old Tay Centre Hotel.

My 'office' was a desk in the Brown and Root general office, housed in a bleach white warehouse and offices unit that stood in the shadows of the Tay Road Bridge. From the day I arrived in Dundee, city of jute, jam and journalism in years gone by, those shadows never lifted. I hated the place. I missed Vera and Leanne every night and knew within days that this wasn't a place I wanted to bring my family to live.

We did make token gestures to check out the possibilities of moving there. A pokey old terraced house in Broughty Ferry was, at £5500, beyond our means and the offer of a horrid flat on the Whitfield Estate by the local council finally made up our minds. Vera came down on the train with Leanne and we went to view the flat; it was awful. The firm weren't too keen to let me come back to work in Aberdeen until I'd trained a suitable replacement and so began the worst year of my life to date. A year spent mostly away from Vera and Leanne and all the things I knew and loved in my home, Aberdeen.

Our own troubles pale in comparison to the world of woe we live in and man's endless lust for conflict was once more to the forefront. A bloody peace was being negotiated in Vietnam but the international peace conference in Paris seemed more intent on dotting I's and crossing T's than saving one life from the carnage that was the end of the Vietnam war.

I always felt that the Vietnam War made a statement that was to the eternal credit of the American people. Whatever the rights or wrongs of their involvement there and the horrors perpetrated by both sides, they chose defeat rather than embroil the world in a nuclear holocaust. The world's most powerful nation could so easily have opened the door to Armageddon but saved the planet from that fate in the moment of their humiliating defeat.

Legends don't come along too often in this life and Cappielow Park on an April Saturday afternoon wouldn't be an obvious place as the backdrop for the birth of one of the biggest. One Willie Miller came on as a substitute against Morton in Greenock that day and so began the tale of the finest Don of all time. Charlie Cooke will always be my favourite player but I'll always think of Willie as the fighting heart and spirit of Pittodrie's greatest days. We Reds have made a legend of Zoltan Varga over the years, great player he was but his brief spell at Pittodrie leaves him standing alongside many others in Willie's giant shadow. The footballing fates were writing copy for the future at Cappielow that day, for as Willie was taking centre stage for the first time Zoltan was making his last appearance for the Dons.

I spent my working life at Dundee arranging the import and export of equipment to all corners of the earth but the finest piece of shipping during my time there was arranged by a tipsy office cleaner just before Christmas—and I was the cargo! We'd all gone to the Unicorn Bar for lunch to celebrate the Christmas and New Year holiday; we were closing for the whole week. We returned to the office with a huge carryout for the staff party. I vaguely recall a knees-up atop the absent Mr McGregor's desk; he was the Brown and Root boss and we all laughed as his paperwork was drenched in vodka from our well filled paper cups.

My recollection of the taxi journey to the station is even hazier but for some reason everyone had decided to come to the station to see me off. However I vividly recall my dismay at being refused permission to board the train—drunk and incapable was the verdict of the man at the platform gate. Enter our cleaner who was having none of it. I had to get home to Aberdeen, my suitcase was full of presents for my wife and daughter and I'd probably sleep all the way to Aberdeen. Where was his Christmas spirit?

So it was that I became the only human Red Star parcel ever to be shipped to Aberdeen from Dundee. The ticket man relented but would not inflict my presence on the other passengers. He and the guard agreed that I could be accepted as a goods item and travel in the guard's van, on due payment of the correct tariff of course. I did sleep all the way home, leapt out of the train into a cab and was curled up in bed before 8pm!

What I didn't know was that the gang had phoned ahead and alerted Vera to my ignominious transportation home to the Silver City. She had dutifully turned up at the station to supervise the last leg of my journey home and we had missed one another. I was amazed to wake up next to her in the morning and could barely mutter in complete confusion, "What are you doing in Dundee?"

I nearly got stranded in Dundee that Christmas and nearly won a lot of money earlier in the year when Richard Pitman's front running epic on the gallant *Crisp* failed by a whisker to prevent *Red Rum* from beginning his five year Aintree odyssey that would re-write the pages of Grand National history. Roger Taylor was a nearly man too, losing in the singles semi-finals at Wimbledon and then coming second to Jackie Stewart in the BBC Sports Personality of the Year.

Funny, but it's only once you've had a child and then hear that a second is on the way, that the full understanding of the timeless magic of pregnancy dawns on you. Then you realise why, since the Garden of Eden, every birth has been the first, the first step on life's highway for all the worldly travellers of the ages. In the summer of '73 Vera and I learned that another journey was about to start and now there was no mystery at the surprise, uncertainty and joy that the news fired through our family.

We talked it through and decided that I would leave Dundee and come home before the baby was born. I'd missed so much of Leanne's early childhood; the miracle was how loving she had been to me in spite of that. It had been so hard for Vera on her own and we both knew then that for the rest of our lives, family would always be more important than work. We were never happier than when we were at home playing with Leanne or later of an evening when she slept Vera would catch up on her favourite drama of the day, *Sam,* or I would listen in to the latest edition of the *Old Grey Whistle Test.*

Marriage is like a bank account, with love the currency used for all deposits and withdrawals. It's hard to admit but just around this time I was somewhat overdrawn. Vera had given so much, no everything, to our marriage and I had so often continued on in selfish ways. She had gladly stepped on to the treadmill of young married life and deposited regularly, yet never taken a penny back. My large overdraft had often left her alone and without the understanding she needed. Happily the Bank of Marriage allows you to be both manager and customer and sound advice can quickly help you to start balancing the books. There would be no more working away from home for me, my finances had to be put in order and love was a resource I had plenty of to give.

This ray of sunshine golden bright,
Had entered smiling through life's door.
For all the tears of day or night,
She laughed as none had done before.
We shared the early nightly chores,
Saw to needs and feeds and such.
For when a child is truly yours,
No effort ever seems too much.
So soon with mother left alone,
As I pursued my solo course.
In search of gold for house and home,
Finding quick the quest a curse.
Weekend father for a while,
Though never loved the least bit less.
Greeted always with a smile,
Gold locks against my heart would press.

My career by the banks of the silvery Tay would end with a bang but although the crash must have been heard in Fife, the first man ever to pilot a fork lift truck through the sound barrier, Ronnie the storeman, was literally struck dumb by his achievement. Apart from their huge pipeyard, which lay between the Rail Bridge and the airport, the nerve centre of the Brown & Root operation was the warehouse and office unit at the docks. The warehouse had somewhere in the region of 9000 square feet of storage space. This housed every imaginable shackle, valve, nut, bolt, bracket and gismo that could possibly be required in pipeline construction. Half of this storage area was given over to Dexion shelving, a grown up version of Meccano. The shelves were filled to overflowing with miniature marvels of engineering wizardry and each item had been logged, tagged and located.

The oil industry always seemed such a stop start business; there was either a mad panic on or we were all left bone-idle. To fill those quiet times with interest, Ronnie and the rest of the lads had worked out a time-trial circuit for the warehouse forklift. It involved a series of intricate manoeuvres, in forward and reverse, in and out and up and down the narrow aisles between the shelving. We office lads would occasionally have a go, but no-one could match the peerless Ronnie.

One quiet Friday afternoon—it was always quiet on a Friday after lunch at the Unicorn—Ronnie was in fine fettle. For reasons best known to himself he was desperate to become a Freemason and at lunchtime he'd had a pint with a guy who knew a guy who was just about to become one. This loose vinculum had convinced him he was now in the know and would soon be privy to the secrets of the dodgy handshake. The other two storemen, Tommy and The Wasp, were attempting to demonstrate how to light a fart with a cigarette lighter; Scotland's drive to become Europe's major oil producer was in safe hands. "Has anyone done the circuit in less than a minute?" someone asked, more out of a need to change the subject than out of real interest.

Ronnie was the top man, he was down to sixty-two seconds and leapt to his feet, "No, but they will today," he affirmed.

As he leapt up onto the forklift there was an aura about Ronnie, it may have been his soon to be granted mystical powers or perhaps he had perfected the secret of Tommy and The Wasp's experiment and now had a cabbalistic method of self propulsion. The truth may never be known, but he drove like a man possessed. In, out, back, forth, up on two wheels, no hands on the steering wheel, his magical display was reminiscent of Paul Newman's Butch Cassidy on his bicycle. He was almost across the line, surely a new record, when suddenly a horrendous, grating, creaking noise echoed around the building. Ronnie had made a mess of the final reverse manoeuvre and the forklift had wedged firmly between the last row of shelving and a roof support pillar, which was also the finish line! But for this, he would have been under the minute.

The ensuing, slow motion, dream-like sequence can only be likened to a giant version of the World Domino Toppling Championship. As Ronnie edged forward an inch to free his chariot the shelves began to topple. Ever so slowly each six foot high stack neatly crossed the five-foot gap between rows and smoothly sent its neighbour off on the same unstoppable mission of symmetric destruction. The deafening noise seemed to follow the devastation like thunder after lightning, then the absolute silence was awesome.

Mr McGregor was first down from the office to survey the ruins. Ronnie sat atop the forklift, to all intents and purposes a victim of the Medusa; not a flicker of life came from him. The rest of us must have presented a strange sight to the boss as we frantically wrestled with one another to get into the single toilet cubicle. There before him lay all the fruits of his considerable labour, now in magnificent disarray. How on earth would he be able to prepare the next desperately needed consignment to the pipe-laying barge? He had imbued Ronnie with all his knowledge of the Vocabulary of Stores but now all was lost, as was Ronnie's voice. Thousands of carefully tagged pieces of equipment lay scattered everywhere. Ronnie was never able to satisfactorily explain what had happened and the boss could never understand how on earth all of us could have been looking the other way at the very moment of disaster. Well he'd seen it for himself; we were all bursting for the loo!

We'd decided that there would be no more working away from home for me, but four weeks before Vera was due to have our second child I had to resign, as the firm dug their heels in on my position in Dundee. This wasn't a time you'd have chosen to be unemployed!

These were dark days in Britain indeed and the government introduced a three-day working week as miners banned overtime and train drivers went on strike. Television closed down at 10.30pm to stop us contributing to the power crisis by burning lights too late and drinking cups of tea as we watched Colditz or a late night edition of Match of the Day.

I was making Vera a cup of tea one morning and marvelling at how well Leanne was now walking when the phone rang. I'd been at home for a week since I'd given in my notice and was surprised to hear Mike's slow cockney drawl, "What are you doing Sid?" he asked.

"Making a cup of tea," I replied.

" Get yourself into the office tomorrow," he said.

"Thanks a lot Mike," I agreed.

I already knew that the oil boom wasn't for me but at that moment Mike had saved us. Our baby was due in just a few weeks and now, thanks to God and Mike, we wouldn't be bringing it into the world with me on the dole. I only once ever walked out on a job again in my life, and on that occasion it was also about what we thought was best for the family. In both instances I count myself very lucky that things worked out the way I wanted.

Vera's high blood pressure had been causing a little concern and on her due date, 15th March, she was taken into the maternity ward at the ARI. Nothing happened for two days but on the Sunday I'd just came home after visiting her, when a nurse called to say I best get back as she'd gone into labour. Lilian was watching Leanne and thankfully I was able to about turn and got back to the hospital just as Vera was being wheeled to the delivery room.

The same midwife who had delivered Leanne was standing next to Vera, a young nurse asked if I'd like to sit down but our old friend advised her, "No, he'll be okay, he's done this before!"

We men are useless. There was Vera about to give birth and all the women, including Vera, were worried about me! Someone asked if we'd allow a class of trainee midwife's to witness the birth and suddenly the room was busier than the Beach End at a home game against the Huns. Vera was in a hurry this time and it seemed only moments after we'd entered the room I was whispering to her, "It's a boy!"

We'd hoped for a boy to complete our family, Vera especially so since the time of her miscarriage. Then we had found out that her 'A' Rhesus Negative and my 'O' Rhesus Positive blood groups were the very combination that could cause Blue Baby syndrome, especially in boys. It had caused the miscarriage, but injections for us both would solve the problem, we'd been told. Despite this, Vera had been convinced she'd never have a boy. She strained to see him and gasped, "Are you sure?"

Unlike Leanne's perfect entrance into the world, Paul was a pug-nosed, wrinkly little fella...well, not that little! So there in front of a room full of strangers I said to Vera, "Hold on and I'll have another look!"

The moment I said it I wished the floor would open up and swallow me—if I didn't know the difference by now, how on earth was I standing there in the first place? A boy it was then, Paul Sidney Robertson, at 1432 on Sunday 17th March 1974, weighing in at nine pounds exactly. The movies had played a part in the name game again; Paul Regret had been my favourite character in *The Comancheros*. We both loved the name Paul and never had one moment's regret about him from that day on.

We did have a scare; those antibodies showed up on his umbilical cord and he was whisked off to the special nursery just moments after. It was all just a precaution, as he was hale and hearty but for two days only I got to look at him and whatever reassurances I gave Vera, she was inconsolable until she could hold him in her own arms.

An audience of nurses was viewing the birth,
My comments must surely have caused them some mirth.
"He's wrinkly!" I think was my throwaway line,
Then to check on the sex I looked one more time.
Well for Vera no words to tell joy or relief,
The achievement of that she thought out of reach.
The heights that she'd reached on the short road we'd run,
Wife in a million, mother of daughter and son.

This was a time for boys, for grandfathers' eyes to sparkle and for father to dream such boy's dreams that the hairs on the back of my neck stood up and tingled. This was a time for boys, thanks to a woman...Vera.

Life keeps its cruellest twists for the most inopportune moments. Vera and I were so happy; yet in our own small family my sister Annie and Bob were coping with the loss of their own infant son. Wayne had been born on the 23rd of January that year and tragically died when only weeks old, a victim of Cot Death Syndrome. All the harder to bear the grief when you'll never understand the reason why. We were uncertain and didn't want to flaunt our joy but Annie and Bob were as happy for us as the rest of the family. Annie seemed to draw some comfort from the times we visited and she held Paul in her arms.

The spectre of Watergate finally put paid to Richard Nixon, who resigned the American Presidency; perhaps history would prove him to be a greater man than a scandal-obsessed world could then admit. India joined the world's atomic powers but surely that achievement would gain no praise in the annals of tomorrow.

History can sometimes be a bore. Celtic's nine-in-a-row championships certainly had made history, but had also made Scottish football the most boring competition of all. It had ever been thus and no doubt ever will be so, but soon a light would rise in the north and for a few years we Reds would bask in the glory of our team's achievements.

Vera was twenty-one that year and our lives couldn't have been happier. She coped so well with the kids, we were at one with our parents again and I was back playing with train sets. Stan had bought Paul a Hornby model railway of British Rail's High Speed Train; he himself had been one of the first drivers to take one into the Joint Station at Aberdeen. The boxed engine and carriages are still up in the loft all these years later.

For me, songs have always marked moments and there were two that year that we would cuddle up together and listen to with a wee dram when the kids were asleep; *She* by Charles Aznavour and Ken Boothe's *Everything I Own* were special tunes for us then. Abba had burst onto the scene after their Eurovision win with *Waterloo* and although Radio One still shared transmission time with Radio Two, Messrs Blackburn and Walker, Diddy David and Emperor Rosko were changing the nation's listening habits and tastes. Vera was still a devoted Elvis fan and I'd taken a liking to the softer sounds of John Denver.

With unseen ease the girl had bloomed into womanhood.
No magic potion poured, just the wave of Father Time's wand.
Life and love had stolen some reckless youthful days.
Cares and woes of family were well known to her.

This woman grown was an angel to me.
All my desires were hers to meet and well fulfil.
A web of love she wove, children safe and comforted.
The girl lived on but woman was now her name.

We three needed so much of her,
I who thought myself the strongest arm.
They who cried for love and care and more.
Each in turn was given all her wondrous love.

Woman, soft but strong in hidden ways.
So giving of her precious days of youth.
Asked nothing of us for all her treasures.
Was all that any hearts' desire could crave.

Steve McQueen and Paul Newman were able to save lives in *Towering Inferno* but boy was I in trouble when I failed to prevent one little two year old girl from leaping to disaster on a Saturday afternoon. Vera had gone into town shopping and I was child minder in chief. Paul had fallen asleep, Leanne was playing with her toys, a cup of tea and Grandstand beckoned.

The poor wee soul's cry had me rushing through to the kitchen, her mouth was covered in blood and she was sobbing her heart out. She'd cleverly used her blocks trolley, which was full of books, to clamber up onto a chair, pulled herself atop the kitchen table and leapt in best Wonder Woman fashion into mid air. She was patched up and comforted much more easily than Vera forgave me when she got home! When two of Leanne's milk teeth started to turn black a few weeks later my name was mud once more. We took her to the dentist who x-rayed her teeth and assured us that everything was okay but in the years to come Vera would always be convinced that moment was the cause of all Leanne's later problems. Into her teens she had to wear a brace and be treated by the orthodontist.

The sporting greatness of Muhammad Ali meant that supreme athletes like the cyclist Eddie Merckx not only had to live in his shadow but also, in most cases, weren't even mentioned in the same breath when talk turned to sporting heroes. This year of all years perhaps best illustrated why. This was to be his finest sporting moment. At thirty-two years of age, *The Rumble in the Jungle*, in Kinshasa, Zaire. The indestructible, unbeatable champion, George Foreman, was the opponent, but Ali was not a man to walk in fear. Skill and grace had brought him worldwide acclaim but guts, determination and the heart of a lion had made him a champion in the toughest sport of all. In typically unorthodox fashion he allowed Foreman to punch him about the body for seven rounds, as he lay on the ropes seemingly unable to prevent the onslaught. Only Ali could have taken those savage blows, and then launched an unbelievably swift counter-attack to knock Foreman out in the eighth round. "Rope-a-dope," he called it; he had allowed Foreman to exhaust himself in delivering those murderous punches. Muhammad was no fool in or out of the ring.

I wouldn't be ready for many of life's challenges until I was well into my thirties but I was ready for a wife and children in my early twenties. Here we were after three years of marriage living a blissfully happy life together with Leanne and now Paul, the centre of all we did. We weren't well off but my wages saw to all our needs. Vera would soon get a little of her own life back by getting a part-time job at BHS on a Thursday night and all day Saturday. I was able to watch the kids and Lilian was a great help with baby-sitting any time I had to work overtime. Vera's job was just pin money but it gave her back a sense of independence and a new world of her own to talk about.

Leanne was racing towards her third birthday and the poor little thing was about to face yet another problem. We started to notice, especially when she got tired, that she had a slight turn in her left eye. More visits to the doctor were called for and the eye clinic diagnosed a lazy eye. It was quite a common thing, they said and a pair of glasses would help correct the fault. So she started wearing spectacles when she was three and, like me, has worn them throughout the rest of her life. Nothing ever seemed to bother her and she took it all in her stride. What with her glasses soon to come and her two black teeth, she certainly didn't deserve her unwanted third birthday present.

She's not been like this these thirty-six months; still all kids catch measles or mumps.

In comes the doctor, "What have we here? Mrs R she's got the measles I fear!"

Four days in a dream, half-asleep, try making her laugh not a peep.

Soon be over it or so we thought, that was before we saw the spots.

But now we're sure the doctor can fix her, the proof of the pudding is in the mixture.

Sure as fate she starts to improve, soon the wee monkey will be on the move.

Now she's at it laughing and leaping, we're sure she was better always sleeping.

Yet truth to tell we're really glad, to see our Wee Pal happy not sad.

The world was a crazy place then and perhaps it ever will be but Jack Nicholson reminded us it isn't always easy to tell who are the lunatics and who's in charge of the asylum. His flawless portrayal of Randle P McMurphy in *One Flew Over The Cuckoo's Nest* was to earn him a richly deserved Best Actor Oscar. That mad world had Britain seemingly a nation in the doldrums; the economy was in dire straits and neither the Labour Government not the Conservative Opposition seemed capable of leading us out of the mire. It was a time for re-invention and the Conservatives certainly came up with the goods. In what might have been seen by many as an act of madness they elected Margaret Thatcher as party leader. This in itself was a political milestone for Britain. Love her or loathe, her she was now only a few years away from becoming one of the most important British Prime Ministers of the century.

We voted on Europe that year and if ever there was a time when the uninformed took a major decision on the unfathomable, this was it. Life's too complicated for things to be boiled down to a simple yes or no, but yes we said to staying in Europe, I think! Henry Kissinger was still a man on a mission for peace in the Middle East but peace, as ever, seemed to be mankind's elusive Holy Grail.

Since Neil Armstrong's giant leap for mankind the manned exploration of space had stalled somewhat and it had been left to James Tiberius Kirk and the intrepid crew of the *Starship Enterprise* to boldly go where no man had gone before. Leanne was now ready to set off on her own voyage of discovery; nursery school was beckoning. I remember that Vera was more excited than Leanne. Overalls, a school bag, pencils, crayons, new shoes and all she'd need for Byron Park Nursery School were on that summer's shopping list. Leanne had grown well and neither the slight turn in her eye nor the glasses detracted one tiny bit from her loveliness. Even the failed attempt at flying which had blackened her teeth took nothing from her impish grin or ever-happy face.

Already Leanne was a mother to her bustling younger brother who had taken his first faltering steps just before his birthday. He was quick at physical things whereas Leanne could have talked your head off from the time she was a year old, and hasn't stopped since. She was interpreter-in-chief of all his demands and she could tell exactly what he wanted no matter what gibberish emanated from his mouth; it was uncanny. Until he was almost two years old we could only ever make out that to him she was 'Knee-Lee-Dan.' It was the only word he needed to know, she did the rest. Leanne was all and more than we'd dreamed she'd be.

So it was goodbye to *Play School* and *Camberwick Green*, the apron strings were sadly snipped and Leanne was off to learn of things other than Mum and Dad. We never know where life's road will lead or whether yellow bricks will pave the way but all we wished for her was that she dodged the grapes of wrath and laughed with life.

A famous landmark disappeared from the dockland skyline that summer. For over sixty years the famous Sheer Legs had towered over Waterloo Quay but the huge tripod crane finally became one giant heap for mankind when demolition experts sent it crashing to the quayside. I well remembered as a wee boy, out walking with my dad and being awe-struck at its size. Oilrig supply vessels berthed in the harbour were the eyes of the modern world looking back at a local wonder of the past.

Vera and I visited our parents often and saw a fair bit of Annie, Bob and their kids in those days, but we were always happiest just being together. With the kids so young we enjoyed weekends at home together, a wee dram and our favourite music once the kids were asleep was our favourite routine on a Friday or Saturday evening. We both loved the Eagles and *Lying Eyes* was always guaranteed to bring a tear to Vera's own. Bob Dylan was never on her play list but she'd suffer *If You See Her Say Hello* just for me. Queen broke new ground that year by using a video to promote sales of their latest single, which just happened to be *Bohemian Rhapsody*, destined to become an all-time classic.

The sporting world found an unusual hero in a grey haired, mild mannered cricketer, David Steele. In a torrid summer for English cricket he alone seemed able to offer resistance against the awesome pace of Lillee and Thomson. My favourite English club, West Ham United, lifted the FA Cup and a charismatic new manager arrived at Pittodrie, Ally MacLeod.

Jaws was the blockbuster movie of the year but the Robertson family had a watery tale of their own to tell. Leanne was out playing in the garden on a lovely late autumn Sunday afternoon. Vera was always at the window checking on where she was and she was off down the stairs in a flash when no sign of her was to be seen as I followed with Paul in my arms. We quickly found her holding court with a group of the local kids. It had rained heavily the previous night and they were all standing around a huge puddle. Having removed her cardigan and socks she was, in best mother mimic mode, explaining to all and sundry how to properly wash your clothes. The puddle was little better than a mud heap; maybe the leap from the kitchen table had done more harm than we thought!

Paul had started his terrible twos in quite an eventful manner when he, Leanne and I were playing a hiding game. He, like all kids, was revelling in the pleasure of the sheer terror of being caught. He would run off at high speed when discovered, to prolong the thrill of the chase. In one headlong flight for freedom he overbalanced and flew headlong into the bedroom dressing table. My name would be mud again, he opened a huge cut on his nose, and the blood was everywhere. The wee man was in tears and Leanne was crying too, upset for her little brother.

I'm sure I should have taken him to the hospital for stitches but after I got the bleeding to stop and cleaned him up I decided to try a piece of clear plaster tape to hold the open wound together. In the next few days it healed well but the faint line on Paul's nose is a constant reminder of that little mishap. My injuries would have been worse than Paul's if Vera had not felt faint at the sight of all the blood on his wee blue jumper when she got home from work. I was firmly told that I was definitely on my last warning, one more slip up on Saturday afternoon baby sitting duties and it would be the hospital for me, at least! We look back and laugh at things like this today and we were both careful, loving parents but bumps and thumps will happen to all kids no matter how cautious parents are.

A new sporting hero arrived on the scene for me when a young Swede strolled through the gates of Wimbledon, clinched the title and began an unsurpassed dominance of the Men's title that would last for the next five years. I still play a reasonable game of tennis in my mid-Fifties and even now try to model my style and court manners on Bjorn Borg. His ability to keep all the explosive emotion of sport's ups and downs within himself and somehow channel them into his performance has always amazed me.

We Reds had learned that our new manager wore his heart firmly on his sleeve and when our run to the League Cup Final was capped by a 5-1 thrashing of Rangers in the semi final, glory beckoned. It was clinched by an old Pittodrie stalwart, Davie Robb, who came on as a sub and scored in extra time to clinch the trophy 2-1 against the other half of the Old Firm. The next day saw 25,000 fans inside Pittodrie to see their heroes parade the Cup; Ally's Army was on the march.

Leanne was doing really well at nursery, she was bright as a button, could count more sheep than it took to send an insomniac to sleep and was making a good attempt at reading the little picture story books she got to take home. Paul was actually beginning to speak to the rest of the world but in times of crisis would revert to his own mysterious language, when it was down to Leanne to act as go-between. In a long hot summer he steadfastly refused to wear his sun hat, which was thrown to all points of the compass whenever it was placed on his head. In the end we had to call in the doctor when he took ill; he'd suffered a mild bout of heat stroke and I think Vera resorted to tying the hat around his ears after that. Much wailing and unintelligible babble ensued!

John Wayne has always been a favourite of both Vera's and mine. He made his final movie that year, *The Shootist*, which would become sadly prophetic of his real-life demise three years later, a victim of cancer. Like many Wayne movies we could watch it over and over and Vera never makes it to the end with dry eyes. She still laughs, fit to burst, whenever we watch an old *Carry On* film; one of the greats of the genre, Sid James, died that year. Wherever he is I hope he knows just how much laughter he still brings to the world.

Harold Wilson bowed out of politics by resigning as Prime Minister. Jim Callaghan replaced him but he was inheriting a poisoned chalice. Mao Tse-Tung died but in the mysterious ways of Communist China then, I don't think we'll ever know how long he really was dead before they told the world. Over the years I've seen so many politicians who appear dead from the neck up, but the scourge of this world are the ones who are dead in their hearts. A monster from the same dark side of politics as Mao, Idi Amin of Uganda, at least received his comeuppance that year. In assisting terrorists who had hijacked an Air France jet at Entebbe Airport he hadn't reckoned on the audacity of the Israelis. Their commandos flew 2500 miles from Tel Aviv and killed the terrorists and twenty of Amin's soldiers whilst freeing the hostages.

Vera and I had been married for five years. Five wondrous years! Children, a home, regular employment and closer and more in love than ever. Rifts with family had healed but we were proud that we'd proved wrong their often not so whispered fears that ours would be a brief union.

Lilian offered to baby-sit on our anniversary. It was a Saturday night but we just wanted to find a quiet pub for a few drinks and be on our own for a while. We ended up in the lounge of the Holburn Bar and had the jukebox to ourselves. All the sad songs got a spin and Vera made sure that Cliff's *Miss You Nights* got an extra play.

We didn't stay out too late and once Lilian had gone home we poured a drink and cuddled up together on the settee. The kids, for once, looked as though they were sound asleep for the night. The late movie was *River Of No Return* with Bob Mitchum and Marilyn Monroe. Like them we'd signed up for the whole trip. We watched it in the dark, our arms around each other. What a lovely day!

The daily toil, the slog and grid,
For money pockets silver lined.
From earliest engagement days,
I had laboured in these ways.
Rewards were more than needs required,
Each item sought we bought or hired.
Never lacking life's rich food,
We revelled then, the world was good.

Back to school and forward to Arnage

It was 1977, the Queen's Silver Jubilee year and Britain was a nation set to celebrate but in truth we had little to smile about, all the preparations were really just papering over the cracks. The economy was a shambles, prices had soared by 70% in the last three years, industrial unrest was spiralling wage demands out of control and the nation had to borrow £2.3 billion from the International Monetary Fund to allow Chancellor Healey to balance the books. The spectre of the IRA loomed large in London with multiple bombings. Yes indeed it was a time for celebration!

This was the world then as Vera and I entered what I always remember as the most difficult time of our marriage. As a young family we were very vulnerable to those economic problems and money was becoming tight. I was already working all the hours I could and Vera had her wee job at BHS. We decided Vera should try for a new job and so she entered the world of the Sport of Kings and took a part-time job with the bookmaker, William Hill. The extra cash was most welcome!

Leanne would be leaving Mrs Lowe and moving on to Westerton Primary School, it was amazing that her proper school days had come around so soon. With Vera working and Paul starting nursery school we arranged with Annie that she would pick the kids up after school on workdays and look after them at hers until Vera or I could collect them. It was all done with the best of intentions but on looking back I don't think it was a great time for Leanne, she was soon to be in the shadow of her three cousins. Being younger and a boy, it was much easier for Paul. Leanne was still only five years old and unable to explain to us how she felt. I always look back and think we could have managed as we were. In saying that we were grateful to Annie for being willing to help and forever sorry if it caused our wee girl any hurt.

Now off alone on life's mad chase,
To learn the wonders of the age.
To school she trips her tiny pace,
Her story turns another page.

Pop videos were all the rage and Paul McCartney's *Mull of Kintyre* was the big seller that led us into the New Year but I absolutely loved Michael Nesmith's *Rio*, my number one of the year by a mile. Vera, like millions around the world, was distraught when news of the death of Elvis Presley came through. At forty-two years of age the King had tragically turned into a caricature of himself and perhaps like James Dean and Marilyn Monroe before him, his memory would be best served by the fact that he never did grow old.

A beacon of hope shone from the Middle East in the shape of one man, Egyptian President Anwar Sadat. He was vilified by other Arab nations as he visited Jerusalem, then under Israeli rule and addressed the Israeli parliament, the Knesset. I sensed that here was a great man, his mission was peace, peace saves lives and he who saves one life saves the world entire.

Saving lives can mean something entirely different to a three-year-old and I had to deal with a grief-stricken Paul one Sunday afternoon. We'd gone out for a walk together and were nearly home when he cried in anguish, "Where's Ted? I've lost Ted!"

He was inconsolable, Ted was his best friend in the world and with more hope than conviction we set off to retrace our steps in search of Ted. The next evening I scribbled down how things worked out.

Yesterday on concrete bare,
My small son lost his teddy bear.
He paled and said he wouldn't mind,
If the bear we couldn't find.
But happily at three years old,
Love lies near the surface...bold!
Not tangled in a web of pride,
And so my boy just sat and cried.

For hope he searched in father's face,
So off we went our steps to trace.
Combing every inch of ground,
Yet Ted was nowhere to be found.
Finally our nerves on edge,
We saw Ted lying on a hedge.
My son regained the smile he lacked,
For being bad Ted's bum was smacked!

In the middle of Britain's sea of troubles the Queen's Jubilee had been a bit of escapism for us to focus on and just a couple of days before we centred our attention on Leanne's fifth birthday, Virginia Wade won the Ladies Singles at Wimbledon. As the Queen presented her with the trophy on Centre Court it felt as if the entire nation had fixed on one of the happier moments of the year.

Leanne was insistent; they had to come off, she was five years old and far too big for stabilisers on her bike. I tried to explain to her that once I'd broken the fixing bracket, they'd be off for good and could never be put back on again. "That's okay I don't need them," she haughtily assured me.

Off they came, off the bike came she seconds later and it was apparent that Leanne had not yet found her balance. Kids are never fazed, out came her dolls and their pram and into the cellar went the bike. Cycling was boring anyway she told me! Later that summer the bike did make a re-appearance— we were amazed to see Paul on it, buzzing around the grass area in front of the flats. Vera had been tidying out the cellar, but how he got it downstairs and found his balance remains one of life's mysteries?

All the grannies and granddads lived in Torry and the 13 bus was our frequent ferry across the water when visiting. One of the Corporation buses had been done up in silver livery for the Jubilee Year. Paul's cry of 'The Silver Bus' would ring out whenever he saw it. He was in heaven if it was on the 13 route and we actually caught it to Torry. It always amused us that he became really scared as we approached the Victoria Bridge; he loved to sit upstairs at the front but hated it when the bus came to cross the River Dee. As ever Leanne was his minder and she would be warning us as soon as the bus approached Guild Street that it was time for us all to move downstairs!

Space fiction and fact vied for the cliff-hanging spectacular of the year; *Star Wars* hit the cinemas and a cult was born. The ungainly space shuttle hitched a ride on a Boeing 747 and satisfied NASA that it would be a success in flight. Vera and I enjoyed a more sinister science fiction movie, *Demon Seed*, all the scarier because a machine was imposing its will on a human being. I still liked horror movies; Vera always needed a cuddle when she was scared!

Paul had sent a stir through the family, being the first grandson to Stan and Lil and, since the tragic loss of Wayne, the only one for my mum and dad. Much fuss was made of this new man about the house and he had quickly changed from the porky little baby into a smart wee lad. Vera seemed to have a special pride in him and the tigress' mothering instinct towards him. Paul in turn gave his mum the same devotion and was always like a cuddly toy to her. For Leanne and I he was a pest, it seemed he could charm us into catering to his every whim. Paul was content to grow up loved and lazy!

When Paul's nursery days arrived, Vera was reluctant to see it as the same adventure that Leanne had set out on. Much was made of him not being as ready as Leanne had been, but secretly I felt Vera was just clinging to her last baby. Leanne was, so quickly, well on her way to growing up and in spite of what Mum thought, Paul looked as though he'd manage well enough.

So close they clung to one another, so close their lives entwined.
The boy a treasure to his mother, the boy who'd eased her mind.
The love between them freely flowed, the love which bound their hearts.
Such times when life with loving glowed, such times when growing starts.
Well he grew her bright young boy, well he earned her praise.
With ease he filled her heart with joy, with ease he'd spirits raise.
Come the day when off he'd go, come the day he'd walk away.
For him at school she whispered no, for him it was with her to stay.
Then off indeed to school he went, then off her lips no word was spoken.
So soon their days together spent, so soon her heart was broken.

With a life so happy and settled Vera and I took a major decision. We felt no need to add to our family and Vera had always had bad reactions to being on the pill. I must admit the thought of the 'snip' terrified me so Vera was the one who went for the sterilisation operation. There were no complications and no regrets, although a couple of years later we did ask about the possibilities of reversal. It could be done but after much thought we came to the same conclusion— our family was complete and was all we needed to build our world around.

As I'd developed a liking for golf, I'd never once thought of it as a dangerous sport. The odd moment of throwing yourself flat on the ground, in response to a hearty shout of 'Fore!' wasn't too bad unless it had been raining. My lack of ability saw me in the trees more often than not and then bees and wasps were my main concern. I was in for a rude awakening when I went on the Glenlivet Bar golf outing, sponsored by mine host Jack Gall, a golfing fanatic and one of life's gentlemen.

We were bound for Braemar and would set off from the pub at eight in the morning. In time honoured fashion we all turned up early, just after six to be precise! The golfers amongst our band helped load the clubs aboard and the boozers made sure the generous supply of liquid refreshments donated by Jack were easily accessible. By the time we reached Braemar we were in high spirits. As I took my bag out of the bus I struggled to lift it, and then I remembered I had a half bottle of vodka and twelve tins of lager inside. My high spirits were buoyed by a solid five at the first, almost extinguished by a meandering seventeen at the second, soared after a three at the next and totally devastated after a thirteen at the fourth. Given my somewhat merry disposition I held my game together brilliantly and covered the remaining fourteen holes in level sixes for a round of 122! The ever-reducing weight of my bag had been a major contributing factor to my improvement.

Discontented murmurs after lunch gave me the first inclination that my two playing partners were less than happy with me. Fate saw the three of us drawn to play the afternoon session together again. Neither of them spoke to me in the afternoon round, save to confirm scores and my impressive second round 97 did little to curry favour with those golfing Goliaths. On the way home we were to stop for a meal and the presentation of the days prizes at the Charleston Hotel at Aboyne. There 'Naughton Wayne and Basil Radford' could contain their annoyance no longer; I was torn off a strip for spoiling their day and chastised over my lack of sporting prowess.

Being labelled a drunk I could take on the chin but me, not good at sports, I was incensed! My ensuing challenge was accepted, I'd take either or both of them on there and then at any sporting contest they wished. The taller of my antagonists declared a race should settle the matter and as one, our party emptied itself into the hotel car park to witness the event. His long legs and sober state did nothing to diminish my confidence that victory would be mine. To loud cheering we took our marks and set off to run the agreed course, out through the car park exit, along the main street and back through the car park entrance for a final sprint to breast the tape at the hotel entrance. Simple enough, I was off like a whippet, well ahead and confident of victory until I fell foul of the fact that we were unknowingly tackling a steeplechase course.

A heavy wooden fence straddled the footpath outside the hotel but in the pitch darkness I crashed straight through it. My cries of pain sportingly slowed the pursuit of my opponent and I graciously provided a soft-landing area for him as he too spilled over the fence, albeit at a much reduced velocity. I guessed he was a tad overweight as he landed on my chest and head. I felt numb as I lay staring at the stars and couldn't move this other man who also lay groaning in pain, somewhat uncomfortably for me, across my chest. The rest of the lads were in hysterics when they eventually came looking for us but sympathetically laid the pair of us out across the back seats of the bus. There was a disco on in the hotel and lots of women; we'd be heading home in an hour they assured us.

Complete anaesthesia by alcohol set in for me and I did make it home in the back of that bus. I also somehow managed to carry my bag of golf clubs from North Anderson Drive to Deveron Road in the process. I realised the next morning that something was wrong as I lay in bed, I could only move from the neck up and only respond to Vera's worried enquiries about my well-being in hoarse whispers. It was the hospital for me!

"What have you been up to?" asked the friendly doctor at Accident & Emergency.

"Well Doc, I was playing this round of golf!" I whispered.

My neck in a collar, a cracked thighbone, a broken toe, a dislocated elbow, countless cuts and bruises and heavily dented pride were my injuries. Golf would no longer figure prominently in my sporting calendar but the wee daft idiot was only back in the bottle until the next time. Four weeks in bed gave me plenty time to brood on my stupidity; day-time TV was still a test-card on BBC and Grampian gave me the *Amazing World of Kreskin*. Now if only I'd been psychic I'd have noticed the bloody fence was there! At least *Happy Days* assured me that there were plenty other idiots like me in the world.

Ally decided to add a tartan touch to his army and his departure to become Scotland boss following Willie Ormond's resignation left the door open for Billy McNeill to become manager at Pittodrie. Ally was off on the first steps of his ill-fated Argentinian adventure and Billy always seemed as if the lure of Paradise would make his stay at Pittodrie a brief one. Two giants of the showbiz world died that year, Charlie Chaplin and Bing Crosby. Chaplin always makes me think of snuggling up to Mum or Dad in the Casino as I started to get tired or the cinema began getting cold. His old silent movies were often shown as a filler before the main features but I was too young in those days to get the humour in his films and as often as not fell asleep when he was on. Bing was always a favourite of mine, the *King of Cool* long before the world had heard of Steve McQueen. Those hilarious *Road* movies with the master of the one liner, Bob Hope, always had me in stitches. Crosby's passion was golf and a fine player he was too, what better final bow than to win his last game by one hole on the eighteenth and then die of a heart attack. A supreme showman to the very last!

We should have come into a bit of money on Derby Day but luck was not on our side. At work Vera placed her annual 10p each way bet on *The Minstrel* and Lester Piggot. She also wagered the same amount on three other horses, their numbers had something to do with the kids and me. They proceeded to finish, first, second, third and fourth! Her boss George was horrified as she delighted in her good fortune at the end of the race.

"Vera, I could have won you a fortune on a forecast bet!" he gasped incredulously.

I had nothing but the fondest of memories of primary school and so wanted my beautiful daughter to experience that same daily joy and happiness. She was five, I was twenty-six; but I could place my heart exactly where hers was then, filled with excitement, expectancy and just maybe a hint of fear. I wanted her to love the world and be loved in return. I saw a boy cry the first day I went to school and it was my turn to cry the very first day Leanne went there.

It's 9.30 on a Sunday morning and I'm in bed wrestling with two kids and trying, oh so unsuccessfully, not to waken Vera up. The phone rings and an American voice enquires where his cargo is. I'm not on call that weekend; I wouldn't have a clue and tell him so as politely as I can.

"I ain't calling any other number boy, get your ass in gear and sort this mess out," he blasts.

At that moment the oil industry and I finally crossed the Rubicon. "Buddy, it's Sunday morning, I'm playing with my kids, in my bed, in my house and you're intruding. At this moment in time I couldn't care less if your equipment is on a slow boat to China or being hauled up Benachie on a horse and cart. Don't call us, we'll call you." I concluded, then hung up.

The thunderous echoes of the oil boom had been rolling around northern eastern skies since the late Sixties. I had attached myself to one of its minor lightning bolts when Vera was less than a month away from becoming my wife and life seemed to be brimming over with new adventures. As the years had passed the job had given us a sound start to our early married life but high demands were made for the good money I earned. There always seemed to be one more rush job to be done, one more family weekend missed, one more night away from home. Dundee had almost been the final straw but now both Vera and I knew this wasn't the work to be involved in for us to lead the simple family life we wanted. The parting of the ways for Rankin Kuhn and me was imminent! We talked it over all that day and decided the time had come for me to move on. I turned up at work the next day and gave in my notice. No mention was made of my American caller but I wasn't required to work a month's notice and was allowed to leave at the end of the week.

We must have been mad, in the economic climate of the time and with two young children, this was probably the most reckless decision Vera and I ever made. I spent seven worrying weeks out of work, the only time I've been unemployed since leaving school, but our family's good luck held and I secured a post as a Fire Control Operator in the Control Room of Grampian Fire Brigade. Accepting emergency calls and mobilising fire fighting appliances to reported incidents was a world away from the oil industry but on life's road it was the right turning at the right time for us. The service was just emerging from the bitterness of the national strike that had seen the old Green Goddesses provide emergency cover in our cities but I had happy times there. I made some good friends, none better than my shift leader Carole Robertson and her future husband Abbey Milne. Carole was a lovely girl to work for and with and I got to know most of her family very well, they were lovely people. Her brother Doug, who was away in the Army in those days, is a friend and workmate of mine today.

I love my son Paul above all men and there is a special place in my heart that only my father and I ever visit. Life however has afforded me the great privilege of knowing three men of whom I can say it has been an honour to know them and call them friends. I feel certain I could have entrusted my very life to them. I met the first in 1978 and it was Vera's sister who brought him into my life.

We'd all teased her about not being married but Lilian was a strong willed girl and as in all things would decide matters in her own good time. When she did it was a rare man she chose, Raymond Baird, a tall, flame-haired, quietly spoken man. He didn't have the temper to match his hair colouring and burned on a very slow fuse indeed. He was a dear friend to Vera and I from the moment we met and adored the kids. I always had the feeling that he lived life just one step behind his dream and somehow that just suited his laid-back approach to life.

They met in January that year at the old Gloucester Hotel, were engaged by May and married in November. Their wedding was at the same church as ours but a much grander affair. Leanne was a flower girl, Vera a Matron of Honour and we all enjoyed a lovely reception at the Atholl Hotel. Paul was my mate the whole day and neither he nor his sister put a foot wrong, Vera and I were very proud of them both that day. Annie took the kids home early and I recall it was a great night with the band's young fiddler the star of the show. Ray and Lilian never had children; they'd have made wonderful parents but life never has shared its treasures out equally.

It was the beginning we all hoped of a wonderful marriage for them and although it wouldn't last as long, this was the year of another match seemingly made in heaven, that of Aberdeen FC and one Alex Ferguson. In the wake of a bitter divorce from St Mirren he had quickly succeeded Billy McNeill, who had indeed taken up the reigns at Parkhead. Fergie, as he came to be acclaimed by the fans, had a quiet first season and it would have been impossible for even the most die-hard of the Red Army to foresee the days of glory that lay just around the corner.

Leanne had made a good and happy start to school, all I had wished for her, and was doing very well. Vera's fears were allayed as Paul took to nursery school like a duck to water. We were amazed but proud when Mrs Lowe told us he'd had a painting chosen to be included in an exhibition of children's art at the Aberdeen Art Gallery. We were even more amazed when we went to see it; none of us could tell what it was meant to be! That didn't prevent us from being as proud as punch that our wee lad's masterpiece had graced those hallowed walls. Kids can get to you with the simplest of things!

Now for the moment tense and dramatic,
Will she solve the puzzle so problematic?
We've tried for weeks it's not been fun,
And still the task's not been overcome.
If only the solution would suddenly hit her,
She'd be proud to go and tell her teacher.
At last she's done it, smiles on our faces,
Leanne has learned to tie her laces!

Leanne had a masterpiece of her own, her hair! It hung down beyond her shoulders and rolled into golden curls at the ends. She was spending a weekend at my mum's with cousin Paula and we went to collect her on the Sunday. Vera and I were speechless! Her hair was shorn to just below hers ears! What on earth had happened? Mum's feeble excuse that Leanne had asked to have her hair cut just didn't wash; it was a long time before we let Mum forget about this little incident. It was as if a spell had been broken; our little girl disappeared and our young daughter emerged. Maybe she did ask for her hair to be cut and she has kept it quite short ever since but I still miss those curls.

I had turned my back on the oil boom but there was no question that it drove the North East's economy, sadly pricing a family like ours way out of the market when dreams turned to owning a home. As oil flowed to Sullom Voe in Shetland for the first time a three-bedroom West End flat in the Mile End area would set you back over £20,000 and £24,500 would get you a detached villa in the ever-expanding Bridge of Don. Vera and I would be dreaming for a long, long time yet at those prices.

My new job and the shifts I worked allowed us to rethink Vera's situation and when the chance of a full-time job at the Mastrick Post Office came along she grabbed the opportunity. I often had four days off through the week and could be around for the kids by late morning when I was on night shift. It all meant less time for the kids at Annie's and we didn't feel we were putting too much pressure on her to watch our kids all the time.

Without I hope sounding too chauvinistic, one of the nicest things about marriage is simply knowing that *she's* there. All the everyday, taken for granted things she handles so well, all the small chores she does that together are so important for a marriage, all the things you never say thank you for. Around this time our family was beginning to spread its wings, with kids at school and me at work. Vera was ready to move to a full working life of her own and certainly we needed the cash. She had been my guiding light these last few years and mothered me every bit as much as she did our children. How strange it was to see her setting off into the world again, how difficult to see her as an ordinary working girl and not just my wife. The loss would hurt a while.

Her bow now has another string,
Her chatter has another ring.
She talks of more than house and home,
She has a new world of her own.
The both she does with simple ease,
A mother still at home to please.
At work she finds a little time,
To be herself and use her mind.

We settle well in this routine,
At home as ever she's the queen.
Now for herself a chance to grow,
A different side of life to know.
To children none the less a mother,
To husband none the less a lover.
Now working girl as well as wife,
A woman with a fuller life.

A man from a faith born out of miracles, and two men who seemed about to offer the world hope of the most precious miracle of all, peace in the Middle East, took centre stage across the globe that year. For the first time in four centuries a non-Italian became Pope with the election of Cardinal Karol Wojtyla of Poland. He would preside over the Church of Rome as John Paul II and show us all how saintly a mere man could be.

Had Menachem Begin and Anwar Sadat's Camp David Agreement brought a prayed for lasting peace, then surely, irrespective of all their previous human failings, sainthood would have been their just reward. They were jointly awarded the Nobel Peace Prize but would discover that the long road to peace is made up of millions of tiny paces. They at least began the journey with a positive step forward.

I became a life long victim of fashion when I fell off my platform shoes as Vera and I hurried downstairs on our way out, one Saturday evening. Why on earth I ever bought a pair I'll never know, but the torn ligaments I suffered, which pain me to this day, remind me constantly of yet another fashion *faux pas* of mine. At least I didn't do any permanent damage to my fingers as I joined in the *3-2-1* craze inspired by the Ted Rodgers quiz show. Vera moved Leanne on from the *Multi Coloured Swap Shop* and *Grease* became their favourite movie. It wasn't for the boys and Paul and I were happy to stay at home—at least he didn't mind me blasting out Warren Zevon's *Werewolves of London*. Telly addicts were gripped by 'Who Shot JR?' fever but *Reggie Perrin* was the show for me. One look at the comically expressive face of Leonard Rossiter and I was gone.

I still dissolve into fits of laughter when I think of an incident one Sunday night shift in the Fire Brigade Control Room. Carole, Morag and I were on the night shift and not long after midnight Carole complained of feeling unwell. It had been a quiet shift so Morag and I tried to persuade her to go home. She wasn't having that but we convinced her to try forty winks in the rest room, then see how she felt. Bob Still was the Duty Officer that night. They usually popped in just after midnight to check everything was okay and leave details of where they could be contacted in case we had a shout. Bob radioed in to say he'd be at HQ in five minutes, which loosely translated meant put the kettle on for a cuppa. Carole didn't look well but stirred in the restroom as the kettle boiled; she was determined to make the report to the Duty Officer herself. I was sent back to the Control Room and she said she'd bring us all a cup of tea. Bob was on the intercom seconds later and I let him in. Only as Carole handed him his cup of tea did I notice that the deep imprints of her fingers were perfectly formed on her bright red right cheek—as she'd dozed she must have rested her head on her hands. Bob never let on if he noticed or not but Morag and I were fit to burst and crossing our legs to prevent accidents as she stood in earnest discussion with him about the night's events so far, for fully ten minutes.

Golf's finest had to give best once more to Jack Nicklaus as the great man

111

strode the fairways of St Andrews to claim his third Open Championship. A pub game took off as a national sport mainly because it was so suited to television and Leighton Rees defeated John Lowe to become the first World Darts Champion. Whether it was a sport or a pastime, it was great fun to watch on the telly and for some reason the kids loved it.

We have a great capacity to leave bad memories behind and the world had largely managed to achieve this with Vietnam but a stunning movie, *The Deer Hunter*, hauntingly brought back the powerful message of how ordinary lives can be torn asunder in times of war.

Bob Geldof and his Boomtown Rats had brought an abrasiveness to pop music, which was making me feel old, but the Commodores proved music was still for cuddling up to with *Three Times A Lady*. Mind you finding a quiet lounge and a jukebox when Lilian or Annie were baby sitting was becoming harder and harder; all the jukeboxes were being replaced by *Space Invader* gaming machines.

Christmas was a wonderful family time; both the kids were old enough to tremble with the excitement of its arrival yet young enough to believe without question in Santa Claus. They'd dutifully leave a carrot for Rudolph and a glass of milk for Santa before they went to bed. Vera and I would stand in for Rudolph and Santa because we knew how busy they were, and our own belief in Santa was always rekindled when we saw the magic of Christmas twinkle across the children's faces the next morning. The living room would be a sea of boxes and when the whoops of delight subsided, when one new wonder was laid aside for yet another and another, those boxes always took centre stage. Lids became helmets; boxes were chariots, dolls houses, ships, cars, cots or prams. All the toys in the world can't compare to a child's imagination and well I remembered, the simplest of things can be magically transformed and wonderland is never more than a thought away.

Cometh the hour, cometh the man? Britain was certainly in need of someone or something. The 'Winter of Discontent' was upon us, the country seemed to be falling apart, yet it was to a woman that the nation turned in May of 1979 when Margaret Thatcher became the first woman prime minister in British history. In the years ahead she would split public opinion in two, the epitome of the Britannia spirit for some and an anathema to others. Love her or loathe her, she was the wind of change that needed to blow across our nation and in the end perhaps she spawned a new brand of socialism!

The waters had already been muddied for me when it came to working out the difference between the Parties. On the run-up to election day Mrs Thatcher had assailed us with the fact that under Labour our £1 was now worth just 50p but had Harold Wilson not solemnly explained in 1964 that the Conservatives had turned our £1 into a ten bob note? I gave up on politics in 1979!

I think the music of the Seventies mainly passed me by but it finished on a high for me as I discovered Bob Seger and the Silver Bullet Band and realised that fantasy women don't always have to squeeze into impossibly small biki- nis. Debbie Harry looked just fabulous in a black bin liner! An old favourite, Dave Edmunds, charted three times. One was a cover version of Elvis Cos- tello and the Attractions *Girls Talk*, and I couldn't decide if their *Oliver's Army* or Neil Young's *Four Strong Winds* was the best track of the year.

We lost a hero that year when John Wayne died. Vera and I have never tried to complicate our liking for his screen persona by trying to evaluate the beliefs of the real-life Wayne. He never failed to entertain us and in his mov- ies you always knew that love would win through in the end and good would always triumph over evil. Oh that those simple values could always prevail in our harsh world.

His own philosophy to acting was simple enough, " I play John Wayne in every picture, regardless of the character, and I've been doing alright haven't I?"

I had to do a bit of acting myself that year but it was a bad decision to be my own stuntman. The kids would often spend a Saturday evening with Lil- ian and Ray and they'd all go swimming on a Sunday morning before they brought the kids home. Ray confided to me that Leanne was doing really well but Paul was a little scared of the water. I remembered how I'd always felt left out at swimming as a kid and determined not to let this happen to Paul.

"I'll need to come and show him myself next Sunday," I boasted.

"I thought you couldn't swim?" questioned Ray.

"Oh I can really," I lied.

So it was, the next Sunday I stood shivering at the edge of the deep end at Tullos Swimming Pool in a pair of black trunks I had borrowed from Ray, two sizes too big. Ray told me it was only 1.8 metres deep, it might as well have been 100 fathoms. I had been telling Paul all week how easy it was to swim and now he stood next to me waiting to witness my expert demonstra- tion. Could he see his hero's knees trembling I wondered? It was the mis- chievous 'I dare you' twinkle in Ray's eyes that finally pushed me over the edge. My ungainly plunge threw water everywhere, my wild thrashing at the surface, when I eventually surfaced, did keep me afloat until I clutched in desperation at the side rail. Lilian, Ray, Vera, Leanne and Paul stood at the poolside in fits of laughter. The trunks I'd borrowed from Ray had saved my dignity and possibly my life—being too large the air inside them had kept me afloat like an inflatable rubber doll and left me bobbing around like a rubber duck in a bath. I'd as much chance of being a swimming instructor as I had of singing Britain's next entry in the Eurovision Song Contest.

The next Saturday Paul and I attended swimming lessons at the Summer- hill Academy Pool and in a matter of weeks a grand old gent by the name of Bert had us both swimming like a couple of eels. Strangely enough another dad and son were at the lessons every Saturday too and their names were also Sid and Paul. Paul went on to enjoy all the fun of swimming for the rest

113

of his childhood and I mused to myself over all the fun I'd missed out on.

What's noisier than one chattering female? Two! Only joking girls, but Vera and Leanne had become a potent double act; getting a word in edgewise wasn't always easy. The problem was solved for a brief spell when they were both struck dumb, but I wished they hadn't had to go through the pain barrier for the short silence.

We got a call from school, nothing to worry about; Leanne had had a little accident. She'd fallen whilst playing in the gym and bitten through her tongue. I'd done the very same thing at her age and knew how painful it was. She was a quiet wee lamb for a week. Vera had a long-standing appointment with the dentist to have a wisdom tooth removed and she was in agony afterwards. An infection set in and she could barely speak for a fortnight. The day Vera went to the dentist I collected her later on and my mum picked up the kids from nursery and school, then got their tea ready. She had pie, tatties and peas prepared for us all, including a huge plate for Vera!

I became aware of the Islamic Revolution for the first time as the Shah of Iran was swept from power and replaced by Ayatollah Khomeini. I'd never claim to understand why it happened but when the US Embassy was stormed and fifty-three hostages were taken, the world once more looked on the brink of disaster. And did that event trigger the Soviet invasion of Afghanistan?

As Paul's fifth birthday approached I thought it a strange twist of fate that the last of the houses in Drum's Lane were being demolished. At his age I had ran to my grandmother's down that narrow street and told her excitedly that I'd soon be going to school. My boy was soon to join his sister at Westerton Primary School.

His little heart will leap with joy, to please his every wish we'll strive.
We hope he'll like his brand new toy, come his big day when he's five.
It's not so long since he was a baby, so round and cuddly and oh so small.
But with some luck, well just maybe, he'll grow handsome straight and tall.
When I watch him run and play, his every movement I can tell.
It seems like only yesterday, being five I remember so well.
I get a very funny feeling, I mentioned this morning to my wife.
Our little baby is now doing, things he'll remember all his life.

We took the movies home with us in 1979 and bought our first video recorder, a bottom of the range Sanyo that set us back three hundred quid, in twelve easy monthly instalments! They were luxury items then and some shops were actually offering a free holiday for anyone buying a new one. Video hire shops sprouted everywhere and now we never needed to miss *Celebrity Squares, The Dukes of Hazzard, Return of the Saint, The Two Ronnies,*

Starsky and Hutch, Mind Your Language, Some Mothers Do 'Ave 'Em or *The Professionals* ever again. This really was the latest 'must have' accessory for the modern home.

Early in the year the world feared an explosive nuclear disaster would engulf Three Mile Island in Pennsylvania as the power station there developed a critical fault. Disaster was averted but we'd a power crisis of our own on Christmas Day. We'd all been in the living room engrossed in presents and play, when Leanne ran to the door to get a toy she'd left in her bedroom. She was met by a wall of smoke, thick, acrid black smoke. The flat was so cold we used paraffin heaters and the one in the lobby was belching out the smoke—its wick had burned out. We managed to get it out onto the veranda and I joked with Vera that we'd have as much smoke from her roast potatoes later in the day!

This was the year of perhaps the most infamous IRA assassination when a bomb blew up the boat of Earl Mountbatten of Burma, killing him, and his grandson and boatman in the process. Following on the earlier assassination of Airey Neave, both a close friend and political ally of the Prime Minister, even deeper lines would be drawn in the sand between the government and the terrorists.

The country's economy may have been in tatters but football, as now seemed the trend, waved two fingers to real life when Brian Clough's Nottingham Forest paid Birmingham City £1 million for Trevor Francis. Where would it all end? Snooker joined darts as a major television sport—or was it another pastime? The unsung Welshman Terry Griffiths became World Champion. He later said in an interview that the highlight of becoming Champion for him, was hearing his two young boys now arguing over who would be Terry Griffiths rather than Ray Reardon when they played on their small table at home.

My father reached his fiftieth birthday; he and mum had moved again but were still in Torry, at a flat near Balnagask golf course, 356a Victoria Road. He was well settled into his job at the hospital but at times could still be as fiery as ever. I thought he andMmum would forever be tilting at windmills but I loved them both dearly.

I may have been dispatching fire engines to douse flames around the North-East but I was unable to put out the fire that seared my skin on a summer Sunday. I had stupidly been working out in the garden stripped to the waist and by evening I was red as a berry and beginning to burn all over. Vera decided the cure was to cover me in talcum powder and in an instant I was lovely and cool. That relief lasted for no longer than the moment it had been effective and then I was wracked by an irresistible desire to scratch all over. I was in agony; Vera tried washing it off to no avail, the torture was unrelenting. I ended curled up on the floor, fists clenched and quivering, as I determined to resist the urge to scratch. It took two hours for the urge to disappear and I'll never forget the lesson learned—talcum powder ain't a cure for sunburn!

We were waving goodbye to the Seventies, a time that would always be the most memorable of our lives, in spite of the music. Vera and I had met, fallen in love, married, had our children and started to build our life together. Poor Vera must remember the Seventies as a sea of terry towelling nappies and for me it had been an era of pursuit, pursuit of a good living for my family. How fortunate we had been in that respect; unemployment was set to top two million, the economy was in a desperate state but we had managed to provide for our family and remain unaffected by the abject poverty that had been the fate of so many decent hard-working people and their families. It was on now to Thatcherism and dreams of a still better life ahead. Whatever lay in store for us, I knew we would face it together and felt sure that things would work out well for us.

Changes were ahead for Vera and I at work. Vera got the chance of a part-time job with the Hydro-Electric in their Mastrick shop. She was going to earn more for three days a week there than she did full-time at the Post Office; there was hardly a choice to be made and the hours would make it easier still regarding arrangements for the kids. I would make possibly the biggest mistake of my working life and leave the Fire Brigade. The money there wasn't great and I opted for a job that Stan got for me at the Railway. I became an Information Officer at the station Travel Centre. The shift allowances were good and there was plenty overtime but hindsight would prove I'd walked away from the fires and into a huge frying pan full of glue!

Mrs Thatcher hadn't shown her true colours to the nation but Europe was soon to become aware of her as she insisted on a massive reduction to our payments into the EEC. Her soul-mate in world politics arrived in America towards the end of 1980 when Ronald Reagan, Governor of California and one-time B-movie actor swept into the White House on a huge majority.

The kids were mostly just going to Annie's at school holidays and Paul had made a great pal. Their dog Flash was his best mate and he'd go walking with him and Bob all over the place. Bob was a cooper to trade but for reasons best known to himself had given it up. He became one of the unemployed army for a while and in a year or so work would take him, Annie and the girls out to live first at Kintore and a few years after that on to Alford. It seems funny now but that small distance would lead to a drifting apart of our families. Neither could then afford a car and in honesty our ways of life were heading off in different directions anyway. Paul still enjoyed his summers with Flash although his tales of Bob shooting rabbits with his air rifle at the allotments off Manor Walk would raise eyebrows today!

I was a year away from my thirtieth birthday and maybe I was getting old! Vera laughed when I told her all the films I wanted to see and music I wanted to hear had been made and written by 1969 but remember, everyone eventually listens to Radio 2. A superb Don McLean version of *Crying* reminded me that music is a timeless thing and will always nurture memories of wonderful moments. I wasn't too hopeful for the future of the movies though—who'd make all the thrillers now that the master of the genre, Alfred Hitchcock, was dead?

One thing I definitely was too old for was mumps! Leanne and Paul both fell foul of them that year and I was, to say the least, a little apprehensive. I'd never had them as a child and certainly didn't want to become a victim now. The crisis passed with no need for me to invest in either soft cushions or a wheelbarrow!

Tensions were running high between America and the Soviet Union over the latter's involvement in Afghanistan, but the Americans had troubles in the region too, as the hostage situation in Tehran dragged on. A disastrous failed attempt at a rescue mission ended in death in the desert for eight American soldiers. These problems undoubtedly contributed to the election defeat of Jimmy Carter and a far more positive and successful handling of a crisis by Mrs Thatcher hadn't helped his credibility with the American people either.

We had been visiting my mum and dad on a Sunday. Vera, Mum and the kids had just come home from the park and they joined Dad and I in watching the World Snooker Championship final, a cliffhanger between Alex Higgins and Cliff Thorburn. A confident Hurricane was beginning to showboat but should have known The Grinder was not a man to take liberties with. Suddenly as the climax approached our television screens were switched to the far more tense and dramatic scenes of a real-life cliffhanger.

Terrorists had held nineteen hostages inside the Iranian Embassy in London for six days. Following the murder of a hostage the Prime Minister ordered the SAS to storm the building. All but one of the terrorists was killed and the remaining hostages freed. The entire drama was presented on television around the world and I think it was then I realised that our First Lady was out of a different mould altogether. We had all eventually headed home on the bus to Mastrick; Vera and I were still amazed at what had happened. The tortoise eventually caught the hare at the snooker and Thorburn triumphed 18-16. It was one of the greatest snooker finals of all time but would forever be a secondary memory of that amazing day.

A great change took place in our family when Raymond and Lilian announced they were heading off to Corby. Ray had come into a small inheritance and his plan was to move south and open a pub or perhaps a nightclub. Ray always had a scheme in mind and although they never quite became the successes he hoped, I don't think he was ever happier than when planning how to make his first million. The kids would miss them most of all and in those days Corby seemed like the other side of the world.

How sad that one of the finest sports writers of his generation and a loyal Dons fan too, James Forbes of the *Evening Express*, died just a few months before the greatest chapter in the history of Aberdeen Football Club began. Courtesy of a great, late run and a 5-1 defeat for Celtic at Dens Park, the

Dons stood on the verge of the championship. A 5-0 thrashing of Hibs at Easter Road was mission accomplished in style and the agonising minutes of waiting to confirm St Mirren's Love Street draw with Celtic, raised the excitement to fever pitch. The title was Pittodrie bound and the world was bathed in red! We hadn't forgotten that a 10-0 defeat by Partick Thistle the next Tuesday would rob the Reds of the championship but even the Jags weren't that unpredictable. A great football double for me that season, as West Ham won the FA Cup.

It was an Olympic year and although many nations boycotted the Moscow Games it was yet another head to head rivalry that caught the public's imagination. Sebastian Coe and Steve Ovett thrilled us all over 800 and 1500 metres and in the end finished with one gold each, strangely each winning the other's specialist event. Scotland had a golden hero too in the guise of a journeyman long jumper who blossomed into the fastest man on earth. Allan Wells took gold in the 100 metres but for me the star of the games was double long distance champion Miruts Yifter of Ethiopia. Yifter the Shifter they called him and the thirty something year old gave me the feeling that I should get back in training, I was only twenty nine and had four years to get ready for Los Angeles.

Coe v Ovett, Higgins v Thorburn, these were the clashes we loved but *mano a mano* nothing could remotely compare to the brutal battle between Roberto Duran and Sugar Ray Leonard for the World Welterweight title. This was without question the finest boxing match I have ever seen. For fifteen rounds these two modern day gladiators went toe to toe with no quarter being asked or given and Duran emerged the victor on points. Maybe the boxing genius Leonard was proving a point to himself or simply learning a hard lesson but five months later he destroyed Duran in nine rounds. Neither had finished writing his sporting roll of honour but nor were they ever better than in that first amazing encounter.

Leanne and I were horrid; we couldn't wait for Saturday tea-time. *Dr Who* was still time travelling and his timeless quest for adventure thrilled the kids as much then as it had me in 1963. Paul and Leanne loved it but he had developed a fear of the kaleidoscopic credits that introduced the show. We would always laugh as he hid behind the settee or under a cushion when the credits ran. Strangely he loved all the monsters and never hid from them. Leanne laughed because she was only eight years old and although there's no excuse for me, I laughed because I've always been a kid with my kids and I was still scared of the monsters when I was twelve!

There were only tears for Vera when Paul came home with a note from the school nurse. "This child is a mouth breather," said the note; Vera was distraught. My expert opinion was sought when I got home and as I'd always breathed through my mouth, with the exception of breathing through my arse when I played football, I couldn't see what the problem was. Paul continued to breath through his mouth and no doubt the school nurse continued to write silly little notes to impressionable young mums. Vera loved and loves the kids to bits and only perfection would ever do for them. She and they were perfect to me and all was well in our world.

Iraq invaded Iran and we became aware of one Saddam Hussein. He was the force that would stand against the rise of fundamentalism—or so we were told, then. Who deals out those truths to us and who re-writes history when a perceived saviour becomes the bogeyman in the years ahead?

Who was Mark Chapman and what had or would he ever achieve in this world? In December he shot and killed John Lennon in New York. That senseless, motiveless murder shocked the world and ended a dream once and for all—the Beatles would never play together again nor would Lennon and McCartney ever again perform those wonderful close vocal harmonies. What a sad side the world can still show as it hurtles through the cosmos.

Is it fate or chance that often gives us great men to deal with the most difficult of times? In the ocean of despair that was Eastern Europe such a man came to the fore, Lech Walesa, a shipyard electrician who became leader of the Polish worker's organisation Solidarity. It seemed to ordinary people like me that here was a man willing to take on the might of the Soviet Union in the quest for freedom. The super-powers postured over Poland and the world waited to see how the dispute would unfold and what the resolution of it would mean in the future.

We finished 1980 with a family New Year party; Stan and Lil came to stay over the Hogmanay holiday. A great time was had by all but Vera was none too pleased when her dad dropped a cigarette on her new living room carpet. The burn mark was tiny but to Vera it was the size of a football! It was definitely time for bed when he nearly crashed through Raymond and Jessie's stereo system. You could never stay mad at Stan for long as he always did everything with a smile on his face and "Who me?" on his lips. I was just glad that my wee idiot had taken the night off and it wasn't me in trouble.

We were approaching our tenth wedding anniversary and although we four were very happy there were still some things that could have made life so much better. I regret with all my heart that we were not closer to our parents. Their was never any real falling out between us but we just seemed to drift into periods of being apart, then always got back together as if nothing had happened. I just felt that the ties that bind should have held us all closer together. I saw no blame on anyone's part and wondered all the more why for that very reason.

Families are such funny things, meant to be filled with love but often so full of conflict. Both from small families, Vera and I had somehow failed to maintain close bonds with our parents. Oh yes, we visited and the like but somehow that close feeling of what I thought should be family always seemed elusive. I never dwelt on who was to blame and never thought to apportion any. In truth we had perhaps all tried our best and it was me who couldn't see that we all had lives of our own to live. Vera's mum and dad had a stubbornness that unfortunately she'd inherited and I felt at times they'd never agree. My mum and dad were like leaves on the wind and would always float in and out of our lives. The love was there and maybe I just couldn't see that you can smother love and we all need our own space.

A safe harbour from the storm.
A shelter snug and warm.
An oak tree straight and tall.
A towering castle wall.
A place where pain is eased.
A sad heart quickly pleased.
A comfort when alone.
A happy house, a home.
A family.

As the kids grew we began to dream of a new home, a room each for the kids, a garden, a home for life. I recalled how nine years earlier, as foolish young lovers we'd clutched at the first offer of a house. Stan and Lil had told me this house, a house they'd never live in, was wonderful. Winter showers had rattled against the windowpanes as we looked around and a neighbour had peeped through tidy curtains as we left to give Vera the verdict.

We were innocents abroad and needed a home for Leanne but now we knew that a home is a living thing and if it isn't loved it feeds black depression. How could you love a house that offered such little privacy? The construction and insulation were so poor; all the neighbours might as well have lived in one big room together. The people were great, a young couple, Marion and George Durkin, had moved in upstairs and we got on really well but oh for a house of our own, a place where you didn't need to adjust the vertical hold on your telly if a neighbour farted. The good times at Deveron Road would always outweigh the bad but we dreamed of something better, we dreamed of our palace, we dreamed the dreams that make life worth living.

Crash bang wallop, clatter bump, the house shook with a mighty thump.
If not loud music from below, from upstairs deafening sound would flow.
In those days stereo wars were fought, a higher-fi each family bought.
When screeching sound abused my ears, Hot Chocolate LP's would appear.

Those flats so old and jerry built, with ringing tones would sway and tilt.
The child above so small and neat, was sadly blessed with thunder feet.

Effects of sound who could conceive, walls paper-thin who would believe.
My television leaps and flickers, when neighbours' wind escapes their
knickers.

But all in all, there's none to blame, each house must feel the noise the
same.
Our torment never any riddle, we're sandwiched in the bloody middle.
Yet time would pass despite the thunder, one day we'd have none o'er or
under.
Then would such stillness make us glad, or sound of silence drive us
mad.

Two tunes ran through my head that year. John Lennon's *Imagine* topped
the charts as the year began but somehow I never could imagine the world
turning out the way he hoped. Elvis Costello might not have matched the
earthy quality of the George Jones original but his version of *A Good Year For
The Roses* remains one of my most favourite records. I fear that posterity will
have 1981 recorded as a far from good year for mankind.

I had prayed for great things from Anwar Sadat, a man on a mission for
peace, but his assassination left the world in little doubt that peace and the
Middle East did not walk hand in hand. Both the American President, Ronald Reagan, and Pope John Paul II were victims of assassination attempts
but mercifully survived the shootings. The Iranians released the American
hostages but to the last sought to make political capital out of the situation,
mainly at the expense of the man exiting the White House, Jimmy Carter.

At home trouble was never far from the headlines, with race riots in Brix-
ton that spread to other areas of the country. There seemed however to be a
general downward spiral into lawlessness rather than a specific racial confrontation at the root of it all. The thin veneer of civilisation can crack so
easily for so many different reasons.

Hunger strikes became a new tactic of the IRA and led by Bobby Sands,
ten terrorists had starved themselves to death before the end of the summer.
I could not understand the struggle in Northern Ireland but was in awe of
those on both sides, who felt so strongly about their cause that they were
ready to lay down their lives for it. I had twice seen the miracle of life take
place and could think of nothing more precious. Life had been kind to me
and I had never known a loved one snatched from me in anything other than
Mother Nature's own good time or by God's own will. In countless conflicts
around the world since time began, could it be the pain of loss and injustice,
perceived or real, that feeds the hate of generations to come?

It truly is a world of hurt and as special as our tenth anniversary was, we
could not hide from the fact that 800 million on the planet still lived in abject poverty. Even our own affluent nation now had about 3 million people

unemployed. We were neatly described as recession hit Britain but there was nothing neat about the lives that those people and their families were now living. I've always felt there's more than enough of everything for us all in this world but it's the lack of the desire to do the sharing that causes the pain. Failure to cultivate that desire will be mankind's downfall.

Dads are cruel, I hold my hand up, I've been a cruel dad. We were all watching the telly on a Saturday evening; the kids loved to sit up late with us and have a wee party. We'd end up with a 'Midnight Feast,' where juice, crisps, sweets and all manner of goodies would be laid out and we'd play games and watch the telly together. We'd all settled to watch a ridiculous horror movie, *Night of the Lepus*. This was basically the story of a giant white rabbit which was taking over the world and hopped along making a silly 'dum-dum, dum-dum' noise in the process. The kids loved it!

Leanne and Paul were now sharing the big bedroom and we'd split their bunk beds down into two singles. I got the task of putting the kids down to sleep after the film. As I switched off their light and closed the bedroom door I slipped to the floor, still inside the room. I silently inched my way between their beds and then mimicked the 'dum-dum, dum-dum,' sound of the movie's monster. Screams and cries for help filled the darkness; they were so loud I got scared myself! Mum came rushing through, I was exposed as the monster but I could see the twinkle in their eyes and the smiles on their lips as Mum clipped my ear and threw me out of the room.

If we saw a big white rabbit that year, we saw an even bigger white elephant when the Gang of Four launched the Social Democrat Party, or SDP. In our crisis-hit land Owen, Williams, Jenkins and Rodgers hardly seemed the dream ticket to future prosperity. I couldn't bring myself to watch the grotesque display of affluence that was the wedding of Prince Charles and Lady Diana Spencer. Britain in 1981 seemed the most unlikely place to write a modern day fairytale.

With darts and snooker at the zenith of their television popularity we had all become fans. Paul even started to call out 'one hundred and eighty' in his sleep; thankfully this strange phenomenon was short lived. Leanne had a shrewd approach to things and was almost guaranteed to win the sweepstakes I ran when the world championships were on the box. She didn't have favourites, just winners. Eric Bristow and Steve Davis were always her first picks. By the time Phil Taylor and Stephen Hendry arrived on the scene we were just giving her the money and tearing up all the other tickets!

Paul became a reluctant train driver on my thirtieth birthday. We'd gone on a day trip to Inverness and on the return journey met Stan at the station; he was driving the engine back to Aberdeen. At Elgin he took Paul up front with him but by the time we reached Keith an ashen-faced seven-year-old was back in the compartment with us. I'd done a run from Dundee to Aberdeen in the cab with Stan and those old diesel locomotives could be a noisy, scary place for any novice, let alone a youngster. Leanne was really miffed she didn't get a shot, knowing her she'd have taken it all in her stride. Charles and Di were holidaying at Balmoral after their Mediterranean honeymoon but we'd had a lovely day as a family and didn't envy a soul in the world.

The video recorder was now a part of everyday life. How could I ever have guessed that one day I'd bring the movies home to my own children who'd thrill to films like *Raiders of the Lost Ark*. I could well remember the days of no telly, of radio programmes and pictures of the imagination. Who was getting the best of it, what wonders did technology have waiting just around the corner?

One J P McEnroe broke the spell that Borg had cast over Wimbledon, but he was no fairy prince who conquered with a kiss and a smile. He was a tennis wizard who triumphed with a snarl and a clenched fist. Aggression was here to stay in sport and none displayed it more than Ian Botham, whose exploits at Headingley gave England an amazing test victory over Australia. A cricketer, who bridged the gap back to a bygone age and none the less competitive in his quieter way, clocked up 8000 test runs for England. Geoff Boycott was a supreme opening batsman but his style of stoic defiance was making way for unbridled passion and raw aggression on all sporting fronts.

Sport of a much gentler nature would lead me to meet the second of the three exceptional men that life has allowed me the privilege of knowing. Vera and I had joined Northfield Bowling Club, which allowed us to enjoy a hobby but also have the kids with us, as they played in the adjoining park where we could always see and hear them. I was reasonably good at it and joined the bowls section at work too. A colleague, Harry Park, was determined to get me to join a private club and so with his sponsorship I became a member of Polmuir Bowling Club. I joined in the last weeks of the season and played in and won the only competition I could enter, the club under 35's championship. I'd win a few more titles at Polmuir but never captured a prize as valuable as the friendship of William Anderson.

I met Bill in the process of winning that first competition and he was to become a friend and sporting companion for life. Bill was a man of wry humour, straight talking and with a sense of fair play and honesty that made him a pleasure to know. His father Jack and brother Ian were men made in the same mould. The boys were indeed a tribute to their father, in all the years I've known them, in the heat of sporting battle, in the flush of alcohol's excess or in the deepest of divided debates I have never heard an oath uttered by one of them. Fine people to know and have had the good fortune to have called friend.

Paul has a little Pittodrie first of his own. The Hamburg match was the first big match I took him to but it was not the first match he ever saw there. That game was a Cup Final in April, the Aberdeenshire Cup Final against Buckie Thistle to be precise. The Dons took the trophy with a 5-1 victory and the game was special for one reason, Joe Harper.

King Joey had long been struggling with a knee injury and made an appearance in the match as he battled to return to Fergie's first team. I think many were like me and thought this could be his last match. I wanted Paul to be there just so he could say in years to come that he'd seen Joey in the flesh. Harper didn't score that night but one moment of cheeky magic reminded the 5000 crowd what he was all about as he crashed an eighteen yarder off the crossbar.

Paul never saw Joey in full flight, scoring and then hailing the Red Army on his knees behind the Beach End goal, but he did see him. The King did play once more in the first team, a meaningless 2-0 home defeat from Kilmarnock; but his legend lives on at Pittodrie. November would bring Hamburg and the Kaiser to Pittodrie and my seven year old son just found it so comical that a football team could be called the Hamburgers—they were something you ate with tomato sauce and chips.

He was cheeky, he was impish, he was funny, he was seven.
When I told him I had tickets, he was really up in heaven.
The occasion for such excitement, in his boyish little heart?
A football match in which he'd play a Dons supporters part.

There would be nothing that could turn this epic confrontation sour.
Hamburg would play at Pittodrie and include Franz Beckenbaur.
The Hamburgers he called them and thought it very funny.
I was slightly less amused; the game had cost a lot of money.

The evening of the mighty match would brim with sheer delight.
If his dazzling, deadly, dandy Dons were best team on the night.
He screamed and yelled and cheered with all his heart and soul.
It must have worked the Dons played well and scored the opening goal.

The action raged from end to end, he thrilled at all the fun.
The joy he showed just couldn't hide; the Dons had really won.
We made for home, we swelled with pride that only victory makes.
Then he in earnest told his mother the Dons had beaten the Fishcakes!

In the early spring of 1982 we as a family were about to make a short journey that would alter the course of the rest of our lives when fate took a hand in a big way for us. With the kids at the age they were, we were hopeful of an offer of a larger house from the council or the Scottish Special Housing Association. When the offer came it was as well that, for the first time in my life, I'd gone to work when I wasn't supposed to.

"What are you doing here on your day off?" questioned my surly boss.

I'd misread the rota sheets and turned up for a 6 am shift on the Monday.

Colin Watt, the British Rail Travel Centre Manager wasn't known for doing staff any favours. I'd been working an hour but was on my way to get my jacket and head home when for once he surprised me.

"Might as well work on and take tomorrow as your day off instead." he said quietly.

So it was that I was at home and not at work when the phone rang on the Tuesday morning. The girl on the line said she was from the Scottish Special Housing Association and was making us a verbal offer of a three-bedroom mid-terrace house at 69, Arnage Drive. She said the official offer would be in the post later that day—but I told her there and then that we'd be accepting!

I ran to Vera's work to tell her and her boss Cathy Paterson let her off for a few minutes so we could go and have a look. The scheme, just on the other side of the shops was our favourite part of Mastrick and we'd always been keen on a house there; it was perfect. The girl had told me the current tenant, Mrs Ingram, would be happy for us to visit and view the house. That's just what Vera, Leanne, Paul and I did that evening.

She was a lovely old lady who'd been the occupant of the house since it had been built, twenty-seven years before. She and her husband had raised their family there. Sadly he had died and she was moving to a sheltered housing complex. This house had been filled with love, you could sense it and we all loved it from the first moment we crossed its threshold.

How strange then that an offer did indeed fall through our letterbox the next morning but it was from Aberdeen City Council. They were offering us a house on Isla Place and had we not known of Arnage we would probably have jumped at it! But fate had lent a hand and although another two days would pass before the written offer for Arnage arrived we knew where we were going. That's life though, our chance now for a home we could build on.

For each of the children a room of their own.
For Vera not only a house but a home.
For me there'd be plenty of painting to do.
A garden out front and at the back too.
We planned the move as fast as we could.
Waiting not one moment more than we should.
We'd prayed for the time when this day drew near.
For Deveron Road shed not one single tear.

As we planned for the future in the home we'd longed for, owning a home of our own was still as much a pipe-dream as ever. Mortgage interest rates were as high as 13% and we felt we'd never be able to achieve our goal of home ownership. But 69, Arnage Drive was far from second best, it was all we'd ever wanted.

Our new neighbours must have wondered about us; my pal Ian Thompson and I carried most of our stuff from Deveron Road to Arnage Drive on our own. When moving day arrived we only needed to hire a small van for a couple of hours. We were too busy to pay much attention to the Budget headlines that Wednesday, but were happy to collapse in our chairs with a cup of tea late in the evening. I think we watched an episode of *Minder* before we went to bed for the first time in our new home. It had been a long hard day for us but Leanne and Paul had been out in the garden meeting all the neighbours' kids. They were well and truly settled in long before their bedtime that day.

We had a holiday planned for the kids Spring break from school, our first ever holiday! My free staff travel on the railway came in handy for our trip to Corby. Raymond and Lilian had settled there; they were running a chippy and were about to take over a pub called the Lantern. We were all looking forward to getting together again and we would be staying the week. The train got us as far as Peterborough and they drove through from Corby to collect us.

This was Thatcher's Britain and perhaps we'd been protected from its worst horrors by the benefits of oil in the North East of Scotland. Corby was an alien landscape! Their chippy and the Lantern stood in the middle of the huge Essex council estate but more than half of the houses were boarded up, vandalised or crumbling where they stood. The closure of the steelworks had created mass unemployment; the living heart had been ripped out of the town. This was a common malaise of many once proud industrial centres in 1982.

Ray and Lilian had bought a house, or should I say the shell of a house, from the local council for around £3000 and refurbished it completely. It was a scheme that formed part of a regeneration plan for the area but without work how could it succeed? We had just moved into a new house in Mastrick, itself a huge yet vibrant council scheme, but some of the streets on the Essex estate looked like scenes from a disaster movie. How lucky Vera and I were and how brave I thought Ray and Lilian were to pursue their dreams in this desolate place. Corby made me realise for the first time how serious was the devastation that was being wreaked on ordinary people by the nation's faltering economy.

In spite of that we had a wonderful time. It was great to all be together again and the kids were especially happy that week. We made plans to return the next summer for a longer stay. They'd have the pub by then and Lilian and Vera talked of their mum and dad coming down too. Stan on holiday at a pub where his son-in-law was mine host! If ever a man thought he'd died and gone to heaven that would have been it for him.

If ever a nation needed a cause to focus on, something to unite the spirit of its people, it was then for Britain. Strange indeed that it would be the invasion of tiny islands 8000 miles across the Atlantic Ocean that would arouse the country's passion. The farcical tin-pot leaders of Argentina's military junta had their forces invade the Falkland Islands. Mrs Thatcher's determination proved more than a match for their medal-laden chests and from the first Argentinian footsteps on South Georgia, to the formation of our Task Force and the Argentine surrender, the conflict lasted only three months. Brief it may have been but 900 men lost their lives and the sinking of the cruiser, General Belgrano, was perhaps pivotal in securing that quick end to hostilities. There are no winners in war but we all seemed to be boosted with the sense of victory and pride in our troops. Maybe there was a winner; the whole affair may well have been the factor that secured victory for the Prime Minister in the next election.

Paul was becoming a big football fan and thankfully at this stage was still both a Red and a Hammer like his dad. A disastrous flaw in the family genes later saw him become a Hibs fan and greater love hath no self respecting Dons fan and father than to buy his son a Hibs top for Christmas...yuk! That was still in the future but then I could still enjoy the halcyon days that were descending on Pittodrie with my son. As his own playing career took off I would desert Pittodrie to follow him but such a power were the Dons in those years that I don't believe we have ever gone to Pittodrie together and seen the Dons lose! Paul will never forget Alex McLeish's famous curler into the top corner in a superb cup final victory over Rangers. We also kept scrapbooks, just like my dad and I had done. Would Southampton or Swansea be English champions that year? There would be no fairytale and Liverpool would power past them both on the home stretch to clinch the title, but I remembered how magical things like that had been for me and knew he felt the same.

I never thought of my niece Paula as a difficult child but I knew that she'd had a difficult life. Annie and Bob were usually a great laugh but always a volatile mix. When they fused with my mum and dad, the sparks were sure to fly. My mum had never given up on the belief that Paula should have stayed with her and for a while she had. Annie, with a husband and two other girls to look after, could perhaps be forgiven for sometimes taking the easy option, but whatever course they followed it was sure to end with Paula feeling torn apart. In the late Spring of 1982 Annie asked if we would be willing to have Paula stay with us for a while. They were moving out to Kintore, Mum was maybe a wee bit too old for looking after a teenager and Paula wanted to finish her schooling at Northfield Academy.

My beautiful daughter was the kind heart that made it all possible. She was almost ten years old and had waited for a room of her own for so long. When we discussed it with her she didn't hesitate and said she'd be happy to share with Paula. So for almost two years Paula became a member of our family. She was in the school brass band and I bet that Eunice and Jim Morrison next door wondered what had hit them when she practised upstairs!

It was a combination of amazing circumstances that led to Paula's stay with us coming to a more abrupt end than we'd ever thought it would.

Bob had been adopted and always believed he was an orphan. Later that year he was to discover that his natural mother had been a young unmarried girl who'd felt unable to cope and had placed him for adoption. She'd later married but never had any more children. In time she was widowed and somehow Annie had traced her. Bob never wanted to meet her but when she died in 1984 she left him everything, including a hotel in Huntly which he later sold. I was never jealous of his good fortune; it had been a sad route that led there; but I was concerned that Paula was then being showered with gifts and possessions that we could never give our kids. We didn't see how we could let it carry on. We talked it over with Annie and Bob; we could understand their desire to give Paula all the things she'd never had and why, and knew full well that Paula was pleased to receive them. In the end Paula went home to live with her mum and dad and share in their good fortune. We hoped that we had contributed something good to Paula's life at an important stage, and her time with us was part of nineteen wonderful years at Arnage Drive.

We settled and felt secure with what the future held, but the death of Russian leader Leonid Brezhnev signalled the beginning of an era of change that would culminate in the end of the Soviet Union and alter forever the fragile balance of world power that had so far dominated the whole of my life. In the never-ending conflict that was the Middle East, the Israelis drove Yasir Arafat from Beirut and the Americans assumed the roll of peacekeepers; but they too would be forced out of Lebanon. A suitcase bomber killed 242 US Marines and it was difficult to see where the madness would end.

Lighter moments are never too far away with kids around, and Paul gave me one of the funniest when he told me the best joke I've ever heard. (Remember that it was being told by an eight-year-old.) He was completely breathless as he entered the living room—he'd ran all the way home from Westerton School.

"Dad, dad, dad, what's the sharpest thing in the world?" he gasped.

He'd obviously had a science lesson at school, I thought, so I offered confidently, "A laser beam?"

"No, no, no, it's not that!" he replied impatiently.

Think Dad; that'll be it, "A diamond drilling bit!" I affirmed confidently.

"No!" he shouted irritably and I could see he was desperate to put me out of my misery.

"What is it then?" I asked shrugging my shoulders in convincing bemusement.

With a wry grin of disdain he clarified, "It's a fart Dad, it goes right through yer breeks without leaving a hole!"

We were both still laughing when Vera got home from her work and I've been laughing at it for over twenty years since.

The charts were good for a laugh that year too. Bucks Fizz, Tight Fit, Captain Sensible and Renee and Renato were hardly acts destined for the hall of pop fame. When a group of kids called Musical Youth hit number one with

Pass The Dutchie, apparently a song about a giant frying pan, I knew I was getting old. Leanne would soon be plastering her bedroom walls with posters of her favourites and it was a bit worrying to see Paul miming the words of *House of Fun* when Madness came on the telly.

Charles and Diana were blessed with their first baby, William, and not for one moment did I envy the life in a goldfish bowl that lay ahead for that innocent newborn. It was a good life for our kids then and as they made friends so did we. Cath and Dave Farquharson were Susan and David's mum and dad and we all became firm friends. We had some monster parties especially at New Year time and we missed them when they moved off to Watford around ten years later.

Leanne finally lost a sweepstake when Hurricane Higgins made a tearful ascent of snooker's highest peak and reclaimed the World Snooker Championship with a win over Ray Reardon. Paul was pleased as punch and bought his first West Ham top with his winnings. We'd many magical moments that first year at Arnage and as we all sat one night watching the kids favourite movie, I felt we were one step ahead of *ET* and had already made our journey home.

The new house overshadowed the other big event in our lives that year. I changed jobs again! My job at British Rail had never been anything more than an exercise in putting money in our pockets and food on the kitchen table. I hated it and was desperate for a change. In response to an advert in the *Press & Journal*, I applied for a post as a Breakdown & Information Services operator with the Automobile Association at their Golden Square offices in Aberdeen.

The money was very good and I wouldn't have to do all the overtime I'd been taking on at the station. The shifts were super, three days on and three days off, 7 am to 7 pm each working day. It wasn't too long after I started working there that Vera went full-time with the Hydro and between my days off and Vera's day off during the week, arrangements weren't any more difficult for the kids. At last we seemed to be moving on to a time when we'd have a bit of spare cash; we hadn't really been in that position since my mad days in the oil industry.

The work involved arranging breakdown service for members, route planning, updating weather reports and giving technical information where possible. It was an interesting job and gave me the opportunity of my Andy Warhol moment, those fifteen minutes of perceived fame he said would come to us all in this life. For a few quid extra each week, it was impressively called our broadcasting allowance, I, along with some of the other lads, did the road reports on *Northsound*, *Radio Scotland* and *Radio Aberdeen*. It was great fun even though we were the butt of jokes by the *Northsound* DJ's and often told to keep it short by the ultra professionals at the Beeb. On those occasions, as we were only on for a minute at best anyway, I simply read my scripts faster and never missed out on any of the information. They didn't know they were dealing with a man who could sing *Sugartime* twice as fast as Alma Cogan! Fame may have been a word that gilded the lily somewhat as regards my broadcasting status. However I can claim to have been a straight man for Nicky Campbell in his Northsound days and Viv Lumsden was on the phone every morning for road report updates before she left the AA and became a top presenter with *BBC Scotland*. The reports took all of thirty minutes to prepare and deliver, during a twelve-hour shift, but the kids would always say that I did the road reports on the radio when anyone asked them what their dad worked at!

We had two teams in the control room who rotated ever three days. Ian Hopkins, Douglas Kemp, Dave Lindsay and myself formed one shift and Hebbie Nicoll had Eddie Murray, Bill Wright and young Pat, who married a patrolman called Wilson Cruickshank, on his team. Dave Maitland managed the control room and they were a thoroughly decent bunch. It was and is still by far the best job I ever had; we were like a group of pals who got together every day for a blether and were lucky enough to get paid for it in the process.

Our happy band did have enemies and like us I suspect many Aberdonians have incurred their wrath. Our arch adversaries were the men of the British Legion who sat god-like in their wee booth in the centre circle of Golden Square and arranged parking for the great and good of its business community. This was done for a suitable donation to their cause but as far as we knew they'd no official authority over the area. Woe betides anyone who tried to park in the hallowed inner circle without their permission and without offering the aforementioned alms. Most of the lads had cars and would be warned off this most convenient parking spot with veiled threats of the dire consequences that might befall their vehicles should they remain within the sanctified perimeter. In hindsight they were doing it for a good cause but boy did they have their jobsworth acts rehearsed to perfection.

Although I didn't have a car I admit I joined the plotters who planned to take them down a peg or two. We turned up very early one morning and filled the lock in the door of their booth with wonderful, fast-setting, rock-like Araldite. Then we watched from our attic control room window as the first arrival puzzled over his key's reluctance to enter the lock. Pandemonium reigned in the centre circle that day. With the cones well and truly secure in the lockfast booth, every Tom. Dick and Harry had their day and parked where they pleased. The little victories are the best!

I would work for three years at Golden Square before they closed the office and made us all redundant. Some boffin in Glasgow finally deduced that if they could service Aberdeen's breakdown needs from 7 pm to 7 am, they could do it all day; downsizing was a must for everyone in the Thatcher era. They gave me almost £3000 redundancy when the time came; we went on our first proper family holiday at last and began to harbour dreams of buying our own home once more. That sort of cash wouldn't make us home owners, we required help from much higher quarters to achieve that aim. Luckily the Prime Minister herself would lend a hand in our quest.

> Times were harder than we'd known,
> But in this we were not alone.
> Millions lost their jobs, their pride,
> We dodged this fate, were always hired.
> Our children grew in pleasing ways,
> In years of woe we knew great days.
> For some this time a poisoned chalice,
> Yet we had found ourselves a palace.

Goodbye Mum

On the nineteenth of January 1983, my last surviving grandparent, Christina Strachan Thomson, died at the House of Daviot by Inverurie. She was eighty-six years old and had been born before the end of the Boer War. Their large family and that family's children's' children had given her and William Lewis Thomson a strong hold on mortality. She had been almost five years old when Queen Victoria died and like that great queen had been a matriarch who'd shaped the daily lives and futures of many.

Even in the deepest chill of a cold sad winter, life shakes you and won't let you dwell on unhappy things for too long. If you feel you've nothing to smile at it'll find something for you. Heavy snow was falling and Arnage Drive was a Christmas card winter wonderland. The local snowball throwers were a pain in the parts though and after yet another thud against the living room window, I could take no more. As I darted across the living room and flung the window open to utter dire warnings to the perpetrators, I was well and truly battered by the second volley. As I turned red faced in anger, speechless and snow covered, to my dear family my hopes of sympathy were destroyed. Vera had fallen off her chair laughing, Leanne was heading for the kitchen to avoid looking at me but she wasn't making much headway as her legs were crossed! Paul, who was still lying on the settee watching telly, calmly brushed the half snowball that had landed near him to the floor and rolled his eyes in dismay as only an eight-year-old can. People who live in snow-covered houses shouldn't make moans!

We got our first £1 coin that year but nearer Christmas a gang of crooks pocketed a whole lot more when they made off with £25 million pounds' worth of gold bars. It was the biggest robbery the nation had ever seen, the Brinks-Mat job at Heathrow Airport. The year had started with the arrival of breakfast television and it's still the last place I'd want to cast my attention first thing in the morning.

The amazing era that Alex Ferguson had brought to Pittodrie was well and truly in full flight and on a Wednesday in May at a rain-lashed Ullevi Stadium in Gothenburg the Dons would pit their skills against the might of Real Madrid in the European Cup Winners Cup Final.

Wait a moment—I had stood on the terracing as a boy when Tommy Pearson managed the Dons, we knew we were a poor side but I remembered the song:

"So bring on the Hearts, the Hibs, the Celtic, bring on Spaniards by the score.
Barcelona, Real Madrid, we shall make a gallant bid,
For we're out to show the world what we can do."

Had somebody told me then that Aberdeen would one day play Real Madrid in a European Final I'd have given them their bus fares to Cornhill Hospital!

We organised a special night at Polmuir Bowling Club for the game. Ian Thompson and I were on bar duty and the place was mobbed. Real Madrid were not of the same vintage as the Sixties sides from the Bernabeu but their name...shouted, spoken or whispered...simply said, football giants! When John Hewitt's match winning header thudded past the Real goalkeeper eight minutes from the end of extra-time, the club was bouncing. Ian and I got ourselves a carry-out and headed home to celebrate but the entire city was having a party and Union Street was at a complete standstill. We eventually walked home to Mastrick and drank the carry-out on the way. I gave up trying to get my key in the lock and fell asleep outside the front door. Vera did rescue me, bless her! What a great night!

In a way Gothenburg marked the end of my days as a Dons supporter. Paul and I went to many games together but his own years on the field of dreams were just about to begin and my allegiance would be to him now and the teams he played for. I still avidly follow the Dons' fortunes but supporters live and breathe the excitement of each match they attend. I had thrilled and spilled with the Dons for over twenty years and loved every moment! The glory of Gothenburg was totally eclipsed for me in a matter of days, oh life you are a cruel lady!

I was day shift on the Sunday after the match, things were quiet, I picked up the phone and called my mum. Dad was decorating their bedroom and I asked her how he was getting on.

"Oh he's had his usual tantrums but is getting on fine now, I'm awa' tae get him a cup o' tea." she laughed.

It was the last time I ever spoke to her and she never did make that cup of tea.

Strange indeed that something so ordinary as a phone call can bring such shattering news. Vera is crying on the other end of the line and all manner of horrors race through my mind before she manages to tell me that my mum had died. No time to think, just go through the motions of getting from work to the hospital. Dad's there and looks as if he doesn't understand what's happened. I go to see her, kiss her and shiver at how cold she is, so soon. In the days that followed I needed Vera very much, for I had no torrent of tears to shed but hurt a deep hurt that bit hard deep down inside. It was good that my father and sister were able to share their overflowing grief and difficult for me to comprehend why mine was not the same. Even now there are things to do and arrangements to be made and this perhaps is the task for me. Vera and the kids are hurting too and through all this we need the love of one another.

This wasn't a time to think of my mother in terms of good or bad, this or that, for reflections did not change the fact that she was gone. We had all loved her in our own ways and would have our own pictures of her to carry in our minds. I saw my mother for the last time on the morning of her funeral and it was not the way I wished to remember her. If only I could have made my father feel this way, but he longed to hold on, have her in his arms once more. His heart and soul had been torn apart and he'd been left completely empty. We would all miss her and always love her. Dad told me later that Mum had put down the phone and called through to him that she was going to put on the kettle for a cup of tea. He heard her cry out in pain, ran to the kitchen and saw her with the half-filled kettle raised head-high. He held her, laid her to the floor and she died in his arms. She had died of a heart attack, which was indeed the third she had suffered. In all her years of poor health she just never would slow up.

I loved her in spite of herself.
She loved me as if without fault.
No raging storm of maternal love.
Yet strong enough for here I am.
Were there two people locked inside?
Sailing always on a troubled sea.
If only she had reached safe harbour.
This woman was mother to me.
Goodbye Mum.

Life perhaps turned out to be a sad song for my mother and although I'm sure she never meant it to be, it often became, *You Always Hurt The One You Love*. In those soft moments which we all encounter, a moment when a smile creases your cheek and a tear at once traces that crease, I think of my mum. When I feel that way the strains of *The Ballad of Lucy Jordan* run through my head and mix with the smiles and the tears. All the great songs tell a story and remember, a great song with a great story will always bring us treasured memories of loved ones.

It was as if the world had kept on spinning but we'd all stepped off for one turn. Day to day things just didn't seem to register or matter for a while. Maggie and Ronnie were working out a great routine together and politics was almost becoming interesting! Daley Thompson and Steve Cram became world champions for Britain at the inaugural Helsinki Games. Not to be outdone, Hollywood gave us another pair of heroes, Stallone as *Rambo* and Schwarzenegger as *Conan* were celluloid supermen for an American nation still recovering from defeat in Vietnam and beset by economic problems.

I had made my saddest farewell of all and now Leanne was preparing for her own long farewell, that rite of passage to growing up, the last year at primary school. Her reports had always been good but I wondered if my desire to ensure that she and Paul enjoyed school was doing them a disservice. Maybe I should have pushed them harder to achieve more? I may have let both my kids down in that respect but I know they have happy memories of all their schooldays. Mrs Taylor held Leanne in high regard and her final year teacher Mrs Balfour would form the same good opinions of her. What greater sense of pride for any parent than to know that other people are so pleased with the person their child is growing up to become?

Life's really a shorter race than you think, time advances unseen at high speed.
Was it not only yesterday when primary you left; now she too is ready to leave.
There she is talking fondly of times gone by, looking on to the challenge ahead.
With a blink you stifle the tear in your eye, wishing still to be her age instead.
Your own childhood days are fresh in your mind, not memories but living events.
Thinking yet of them as your freshest hours, confused at how fast time went.
So nourish her dreams of excitement to come and cherish the seed you have sown.
Understand as she lives them in life, as you love her you'll relive your own.

Paul had convinced Mr Innes he was silly, trying hard to improve but finding concentrating difficult. Chip off the old block there then! Mr Paterson however found him pleasant and helpful, especially to Mr Johnstone the janitor. John Johnstone ran the school football team and this was Paul's first year of training with the squad. Paul would have cleaned his windows, cut his grass and washed his car... twice a week, for free!
Our world did seem all about the kids then and a daily pleasure it was. They both had little blips that year, Leanne had her brace fitted, the first step in straightening all her teeth. She had to have two removed to allow the rest to be fixed and every visit to the orthodontist with Mum ended in a scolding for me, the cause of the problem all those years before.
Paul came home one day swathed in more bandages than an Egyptian mummy. A kind old lady had taken him in and done running repairs after he had a Brian Muir moment and got the brakes wrong on his bike. His pride would have needed a bigger bandage than his head for like Brian, the unkindest audience of all, his pals, had witnessed his acrobatics. Their laughter had hurt more than the tarmac he'd crashed onto.

135

A crash of another sort nearly did Vera a lot of harm. We'd bought new bedroom furniture for Leanne and Paula and were to give the old bedroom unit to my workmate Ian Hopkins. Full of good intentions Vera had tried to move the old one to the landing to make it easier for Ian and me to collect after work. Timber! The whole thing had toppled over and smashed through the new units. A distraught Vera had called me at work and graphically described the scene of devastation between sobs! Thankfully she was unhurt and the old unit had sustained surprisingly little damage and was still of use to Ian. The new bedroom suite was in bits but Ewen & Co. saved the day. The next day they delivered a replacement and told me they'd send the bill once they had salvaged what they could. They'd impressed us years before and they did again—I never did get the bill and we still shop with them today.

Leanne and Paul were the envy of their pals; my dad had laid out a putting green in the back garden for them and all the kids would come around to play. The bright red, metal, numbered flagsticks and plastic pipe lined cups made their six-hole course just like the real thing. Leanne began to learn that a growing brother was a real pain. He and David would hog the course for hours leaving Leanne and Susan more than a little annoyed. The girls were not easily put off though and their strategically placed dolls and prams would eventually prove too big an obstacle for the boys to play around. Then they'd let the girls have their long overdue turn and retire indoors to study the *Wee Red Book* or the *News of the World Football Annual*. Paul was now an avid fan of those annual football fact feasts, just as I had once been.

The saddest year of our married life was ending and we had all helped each other through it. Vera especially had kept my spirits high, and the Flying Pickets' *a cappella* delivery of *Only You* said it all. It was sad that none of us could pull my dad out of his terrible despair. His grief had made him give up his house; it held too many memories for him to face alone. He went to stay with Annie and Bob for a time yet somehow the easy comfort of a dram and a party would only ease the pain for a moment and then deepen his depression in the cold light of day. This was a lonely hard time for him and I was so wrapped in my own good life that I failed to help him as much as I could have.

It was as well I was with him on one of his final days at the flat. We were just tidying things up before he moved out. He was far away as he looked around the rooms and as we made a cup of tea in the kitchen I could sense all his pain welling up inside him. In sheer frustration and despair he smashed his fist through the kitchen window, and suddenly there was blood everywhere. The cut on his wrist was through to the bone; I tied a tourniquet on his arm and got him to hold it straight up. He didn't seem to feel any pain or be much concerned over the terrible injury that he'd inflicted on himself. The phone had been cut off because he was moving so I had to try several neighbours' doors before I found someone in to let me dial 999. I was proud that the ambulance men said I'd done all the right things, and happy that dad was fixed up at hospital but the sense of hopelessness that had driven him to do it should have rung louder warning bells for me.

I had thought of the arrival of 1984 since I was sixteen, when I had first read the book of the same name. The horror of an Orwellian world had not befallen us and Thatcherism was taking our nation away from state control. The Establishment and the workers did do battle however. In the guise of our police forces and the miners, thousands of men fought one another tooth and nail over job losses and wage demands. The miners were eventually beaten by a Government hell-bent on seeing their policies succeed; but their methods could easily have been those of the sinister *Big Brother* of the novel.

The country was in a mess but faults lay on both sides, a Government using its police against its people and a Union selfish in its demands. As a boy I remembered how my father had worked long hours in physically demanding jobs for a pittance. It troubled me as I grew that Trade Unions always seemed to grab the moral high ground, but I don't recall any powerful Union voice ever say that *he* deserved a penny more. Aye, there's more than enough for us all in this world but it's doing the sharing that's the hard bit.

I said goodbye to my baby that year as Leanne set off to Summerhill Academy. Until that first secondary school day you can still tell them that the world is made of green cheese. She came home for lunch that first day and said, "No it's not dad!"

Goodbye baby, hello Leanne!

So that's it Lee, off you fly.
No stopping now, the limits the sky.
You'll swim in a much bigger pond.
No nursery rhymes, no magic wand.

If success is unexpected then it is surely all the sweeter smelling. That's exactly how it was for me in the summer of 1984. George Orwell's year of gloom certainly turned out to be a fine time for me. I rolled with seeming ease from one success to another and achieved what amounted to a lifetime's ambitions at bowls in four short months. Immediately I learned that the pleasure of winning only has value if you have someone to share it with. I had three people, in fact four, for Paula was still with us then, who let me share my victorious days with them and thus gave them a real meaning. The tide of success flowed on to what for me were tidal wave proportions after that summer. Paul had started to play for his school football team and although not one of the star performers, he brought a dedication and effort to his matches that I was so proud of, that I, at his age, could never have hoped to match. The team's pinnacle of success came at Pittodrie as they clinched the Cup and we were all so proud of him. My dad was at the final and I wished that my mum had witnessed my success and been able to feel for me as I did for Paul then. That strange music for the moment syndrome warned us all not to get too carried away when *Yesterday's Men* rang out in the charts just after the dust had settled on our successes.

My summer of success at the bowls started with my first attempt at skipping a rink. Davie Pattillo, his son Davie and son-in-law Bob Logan travelled the victory road with me to Dyce where we upset the holders, John Forrest, Peter Jappy, Jim Fowlie and Davie Mellis in the final. Playing at lead, old Davie was our star man that night. A county title...most players never win one—I was delighted!

The next Bon Accord Championship was the singles and I started with little expectation, but four wins in the qualifying at my own Polmuir green saw me through to the last sixteen. My opponent was Balgownie's Les Donald, a young man who was already a county player. Paul came to support me and his bright smile shone through the glass front of the Bonnymuir clubhouse as the game began. It dimmed to an almost invisible peep as Les powered into 9-1, 14-3 and finally 19-6 leads and as I slumped, less and less of his unhappy face was visible. I looked for Paul as we prepared for the next end and apart from his hair he had completely disappeared! Watching your dad being thrashed is hard going when you're ten years old.

At that moment a man and a young lady entered through the clubhouse gate and walked to the side of our rink. I guessed they might be Les's dad and his girlfriend. The man quietly asked Les who was ahead, a thumbs up from Les confirmed the situation and then, although he whispered it, I clearly heard Les say, "I'll only be a few minutes."

I'd have thought exactly the same in his shoes, but the fat lady was only gargling, not singing, and the words chickens and hatched would come back to haunt poor Les. As the tide of the match turned my comeback was confirmed by the re-appearance of firstly Paul's eyes, then his nose and finally his smile at the clubhouse window. Forty minutes later we shook hands as my 21-20 victory saw me into the quarter-finals.

Val and Gladys Henry and their sons Steve and Roy, are one of Aberdeen's best known bowling families. All super players, Roy a national champion. Vera had been best pals with their daughter Valerie through secondary school. The competition would finish at Cults Bowling Club but the Henry family blocked my way to further progress.

Steve and I played an acrimonious quarter final and he walked off the green after my 21-17 win accusing me of playing the unplayable hand all night and being even luckier against him than I'd been against Les. We did shake hands and have a blether in the clubhouse later; I've always envied Steve his ultra competitive edge.

Fate pitted me against Val in the semi-final; it was a match worthy of being the final. I don't think that either of us could have played better. The only odd thing about the game was Val whistling *Oh How I Miss You Tonight* all the way through. Val can be a little hard of hearing and probably wasn't even aware he was doing it. I didn't mind, he was a good whistler and I liked the tune. The match went to the very last bowl, was the finest I've ever played in and another 21-20 win saw me into the final.

My final opponent, John Clark, was a Cults member and would have the added pressure of playing in front of his home crowd; we were both appearing in our first major singles final. John was an absolute gentleman but the night of the final I was, as they say, in the zone. I have never, before or since, played as well and remain convinced that I would have beaten anyone that night. The 21-3 scoreline in my favour reflected how good I was feeling about the game on that summer evening over twenty years ago.

My Bon Accord saga for that year was completed when I was selected by Polmuir to skip the triples rink at the end of the season. Graeme Stewart, Charlie Walker and I recorded an undeserved 13-12 win over Ian McFarlane's Cults triple in the final at Culter. One of my opponents that night, Colin Mearns, became a firm friend and as my game disintegrated in the years ahead it was a few coaching tips from him that helped keep me on the green with so many wonderful people. What happened to me in the pairs that year? John Gallon and I teamed up and I honestly can't remember if we lost in the last sixteen or the last eight. The Grand Slam would have been too much to ask but I treasure forever the memory of the few weeks when I stepped out of the sporting shadows.

Les, Steve, Val and John went on to have far more successful bowling careers than I and I plumbed the depths as quickly as I had scaled the heights. I still play and enjoy being just another ordinary club player. I've learned that the companionship of the game is more important than any brief moment of glory. The essence of that companionship was highlighted by my blossoming friendship with Bill Anderson. Vera and I became great pals with him and his wife Nancy and we'd many super social evenings at Polmuir and each other's houses. Bill and I also discovered that our passion for sport included tennis and our weekly game became and still is a much-enjoyed ritual for us both. How better to spend time than with a great friend in the pursuit of a great pleasure?

The world spins ever round and round,
As we our pipe dreams chase.
From dark days an escape is found,
And glory takes their place.
So with success the briefest brush,
Was mine's to have and savour.
The nicest part of victory's rush,
Paul too would share the flavour.

Paula had given us an instant teenager but she had settled in well. Her one annoying habit was to constantly sing *Relax Don't Do It* by Frankie Goes To Hollywood. I might have enjoyed the whole song but she only seemed to know the first line! The Boss was more to my liking and I got my first Springsteen album that year, *Born In The USA*. The music world led the way in raising funds for famine relief in Ethiopia. Bob Geldof was brash, wore his heart on his sleeve and brought the F-word into our living rooms on a Saturday evening but his amazing efforts in organising the Bandaid concert were astonishing. We all rushed to the record shops to buy the anthem of the cause, *Do They Know It's Christmas?*

The Dons won the Scottish Cup for the third year in succession and how easily we began to take success for granted. No-one in Scotland had ever taken rugby success for granted but after a gap of almost sixty years we finally won the coveted Grand Slam again. Paul and I became cycling fans and thrilled as Robert Millar became King of the Mountains in the Tour de France and finished fourth overall. Vera and Leanne preferred the more graceful perfection of Olympic Ice Dance Champions, Jayne Torvill and Christopher Dean. Their *Bolero* routine was as flawless as the gymnastic brilliance Nadia Comaneci had displayed to the world in Montreal eight years earlier. At the 1984 summer Olympics one Carl Lewis emulated the quadruple gold medal haul of Jesse Owens. How different the acclaim for those two wonderful athletes—Lewis adored by his own nation in Los Angeles and Owens a man alone in Nazi Germany at the 1936 Berlin Olympics.

There was nothing to smile at in the bitter miner's strike but we had a little wage dispute of our own that year. Paul had walked to the shops with me; one of the things I had to do was cash our Child Benefit at the Post Office.

"Why do you get that money, Dad?" he asked innocently.

"Oh it's you and Leanne's wages," I replied casually.

"What happens to them?" he quizzed curiously.

"Mum spends them," I waffled.

"Do you always get them?" he enquired gravely.

"Ever since you were born," I said smiling.

Vera wasn't smiling later that night when Paul asked her what she'd done with his £2500 wages, as he'd not received a penny of it his whole life! I was impressed by his cheek and would have been overawed at his maths but guessed that Leanne had been his financial adviser. He was quickly put in his place by his mum and declined her offer to run his own affairs from now on with a £5 a week budget. I'd set him up and he was not a happy chappy for a day or two.

The IRA struck a blow at the very heart of Government as they blew up the Grand Hotel in Brighton during the Conservative Party conference. I felt no affinity for the Thatcher Government but they were my country's elected one and for the first time I began to believe the IRA were against me. Solutions would need to be found in Ireland but they would have to come through the rule of law and not because of our fear of the gun and the bomb.

A town called Bhopal in India was the scene of a disaster that brought home to us just how susceptible we could be to our own scientific development if it is not safely managed. A chemical storage tank at a Union Carbide factory leaked and more than 2000 people died, with thousands more injured. Ever since the industrial development of the nineteenth century scientific advance had appeared to be the genie in the bottle that had provided all that a developing world wished for. This had often been at high cost to those nearest the coal-face and showed that we needed to be careful that we knew how to keep the lid firmly on the bottle at all times.

By the end of the year Paula would have left us to go home to her mum and dad. We hoped it would work out well for them all. Secondary school teachers made Vera and I as proud as punch as they reported our own daughter was hard working, attentive to her lessons, a pleasant girl to know, friendly and well behaved. Her year teacher, Mr Walsh, was only confirming what we already knew but we all have that blind love for our kids and it's so good to know the world thinks well of them too.

I'd had a brief moment of success but it paled in comparison to Paul's road to glory, which would end with him playing at my boyhood sporting Mecca, Pittodrie Stadium. John Johnstone had a wonderful football team at Westerton that year. Like all great sides they had that solid spine that held them together and all the others, Paul included, played their roles to perfection.

Goalie Michael Mulloy, centre half Don McIntosh, midfield maestro Paul Vettese and the incomparable Colin MacRonald in attack were that solid spine and the edge that carried the boys to the Willoughby Cup Final at Pittodrie against Abbotswell.

Paul played that whole season at left back and as Vera, Leanne, my dad and I sat in the main stand one little cameo stays in my memory. He chased back after a long ball over the top; under pressure from the winger he feinted a back-pass to Michael in goal. The winger moved inside, Paul turned to the touchline and sent a lovely ball up the line to Colin. The Cup was sealed with a 3-0 triumph; the pride on the boys' faces as they received their medals was a joy to behold. But there's always a fly in the ointment; I was the only dad with a Betamax video recorder. All the dads had chipped in to have the game recorded and my copy of the game became obsolete in a couple of years. It's become my Holy Grail these last twenty years to find a copy of that tape and watch those magic moments once more.

Oh life, you are a strange joining of happy days and sad, sad times. After giving us such a wonderful year the dreaded word redundancy was about to bring much uncertainty into our lives. Phil Smith was a tall, silver haired, well dressed, imposing man and also the AA's Scottish Breakdown Services Manager. He was uncharacteristically subdued that spring morning when he arrived in Aberdeen to talk to all of us.

It certainly was a bolt from the blue when he advised us all that the Aberdeen Control Room was being closed. A few of us would be offered jobs in Glasgow but there would be redundancies and the closure would be phased in over six to nine months. I was offered a post in Glasgow but moving there was never a serious option for us. I didn't want to hang around under a cloud and within weeks found myself another job with the council as workshops receptionist at the Cleansing Depot at Kittybrewster. It was a temporary post but perhaps it might lead to other things. At least it had possibilities; the AA was now a dead-end. If I'd known what those possibilities were perhaps I wouldn't have jumped ship so quickly.

The Government finally beat the miners and their return to work signalled a change in industrial relations that seemed to turn the country back to the days when employers had all the power. My grandfather had spoken once of returning to 'a land fit for heroes' and having to fight other men for a single day's work as a slapdasher at the Hall Russell's shipyard. The Iron Lady had seen off Arthur Scargill—but who were the real winners?

Mikhail Gorbachev came to power in the Soviet Union and began to implement programmes of reform that would alter the shape of our political world forever. He did not complete the political journey to see them to fruition, however and in the end the mighty power of my youth, the Soviet Union, crumbled under a landslide of corruption and economic mayhem. Perhaps if the West had accepted Gorbachev at face value much sooner, the transformation of the Soviet Empire would have been more orderly.

The bikini-clad girls of the earliest Bond movies had been my first pin-ups, and at the age I was then I smiled at the thought that Madonna may have been Paul's first fantasy lady. She reached number one for the first time in 1985 with *Into the Groove*. Madonna would have looked as good as Ursula in that white bikini but she'd never sing *Love Letters* like Ketty Lester!

Paul and I had two new sporting heroes that summer. We were amazed at the power, aggression and stamina of Bernard Hinault as he swept to his fifth Tour de France victory and spellbound by a seventeen year old German at Wimbledon. Boris Becker exploded to the title and looked like a circus acrobat as he leapt and dived over every blade of grass on Centre Court. In the most dramatic piece of television entertainment, Dennis Taylor defeated Steve Davis on the last ball of the last frame to win the World Snooker Championship. Nobody had expected Taylor to win but guess who had him as their second pick in our sweepstake...Leanne!

I got two things badly wrong that year; one of them broke the kids' hearts and the other might have broken the lifelong bond of harmony I've had with my son if I hadn't quickly remembered I was the adult and he was the eleven-year-old.

Vera and I decided that we'd get the kids a dog and a bundle of brown and white mischief entered our lives. I'd told the kids all about my boyhood adventures with my dog and their little Springer Spaniel would have the same name, Rogie. The kids loved him and for a while things went well. It was difficult with Vera and I at work and the kids at school all day. Perhaps if I'd still been on shifts it might have worked but I know I didn't try hard enough to keep him with us. The day I left him at the Cat and Dog home I slunk home along side streets, ashamed of myself. The kids never made an issue of it with me and that's to their eternal credit, it just took me a long time to look them both in the eye again.

Paul was in his last year at Westerton and was now centre-half of the school team. A twenty-five yard scorcher in their pre-season trial at Sheddocksley gave me hope of more great days ahead, but they were not the team of the previous year. After a defeat at Harlaw I berated Paul about how poorly he had played. I saw the confusion and disappointment on his face and immediately felt a fool. Wait a minute Dad, the pleasure of this is watching your son do something that gives him pleasure. Every time he does that makes it a great day for you. The winning or losing means nothing, I shut my mouth and have kept it closed for twenty years since, except for voicing my thanks for all the great days he and all his teamates have given me over the years... win, lose or draw.

An epidemic was brought to our attention by the World Health Organisation and the world became familiar with the Human Immunodeficiency Virus, HIV. Initially dismissed as a disease that only affected homosexuals, it would become a major concern around the globe and twelve years later over two million people were dying annually from HIV/AIDS. That year the high profile death of Hollywood star Rock Hudson raised awareness and sympathy, but the battle to find a cure for this mass killer continues.

Two disasters befell the world of football when over forty fans died in a fire at Bradford City's Valley Parade ground and then a similar number perished amid scenes of senseless crowd violence at the Heysel Stadium in Brussels prior to the Liverpool-Juventus European cup final. The meaningless sham of a game that followed in Belgium that night brought no credit to anyone.

Since I first saw that beautiful, sleeping, orange face I had believed in miracles. The years that followed had done nothing to dissuade me from that belief, but my how time had flown, and here was my baby about to join the ranks of teenagers, when children become an alien species and parents struggle to find a way to talk to someone who days earlier would have been smothered in a loving hug to cure all ills.

Now when I did that an indignant young lady would cry, '...leave my property alone...' in reference to the new woman she was growing into and her need to now be oh so personal and private. Bear hugs from dads were out for young ladies! As I had done, Leanne would soon sort out all her teenage selves and I would learn to know and love each one.

The downside to Leanne's teenage days were a Norwegian pop group! How could a country that had produced more Eurovision noughts than a pools winner's cheque come up with a group to conquer the British music scene? Leanne would sit quietly in the living room but the mere knock on the door from her best chum, Maureen Cruickshank, would galvanise her into action and strangely, simultaneous fits of laughter. Then off upstairs they'd run to that secret teenage world of whispers and giggles, then the melodies of

A-HA would fill the house. What did *Take On Me* mean and how could *The Sun Always Shine On TV*?

In spite of the Viking invasion music still had something to offer me and Chris Rea's *Stainsby Girls* introduced me to his great voice and music that would be a pleasure for years to come. Live Aid concerts in London and Philadelphia helped raise £40 million for famine relief in Ethiopia and 1.5 billion people world-wide were said to have watched them on television. These efforts were fantastic but our sophisticated modern world still seemed as far as ever away from finding permanent solutions to the horrors that afflicted its poorest people.

So special that first moment, so special still today.
How quickly all those years went, how quickly came the day.
My daughter then a baby, my daughter now so grown.
Leanne soon to be a lady, Leanne will ever stay my own.

Is it possible, can it really be, have fifteen years slipped by so quickly? Regret perhaps at the passing of them but no regret for the living of them. Such heady days indeed with any lows along the way, mere pinpricks on the beautiful tapestry that our life together had become. Two lovely children, the daughter so sure of life, so honest and the son, so much the boy that we always hoped he would become. A rare bargain indeed, those fifteen years, so much gained, it seems for so little given. What of times ahead, could fortune's star shine so bright for another fifteen years? We lived in hope! Soon another life would begin with children gone and we two left alone to learn even more of each other. Then would there once more be the miracle of birth, would tiny steps on shaking legs again be watched with wonder? Yes there was much to look forward to and many happy memories to treasure. That magical musical time clock that seems to chime at every happy moment in my life was sure to be ticking away and as always summed up my situation perfectly. I knew as well as Sam Cooke that it was indeed a *Wonderful World*.

My love for you shall truly last,
A bridge to the future from the past.
However long our days may be,
You shall I pray remain with me.

From happy days we travel on,
And more shall follow those now gone.
The road we walk may twist and turn,
But my love will forever burn.

A comfort many times through life,
A friend, a lover and a wife.

144

Be sure I search for nothing more,
Than we continue as before.

Those many times I let you down,
Or stirred a tear or caused a frown.
For these forgive me if you choose,
Be sure my love you'll never lose.

Like Eric Clapton we were at the crossroads, Vera and I. It had been almost two years since I'd been made redundant and the temporary job I had with the council was getting me nowhere as fast as an elephant tap dancing on quick setting cement. We felt a change was needed, but there's always a fire burning just outside the frying pan. During the summer of 1986 the chance of a move came along and so I took the plunge into the Control Room at our local Police Headquarters. It wasn't easy for Vera or the kids because in honesty the job was a bitch and the shifts were the pits but the *Catch 22* of good job security and good wages kept me going. I was a pain to live with in the run-up to Christmas that year, the job often got to me and as always I took that out on the ones closest to me; as always they stuck by me.

Jack William Nicklaus just couldn't stop trying to close the gap on Muhammad Ali in my fantasy race along Union Street. At the age of forty-six he claimed his sixth US Masters title at Augusta. His demeanour in and away from the sporting arena marked him as a special man and he always gave the impression that life had blessed him with something much more important than sporting greatness, his family. The Greatest must have heard Jack's footsteps fall ever closer as they entered the home stretch.

Leanne became a working girl as she took on a delivery round for the *Aberdeen Advertiser*. Talk about slave labour! She, David, Paul and Susan could all fill a bag of papers and still not have a straight back between them! Vera even took pity and often went out with her to lend a hand. It always seemed such an awful lot of effort to deliver a paper that as often as not hit the rubbish bin in pristine condition.

There didn't seem to be much opposition being delivered to our government back then and the first signs showed that their own in-fighting might eventually bring about their downfall. The Westland Affair let the public see what a murky, treacherous world our politicians operate in.

The world learned neither peacetime nor neutrality could save a nation from the threat of nuclear power. The Chernobyl nuclear disaster saw fallout carried around the globe and the effects would be felt into the next century.

Going to the movies was almost a thing of the past but a video, a Chinese take-away and a glass of wine were a great way to spend a family night in. Leanne and Paul never had the wine of course but they always disagreed about which film we hired! *Crocodile Dundee* was the big favourite that year and Vera did become just a tad scary as she brandished her tattie-peeler in the kitchen, telling us all, "Now this is a knife!"

Bob Hoskins stole the show for me in one of those superb British movies, *Mona Lisa*. The hard-boiled tough guy with a soft centre is finally a victim of love, in a tale that looked at the dark side of a world devoid of morality.

I was determined to keep up with the kids and I listened to all the music of the day but if I hinted at a liking for bands like Dire Straits or the House-martins it compelled the kids, in time honoured fashion, to say they didn't think much of them. Whoever the kid's favourites were, neither Five Star nor Nick Berry were ever going to make it into my record collection. Vera and I went to a Sixties night at the Beach Ballroom with some pals, I think it was Stan Fraser first half and Tommy Dene after the interval. Memories came flooding back of years gone by, especially as they played Chris De Burgh's current hit, *The Lady In Red*, before things got started. I looked across the table at Vera and there was the girl I'd met at the Palace looking back at me.

They announced there was a wee surprise for us at half-time; Bobby Vincent was going to sing us a song. I hadn't seen Bobby in years but had heard that his health was failing him. It was sad to see him limp up on to the stage; he held his mouth organ in his hand and looked a frail and lonely figure as he stood at the microphone. Bobby had always been the real deal and when he started to sing the joint was jumpin'. His delivery of *Down At The Club* was perfect and there was no way he'd get off the stage after just one number. He gave us *Save The Last Dance For Me*, smiled, waved and then left the stage without a backward glance. I could have kissed Vera and gone home happy there and then.

Our favourite TV sports gave us an amazing contrast in 1986. Eric Bristow, the Crafty Cockney, took his third World Championship in a row and looked unbeatable. Joe Johnson arrived at The Crucible a 150-1 outsider; he had never even won a match there. Time after time Joe smiled his way through games, making frame winning breaks in the process, usually when he was behind and the frame looked lost. His penchant for winkle-picker shoes and his 'what am I doing here' expression made him a lovely character to watch. He was superb in his shock final victory over Steve Davis. Yes Leanne had picked him in the sweepstake...she liked his shoes!

My job in the Control Room at Police Headquarters remains the most unpleasant, difficult work I have ever undertaken. The management style always seemed to be, "We've got a difficult job here, how can we make it harder?" Dave Leitch started on the same day as me; his dad Stanley and Vera's dad had been drivers and workmates together since the days of the old LNER. Vera had known him since they were kids and he and I would become firm friends. We see a lot of things in life the same way and don't take ourselves too seriously. Dave got a raw deal at Grampian Police and left before his probationary period of six months was up. He seemed to be getting the hang of things okay but was always being pressurised to do better; I never quite understood that and I've seen some real duffers be carried along in my time. He left to join the Royal Mail and I stayed at Queen Street, we're still great friends and work is still the bane of both our lives!

The death of two great football men, Jock Stein in 1985 and Chris Anderson in 1986 were pivotal in Alex Ferguson moving on from Pittodrie. His shared roll as Aberdeen and Scotland manager after Stein's death made it clear he was looking for a bigger challenge. The loss of Chris Anderson, the man who made Pittodrie tick behind the scenes, perhaps made him feel all that could be achieved there was now behind him. In the years to come Dons supporters would be in no doubt that it had been two men, Ferguson and Anderson, aided by a superbly gifted group of young footballers, who had made the club the power it was. Would we see their like again? Certainly not in 1987 with Ian Porterfield now at the helm and the club seemingly losing direction.

Paul would join his sister in the teenage ranks and Vera and I were beginning to feel that our life clocks were ticking just a wee bit too fast. Where were all the years going to? I thought of us having come all this way together and wondered just where our children had gone.

Sparkling, impish, loving eyes, the pricked up ears that hear no lies.
The softest heart so quickly broken, lips from which just truth is spoken.
This a treasure, this a child, a wondrous person meek and mild.
Believing all and trusting others, blind in faith to fathers...mothers.

Such a pleasure quickly lost, the loving heart feels icy frost.
The many times when they're not there, the secrets we no longer share.
So on in life they quickly travel, all its mysteries to unravel.
In time themselves to take their lovers, then play the role of fathers...mothers.

Vera has a thing about living room suites and the new one that we'd bought in the January sales meant we'd had almost as many of them as we'd had anniversaries. Maybe this was number thirteen because a week after we bought it a mysterious tear appeared on one of the chairs. Paul was the culprit, having sat down with a sharp pencil in his back pocket, but the confession didn't come until a week or two later when the heat was off and I'd calmed down a bit. Vera was never going to live with a suite with a patch on it; its days were numbered from the moment the rip appeared!

Whilst on a mission to Beirut to try and arrange the release of hostages, Terry Waite was himself taken hostage and would remain a captive for the next five years. Most of us were unaware of the problems that plagued the Lebanon but Terry's plight changed all that and the story of his own marvellous spirit and courage would be an inspiration in the days following his eventual release.

Leanne had taken on a newspaper round at R S McColl's and then moved on to a weekend job in the shop. She was never afraid of hard work and her school reports echoed that fact. Paul was getting reports every bit as good and went through his entire Autumn term of 2nd year without a single absence. In a world that was so difficult for youngsters, Vera and I were delighted that our kids seemed to be so well adjusted to life. Leanne was looking forward to a school trip to Tomintoul; the break from work would be good for her. Summerhill didn't have a football team; none of the teachers were willing to volunteer their time to do it, changed days indeed from Westerton! Paul was playing all his football with ALC Spurs so wasn't missing out. The Lads' Club had long since moved from their Hutcheon Street base of my youth, it had been demolished to build a roundabout—the god Car had to be appeased at all times. Paul went to their new premises at Tillydrone once a week for training. Another childhood friend of mine, Davie Johnstone, was now in charge there. In June that year Paul did at least have one sporting memory to treasure from Summerhill, when he won the 100 metres, 400 metres, and high jump and was in the winning relay squad at the school sports.

My namesake Sid Waddell was the totally over the top commentator at all the big darts events. Sid would assault our ears with some awful drivel but still came up with classics like, "That's the greatest comeback since Lazarus." Vera, a rival for Mrs Malaprop on her day and always willing to mix a metaphor with the best of them, simply loved Sid. At that year's World Championships Sid was brutalising the English language in fine style. Vera could take no more and put him to the sword superbly.

" If that eejit opens his moo and spiks ony mair shite, he'll swallie his ane heid!" she proclaimed.

Paul didn't swallow his head but he certainly re-arranged it. We didn't know whether to laugh or cry when he walked in with a *Max Headroom* haircut, but I pointed out to Vera that he'd come in handy as a toilet brush for her or I could make use of him if I ran out of sandpaper when I was paint stripping all the woodwork. This was just the beginning of Paul's proclivity for hairstyles that were weird and wonderful to say the least. Vera has all the mug shots and they will be used in evidence against him when the day comes that he tries to talk sense to his own kids.

We had a bit of bad news in May when Vera was diagnosed with an ovarian cyst, which was so large that the doctors would have to perform a full hysterectomy to remove it. She was only 32 years old and the operation could not be done until November that year. We were thankful however that there were no signs of anything malignant. After the operation she had complications with an infection and it would be the end of March the following year before she got back to work. It was a very difficult time for us all.

These loving times we hold so dear, I pray you will be ever near.
So we in life can always share, the fruits of love abundant there.

My friend, my lover, mother, wife with you I'll spend the whole of life.
All words of love to you I've spoken, these few lines another token.

Apart from visiting Ray and Lilian, we had never had a family holiday. My new job in the Police Control Room was not the sinecure I'd looked for in life but I was at an age when I valued the security and they threw more overtime at you than you could shake a stick at, so the money was very good. Before Vera went into hospital we planned to have a proper holiday. The Isle of Man would be our destination. A sun that shone for days on end, such was our summer. The clear blue Irish Sea was crossed and Columbus like we disembarked. The Isle of Man was all we had hoped it would be and more. We had caught this island jewel at its most beautiful. Friends were easy to make and having fun became commonplace. It would be a great memory for us all to treasure.

The sporting highlight of the year for me was Jimmy Connors' amazing Wimbledon comeback against Michael Pernfors. The thirty-four-year-old recovered from 1-6, 1-6, 1-4 down to win in five sets. Now there was an event that Mr Waddell could have done justice to!

Two strangers were about to enter our lives and change our ways forever. I had failed abysmally in our first attempt as pet owners and to their credit Vera and the kids had never showed how much they missed Rogie, which I knew was for my benefit. It was with some apprehension that I awaited our new arrivals. The two intrepid travellers arrived with Vera; she had got them from one of the girls at work. So we had them, two fluffy bundles, one a bold, inquisitive but obviously loving ginger tom and the other a tiny, fretting and timid creature that would need much loving. Paul claimed the ginger tom as his and named him Tinker, Leanne just wanted to mother the wee one but the name she chose, Spike, seemed a little out of character. Cats had features I quickly came to admire, their independence was total and their eyes never left danger when it threatened. Curtain climbing was one of their less endearing traits and Spike took to sleeping atop the gas fire on the living room wall. Her tail would droop down but when the fire was on it would overheat and shoot straight up in the air. Smoke would sometimes be coming from it but it never seemed to disturb her slumbers! Their feet were soon well and truly under our table so I'd just have to live with it.

Over the years we had kept in touch with Stan and Lil but it was a looser contact than I'm sure we'd all hoped for. It often centred on a few drams at their local and only in the years ahead would we discover what a strong hold the demon drink had taken on their lives. Vera and her sister seemed resigned to this permanent rift, it was all so sad. I met up with them one day for a couple of beers; Stan had taken early retirement and Lil was organising a party at the Lorne Bar. We planned for us all to get involved and it happily became more of a family re-union. The party was a great success and it gave Vera a chance to re-new ties with her mum and dad and for Leanne and Paul it meant they'd know more of their grandparents, for fate had robbed them of their chance to really know my mum.

So in a new spirit of togetherness we approached Christmas and New Year. Ben Johnson astounded the world with his speed at the world athletics championships but was only a year away from disgrace at the Olympics. Closer to home a siege at Peterhead Prison was rumoured to have been ended by the SAS; I knew but couldn't tell! Much to Leanne's liking Stephen Hendry won his first major snooker title; much to our liking it wasn't the World Championship so there wasn't a sweeper to lose. As always I foxed the kids with cryptic rhymes on their Christmas presents but sadly spent my first ever New Year away from home at work. Paul looked after Mum and Leanne, fast growing up, was out first-footing.

From the time I'd been made redundant from the AA we'd been sensible with the bit of money I'd gotten and had now set the wheels in motion to buy our house at Arnage Drive. With our 'right to buy' discount the house would cost us £15800 and we planned to run a mortgage of £23000, which would let us put in a new kitchen and bathroom and fit double glazing. We were so keen to become homeowners but the Black Monday stock market crash in October did have us wondering if we were doing the right thing. It would take a year for all the legalities to be sorted out, so we had plenty of time to wait and worry.

I was hospitalised too that year to have my four impacted wisdom teeth removed. I was a bit uncomfortable for a few days but nothing more. On one of the days I was off work I met my pal Ian Thompson. He was now working for the Cleansing and swept the streets around the Mastrick Shopping Centre. Ian had the cure for my pain he said and popped up the lid of his barrow to reveal two whisky bottles neatly mounted in their optics.

"A wee dram for the pain, sir?" offered Ian.

"You know I'm a beer man Ian." I declined.

Quick as a flash Ian opened a thermos flask and poured me a beer. Ian was a lovely lad but did have to admit to a drinking problem—and that illness would cost him his marriage as well as his job. Such a nice man deserved fate to deal him a better hand.

Great music from the present and the past stays in my mind from that year. Ben E King was back in the charts with *Stand By Me* and the Christians beautiful song, *Ideal World*, certainly had me thinking about the many inequalities that existed within it. When Vera was in hospital and the kids had gone to bed, I'd play Judy Boucher's *Can't Be With You Tonight*, over and over.

Working at Queen Street was hard work and the whole experience was a culture shock in comparison to the Fire Brigade and the AA. The answering of 999's, acceptance of normal calls and mobilisation of police responses was non-stop; no wonder air traffic controllers burn out in their mid thirties. Vera and I seemed to have no life together at all but needs must when the devil drives and I was in for the long haul now. The work moved constantly from life's most serious events to the most ridiculous requests for police assistance.

Late in the year, in the early morning hours of a reasonably quiet night-shift, a man called on the 999 line and told me he had killed his wife. Denis was his name and I believed him. I was still talking to him when the police arrived at the call box he was in. He had indeed killed her, a terrible tragedy; a loving couple, a moment of madness. Her life lost, his as well, and their family devastated.

The other side of the coin: a drunk female on the 999 screams repeatedly for a can of coke. Ignoring all warnings to clear the emergency lines she finally managed to clarify, 'I cannae cope!'. Well if she'd had more coke in her vodka then I'm sure she would have managed.

If one man wanted to see the end of 1987 it was BBC weatherman Michael Fish. On the night of October the 15th he assured us all there was no hurricane on the way. By morning it seemed as if half of the trees in southeast England had been blown down. Over quarter of a million homes were without power for a week and it was a blessing that only twenty people died during the storm. Thankfully it had unfolded whilst most of us were safely tucked up in bed.

1988 would be a determining year in our lives, the legal process of buying our home would drag on until August but I was already stripping paint and wallpaper in preparation for the transformations we'd be making after our new windows, kitchen and bathroom were fitted. We were looking forward to it all but for almost fifteen months the house was like a building site.

I'd not been with Vera as the bells rang in the New Year but made it home around 3 am. Dave and Cath Farquharson came round and we still managed a bit of a party. The kids loved it, they could have their own party in one house whilst the adults hit the booze in the other. Vera was getting back on her feet and had been given the all clear at the hospital but a return to work was still many weeks away We toasted in the New Year and looked forward to the exciting year ahead.

Paul was coming to the end of his ALC Spurs days. He'd brought all his commitment and determination to their cause but I'd never been convinced that he'd been fully appreciated there. Before the new season started he had signed for Dod Bennett's Aberdeen Boys Club and a great new chapter opened in his footballing life. His Lads' Club days ended with a lovely memory for us but it wasn't a victory on the pitch. In mid-January we set off to Ayrshire for their Scottish Cup-tie. The Club had planned a wonderful trip for the boys, including an overnight stay at the Inverclyde Sports Centre before the match. A few dads made the trip and the highlight for me was the impromptu seven-a-side match on the Astroturf on the morning of the game. Paul played at centre forward that day and was robbed of a goal in the opening minutes by a wonder save from the opposing keeper from his six-yard thunderbolt shot. The boys slipped out of the cup 3-2 but the fun wasn't over.

Our bus broke down at Fordoun on the way home and I bet the chippy and pub there haven't ever been so busy again on a Saturday night. A great trip!

The song says, "Do you recall when love was all and you were seventeen?"

Vera and I could remember that time for she had been just seventeen when we met. Now we had been married seventeen years and for Vera it meant she had spent half of her life with me. They had been happy times and we had prospered well, although we were rich in family rather than material wealth. We had a stronger deeper love now and I was certain in myself that it would be everlasting. Around this time my dad was really getting himself back on the straight and narrow and now had his own flat on Huntly Street, but it had been a painful road. Still it was good to see and he spent a lot of time at the house with us. In the late spring he laid out a patio in the back garden and put up new washing green poles for Vera, another step on the way to her dream home. He also planted a cherry tree in our back garden, though I suspected in years to come it might bring a tear to our eyes as it reminded us through him of many other things.

A strange twist of fate saw two murders occur in Aberdeen on the same day. A nun was horrifically stabbed at a church on Huntly Street where Dad lived and a husband killed his wife in the flat through the wall from Stan and Lil at Girdlestone. We were now spending a lot more time with Stan and Lil and it was nice to see them both enjoy themselves so much when we went for nights out at the Caley golf club.

Leanne had achieved so much at school and had given it the one thing I had never done in my school days, her best efforts. In remembering my own unhappy times at secondary school I think I let my children down by not pushing them a little more academically. I was always pleased just to see them enjoying themselves but kids do need to be driven sometimes. Leanne always struggled with Modern Studies and though I recall us tackling it together, it was oh too little far too late from me, I'm sorry Lee!

"Methodical, conscientious and reliable— a description of Leanne. Notwithstanding these excellent comments, Leanne also works very hard and has a lovely attitude. Leanne is easy to get on with and I hope she pursues her aim of doing a 5th year." Her fourth year guidance teacher at least saw the woman my daughter was becoming.

Leanne filled my heart on her sixteenth birthday but was disappointed weeks later with her haul of four 'O' levels. I wish I'd given her more of that most precious gift...time!

How could I have known that those grey granite towers which had, sentinel like, stood guard on all the paths my boyhood dreams had trod, would have led me to a moment of such pride and pleasure.

My lovely girl now sixteen,
A woman grown I'm told.

No longer just a bonnie bairn,
In my arms to hold.
I wished a treasure I could find,
For this special day.
But my daughter is the treasure,
In her young woman's way.
My lovely girl now sixteen,
Still a child to me.
Defying all the years that pass,
Ever more will be.
A child for me to cuddle,
In a father's arms.
Blinded always by the child,
From the woman's charms.

Dad, Paul and I were spending a lot of time together. Dad came to a lot of Paul's football matches and we spent time playing pool and snooker together. He was beginning to look more like the man he'd been prior to my mum's death and I was happy for him. A funny little story of Stan and Lil makes us laugh to this day, but was perhaps a pointer to darker days that lay not too far ahead.

We had all been over to Girdlestone for Sunday lunch and as was the way there, a good few libations had been partaken of. Stan had gone to the loo and after a while we could hear a choking cough coming from the bathroom. I managed to push the door open and there he was on his knees being rather sick. A few hard slaps on his back seemed to help but then enter Lil...calamity was just moments away! She's had a few and was on wobbly legs but she was determined to help Stan. As she entered the smallest room she tripped over his feet and feel backward into the bath.

In those days Lil was a little larger than she needed to be and she became firmly wedged in the bath, in a most undignified position. At the very moment my efforts to free her were about to succeed, Stan began to choke once more. The only recourse was to drop Lil back into the bath and once more attend to the choking Stan. This comic routine repeated itself three or four times before firstly Stan rose unsteadily to his feet and secondly poor Lil had her dignity restored and was extricated from the bath. Stan's face however seemed to have changed shape and his speech was unintelligible. To Lil's credit she was the first to reason what had happened. In my over zealous attempts to aid Stan I'd hit him so hard on the back that I'd knocked out his false teeth. There was only one place they could be and in the venerable tradition of a devoted wife Lil retrieved the absent gnashers and moments later we were all enjoying a laugh and a dram in the living room.

Drink sneaks up on you and you never know there's a problem until it's too late. Stan and Lil were as hard working a pair as I've ever known, and so full of life. We didn't know then, but alcohol was to lead to a final tragedy for them—before the end of the year Lil had suffered a bout of pleurisy and their struggle was only just beginning.

Parliament had been both a mystery and an inspiration to millions since its birth and now it would come straight into our living rooms as it was broadcast live on television for the first time ever. The antics within those long closed halls of power would make us wish we'd never been let in on the secret. The Crazy Gang at Wimbledon FC were the sporting inspiration of the year as they defeated hot favourites Liverpool 1-0 in the FA Cup Final, only eleven years after being elected to the Football League.

Kylie Minogue began her journey to pop super-stardom and one of my all-time favourites, Roy Orbison, passed away. As an eleven-year-old on school holidays I had ran from home to the record booth on Aberdeen beach to ask the man to play Roy's *In Dreams* and Buddy Holly's *Bo Diddley* and thrilled as the sound boomed out of the loudspeakers across the sands. I laughed now as I sneaked upstairs to pinch Paul's Aztec Camera CD—*Killermont Street* was the best number I'd heard in a long while. Music's a time traveller too!

Paul was building up his collection from his new-found wealth earned as a paperboy; at last he was getting his wages! The first day he came home from his round he casually mentioned how much he'd enjoyed it and bet being a postie would be a good job. Just like his dad, a man of high ambition! Little did he know how prophetic that statement would be.

He was getting good reports at school but school was the one getting the bad press. Our local politicians had set in motion a course of events that would see the school close in two years. The lies parents were told at meetings beggared belief. We were told the building was structurally unsafe but months after the school eventually closed the council took it over as a training centre and it still operates in the 21st century. Were they trying to save money for the refurbishment of Aberdeen Grammar School? Whatever was going to happen the kids both wanted to stay there and I as always wanted them to be happy, so stay they did. Paul may have claimed a sporting record for posterity that year as he broke the school high jump record for his age. I can't remember any more sports days at beleaguered Summerhill Academy after that so perhaps he's still the man.

Just before Christmas all 259 passengers on a Pan-Am jumbo jet died as it fell victim to a terrorist attack. The tragedy was heightened as the stricken aircraft plummeted out of the darkness and ploughed into Lockerbie, killing eleven residents and wreaking havoc on that quiet border town.

We became homeowners on the 26th of August 1988 and although we'd run out of cash we continued with our renovations. A loan of £800 from my dad let us fit new interior doors throughout and built-in cupboards and a TV unit in the living room. More woodwork for me to stain and varnish! We put £75 a month into a building society account and gave Dad the passbook with a £900 balance just before Christmas the next year. Our solicitor charged £450 for the conveyancing and we paid that up at £50 a month. Nothing changed with home ownership, we were still robbing Peter to pay Paul and as interest rates soared towards the end of the year it was a worrying time. However we were both thrilled that we had realised a dream: we had finally bought our own home.

Hold a memory tightly, never let it go.
For we all in life's living will surely sadness know.
Treat a memory kindly, hold it in your heart.
For the remembering of a loved one will mean you never part.
Dream a dream boldly, plan it every day.
For in that dreaming high hopes will never fade away.
Dream a dream together, a hope for me and you.
For a time will come when dreaming eventually comes true.

A double tragedy and sadness in the snow

We were on the last leg of our journey through the Eighties, a journey that had taken us from the sadness of my mother's death, to the joy of owing our own home and had seen both of our children to the brink of adulthood. My dad and Vera's mum would both see their sixtieth birthdays before the year was out and more amazing events would unfold in Eastern Europe.

The year started in the company of good friends. Cath and Dave and Bill and Nancy were guests at our New Year party. The marathon effort to completely transform Arnage was almost complete and by the end of the spring I'd finally hung up all my paint and wallpapering brushes, at least until Vera's next plan unfolded!

There was a little dampener, or should I say a deluge that extended my efforts. A call at work from Vera informed me of the great calamity. A tap had been running in our new bathroom sink, Vera had ran to answer the telephone and in her subsequent rush to see the latest episode of *Coronation Street*, she'd forgotten about the tap and left it on with the plug firmly fitted in the plughole!

Oh calamity and consternation,
What had the woman done?
After quick telephone conversation,
To the telly she had run.
Coronation Street was gripping,
Viewing ratings were the proof.
A forgotten bathroom tap was running,
And flooded our new kitchen roof!

Now that version of the truth was the one intended to and which indeed, but barely, managed to keep me from blowing a fuse. Months later when they felt it was safe, Vera and Leanne told me the undiluted version. Vera had been glued to *Corrie* but Leanne had answered the phone whilst in the middle of washing her hair. Young ladies are never on the phone for a moment, flood guaranteed! Most of the water damage was to our kitchen roof and I had it replaced and sorted in a week or two. Was I really that scary, girls?

Leanne was a young woman with a bit of world shaking to do that year.

Her first serious boyfriend, Mike, appeared on the scene just after New Year. On the 22nd of May she left school behind after five years of hard work at Summerhill Academy and began work with the builders, Hall and Tawse at Granitehill Road on the 26th of June. She left behind the hard slog of studying for her Highers and was about to find out that work was a lot like school but instead of homework you did overtime and didn't get paid too well for it either.

With her new-found wealth Leanne did get herself her first set of contact lenses and was soon out enjoying herself as often as she could. Mike was a nice lad but very serious about Leanne at a time when she just wasn't ready or looking for that kind of relationship. They'd be together for more than a year but by Autumn 1990, after several splits, they were just good friends. Leanne moved jobs quite quickly and in October she started work at Woodhill House in the Assessor's Office. None of us could have guessed it then but that would be a life-changing move that would have nothing to do with work.

Heartache is always ready to reach out to us in life, as unexpected as summer snow. In the short time we had them Tinker and Spike had become a pleasant fixture in our lives. We loved them in that excessive way that humans reserve for their pets and they, as pets do, revelled in our adulation. Tinker was a free spirit who happened only to share the same address as us and required humans only for such mundane tasks as opening doors. He did have a great affection for Paul and possibly no sense of smell, he always spent each night curled up around Paul's feet at the bottom of his bed. He was a beautiful cat. Spike was an edgy, cautious character who loved the comforts of home to the extent of being in seeming oblivion to her smouldering tail as she slept atop the living room fire. We all loved her for her homely ways and Vera especially prized her. She was a loving cat.

Their deaths were the more difficult to understand because we could see their pain and suffering but never know the source from which it sprang. The vet put it down to some type of poison, possibly slug bait. It inflicted on them both slow lingering deaths, which completely paralysed their hindquarters. Tinker fought bravely for three weeks but in the end the kindest thing to do was to let them both go.

A song, *The Living Years*, reminded me all the things we should say and never do. I bought Dad a copy, popped in on the way home one night and asked him to listen to it when I'd gone. He liked it and maybe it helped him know that on his journey through the dark tunnel he was just emerging from, I'd always been there for him.

The work sent me off to Durham on a Police National Computer course for two weeks. I hated it! I was a confirmed home-bird by then. We had a lovely party at home, a Bruno Party at Cath and Dave's. Frank was heroic in defeat against Mike Tyson and we were all heroic in the face of serious hangovers the next morning. Not long afterwards Cath and Dave moved, I believe they weren't getting on too well with a neighbour but happily they only moved to Gillahill Road, not too far to spoil our little get togethers.

We'd had ten years of Maggie Thatcher and then she gave Scotland the hated Poll Tax. We had to grin and bear the pain of it but its introduction was another step along the road to her ultimate demise.

Annie and Bob were out at Alford but both were having a battle with alcohol addiction and each had a spell in hospital in an attempt to find a cure. Perhaps their good fortune of a few years earlier had proved to be more of a curse than a blessing. A stabbing incident sprang from the domestic turmoil their life was lived in, but thankfully there were no police proceedings and they somehow managed to overcome that and stay together.

Two amazing episodes astounded us all, as firstly we witnessed the student demonstrations in Tiananmen Square in Beijing. They were ended by troops and tanks, and hundreds died, but I doubt if I'll ever see a more vivid image of man's quest for freedom in my lifetime. One solitary student, defiant in the face of an advancing line of tanks! Then in November the Berlin Wall came down, that symbol of all the political and ideological differences of my life, felled by men with sledgehammers, and not a gun in sight!

After the loss of Tinker and Spike we decided to take on another two kittens and so Theo and Jet joined the household. Both were easy to like, Theo a fluffy sprawl of black and white fur and Jet a sleek, pitch black shadow of feline grace. They settled in well but it took time for them to come out of the shadows of Tinker and Spike's memories.

We thought we had another boy and a girl but at their first appointment with the vet he pointed out that Jet was a tomcat. He was a very naughty boy too! Just before Christmas he laid a beautiful robin at my feet. The poor wee thing had been feeding at my bird table. I'd hoped to provide him with succour through a long hard winter and had lured him unsuspecting to his death!

Vera had made all the arrangements to get Dad central heating; the council and the Hydro were partners in a discount scheme. Dad's short fuse was well and truly lit when he received his first bill; he was on the phone furious! In light of his threats to smash all the heaters to bits I nipped down to see him.

"Faithe, Faither, why are ye greetin?"
"Well son it's this damn central heatin."
"Just look at the bill I got the day."
"Its' far too dear I cannae pay!"
"Dad it's worth it for the heat ye've got."
"Nae fear, I'll smash the bloody lot!"
"Faither, Faither, you silly loon."
"Ye've read the meter the wrang road roon!"

Paul would be moving into his last year at school and had agreed a deal with his mum and I. His reports at the end of third year were good but he simply didn't want to stay at school. What could I say? He would put in his best efforts through O Levels and leave as soon as possible afterwards. Like his sister he always appeared to be held in the highest regard by his schoolteachers.

His football was also improving. He was enjoying playing for Dod Bennett and it showed on the pitch. There were more defeats than victories in the early days at ABC but win, lose or draw, football is about playing and being appreciated. Knowing Dod was another stage of the character building that sport can give a youngster, getting to know views of the world and life that are not just their father's or mother's. Paul hasn't scored many hat tricks in his career but did that February, football was fun!

In November 1989 Paul had responded to an advert for a job with Royal Mail in Aberdeen as a Postal Cadet. A test followed in December and by February he'd been told the job was his and he could start after his exams were finished. It took a lot of pressure off him.

Rangers were out to prove that they could make Scottish football every bit as boring as Celtic had done in the Sixties and Seventies by winning the first of the titles that would set them off on their nine-in-a-row run to equal their great rivals record. Wee Jocky Wilson's darts win over Eric Bristow and Nick Faldo's first US Masters were sporting highlights but a sporting disaster was to overshadow all that year. Almost one hundred fans died at Hillsborough Stadium with hundreds more injured as crowd control failed and a deadly crush ensued at the Liverpool end of the ground.

A sign of the changing times was surely the passing into liquidation of the Aberdeen Stevedoring Company as the Government scrapped the National Dock Labour Scheme. Vera had gone into the New Year with a new hobby, ceramics—we had ornaments everywhere! I had a lovely re-union with Jackie Christie and we caught up on all that had happened in our lives. On his sixtieth birthday Dad had a tearful re-union with his sister Gracie. She'd gone to live with an aunt as a youngster, moved to England, married and lived most of her life in Stafford. He hadn't seen her for almost fifty years!

Paul was making a hexagonal table at school for his mum and she cherishes it still. I wish I'd kept the birthday card Stan gave me that year, 'Happy Birthday Cousin,' it proclaimed. He didn't have his glasses on when he went to the shop! That was perhaps the one amusing memory in a year of sad decline for Stan and Lil. They seemed to be tottering into a meaningless old age, pride seemingly washed away on a tide of whisky.

As we had become regular visitors to Torry once more, the signs of years of personal neglect were everywhere. Lil's health was slipping fast, she was in and out of hospital and often seemed to lose touch with reality, perhaps inwardly retreating from the horror that real life had become. Watching her hobble around with a zimmer was a sad sight. They were still the purveyors of fine hospitality but now in a singular fashion that revolved around their passion for a dram. At rare times before the demon shrouded their day in dark fog they could be as I had first known them. We all greatly enjoyed and would remember Lil's sixtieth birthday party. Vera was trying her best to get them a move to a more suitable home and in a daughter's way she hoped she could lead them to better times. Lil had fallen in with a neighbour, a woman of Vera's age and they shared a liking for a dram. Vera found it harder to overcome her influence. Our futile attempts at cleaning up Girdlestone just before Christmas did bring an offer of a pensioner's house near us in Mastrick but fate would rule that out as an option.

Stan's face mirrored much confusion, as his days of golden retiral seemed to have consigned him to a roll of nursemaid and messenger boy. As Lil had slipped, Stan had maintained his health, it seemed his 'Whau's like us?' attitude would never leave him. The shock was all the more numbing when he suffered a massive stroke on the 22nd of December 1989. To see this strong man brought irreparably down was beyond us all. It was all Vera and the kids could face to see him in hospital and I had to wipe away a tear as I shaved him in his hospital bed. Lil, perhaps understandably, refused to accept or believe this devastation of her life but did become more of a concern as she fell even deeper under the influence of drink. Sadly she became almost a caricature of her real self, becoming the sad old lady that Squeeze sang of in *Labelled With Love*.

One day I watched the shell of Stanley Fraser struggle vainly to steer a wheelchair along a hospital corridor and I prayed that soon he would be sleeping the big sleep. They had lived, perhaps a selfish life, but always together; now fate seemed to conspire to force them to end it apart.

The Nineties would open for us all with a double tragedy, which had a bitterness attached to it that would live in our hearts and minds forever. It came at the end of the year but we did have some wonderful moments before that.

Paul turned sixteen and in a poignant moment at the hospital, his stricken grandfather passed his retiral presentation watch to him. Paul left school on the 23rd of May and started work with Royal Mail on the 4th of June. On his final school report his Guidance Teacher wrote, 'Paul is a very mature and well-adjusted young man. He will do well in whatever he chooses to do.' He enjoyed working life from the start and we were so happy for him. Paul did better than he had expected at his O Levels and would ask me later if I thought he should have stayed on at school?

All I could think to say to him was, "Son, 'what ifs' just don't matter in this life. Don't waste it dwelling on them just live it in the best way you can."

Around about then he couldn't have enjoyed his football more either. In a super Cup semi-final the lads were down 2-0 at half-time to Deeside but fought back for a superb 5-4 win and Paul chipped in with two of the goals. The final against Albion Rangers was, unbelievably, an even better game but in the end a heart-breaking near miss for Dod and the boys. Playing brilliantly they went 3-0 ahead but Albion, who would end the season as Scottish Under-16 Cup winners, were a good side and battled back to level terms. Their 4-3 win after extra-time was a blow for everyone but they had all played so well, there was no disgrace in this defeat.

My dad suffered a bout of Bell's Palsy and after the initial shock of his appearance he quickly came to terms with it and would have us all in stitches by popping a cushion up the back of his jumper and doing Quasimodo to a tee. "The bells, the bells!" he'd wail.

As the doctor had foretold he was back to normal in six or seven weeks but kept up his Quasimodo act for months! Sadly an old hero looked almost as strange as Dad, poor Alex Higgins. The Irishman's 'No more snooker for the Hurricane' interview on telly was pitiful to behold as, under the influence of alcohol, he unravelled in front of the cameras for all to see.

The Bon Accord Centre opened in Aberdeen, a shopping mall, nirvana for the modern consumer. Somewhere within its precincts dwelt the ghost of the Rubber Shop. Even today as I pass through it I sense all those glorious toys of my boyhood are about to appear at any moment in one of the large glass windows of the many shops that line the mall.

Vera moved on to a new job within the Hydro and became the trainer for their state-of-the-art in-house computerised accounts and sales receipts system. She was taking it all too seriously, I thought, when she started reciting the security access codes of all the stores she visited, in her sleep!

Stephen Hendry took his first world snooker championship title with a win over Jimmy White, the first of five consecutive final defeats for White, four of which would be at the hands of Hendry. We were also on a run of consecutive defeats as Leanne took the sweeper again! I announced the end of my sponsorship there and then. Martina Navratilova was no first-timer as she took the ladies singles at Wimbledon for the ninth time!

Leanne's pals had a surprise in store for her eighteenth birthday; they set her up for the early morning quiz call on *Northsound*. Robin Galloway duly called and totally embarrassed her but with the help of the background whisperers, Mum and Dad, she got the questions right and won the breakfast set! She had her wisdom teeth removed that year but was lucky like I had been and didn't suffer too much discomfort. She and Maureen were still great pals and Maureen got engaged in October. Then just before New Year Leanne introduced us to her new boyfriend, one Stuart Lundie.

I made a fatal mistake with Stuart, I didn't like him and I'm sure he wasn't too keen on me. I just forgot that whether I liked him or, I loved my daughter and needed to go with the flow a little more. He always struck me as a Walter Mitty character who dreamed a bigger dream than he lived. Perhaps there's no harm in that when you're young and maybe the next year proved me right but my daughter's heart would be broken finding out.

Vera and I were planning a dream trip, our first journey abroad, a trip to the Rhine Valley. The fact we'd get there by bus and ferry didn't lessen our expectations. By the time we got our passports in April, excitement was at fever pitch!

Germany: the excitement of our ferry crossing, the unforgettable magnificence of the Rhine Valley as it is joined by the Moselle at Koblenz, my stuttering attempts at idle chit-chat in German with an old man in a pub in Bad Kreuznach, the quaint streets of Rudesheim...Drosselgasse and Oberstrasse, the quiet beauty of the village of Cochem, an evening strolling on the banks of the Rhine, the sheer size of Frankfurt, the fun of an evening cruise up the river, the beautiful weather and the good friendship of Ian and Margaret. Such was Germany; we had loved it and would return.

By 1990 Scotland were in their fifth successive World Cup finals but as ever we shot ourselves in the foot by losing 1-0 to Costa Rica in our opening match. A poor competition was more memorable for Gascoigne's tears after being booked against West Germany in the semi-finals, he was out of the final and so were England after extra-time and penalties. He did win *Sports Personality of the Year*, we Brits all love a loser!

Scotland were amazing as they took rugby's Grand Slam in a winner takes all match against England. The famous slow march and *Flower of Scotland* match is a treasured memory as Paul, my dad and I thrilled to every pulsating moment together. The Dons won the Cup under Alex Smith and Fergie saved his Man U career by winning the FA Cup. Two former St Mirren managers winning the national trophies in the same season; how often has that happened I wonder? Smith had done well at Pittodrie with the resources available but modern football finances would dictate that the glory days of Gothenburg could never return. Fergie was just beginning his trip to even more unbelievable management successes.

Maggie Thatcher finally walked but battled to the end to ensure that a man who followed her creed would succeed her. John Major became Prime Minister and we wondered what troubled times might lie ahead. In that tragically troubled region of the world, the Middle East, Iraq invaded Kuwait in August and there seemed no way that conflict could be avoided. The Americans were determined to reverse this act of aggression and wanted UN backing for their actions. Months of negotiations would follow but we all felt the world was on the road to war.

My pal Ian and his wife Irene decided to separate, his drinking the main cause. In contrast I was sending Vera twenty red roses to mark the twentieth anniversary of the day we met. How lucky we were!

Ray and Lilian had sold up in Corby and chose Crieff as their new home. We went to visit them after our German adventure and were a little confused at their new lifestyle. A trailer home at a holiday park in Crieff and a stall at an indoor market in Perth didn't seem to fit in with Ray's plans for business success. He always was a bit of a *Don Quixote* and was never phased at what life threw at him next. We never did discover why they left Corby so quickly but it was great to have them close by again. So began happy years of what the four of us called our Perthshire Weekends.

Leanne and Vera were trying to create a world record for watching a movie; they must have learned the entire script of *Pretty Woman* by heart. God help us when it was released on video! *Total Recall* was a clever movie but Paul, who was now doing a delivery round in Rosemount, had no recollection of what had happened to his shoes when he woke to go to work one morning. They never did turn up!

> Lost without trace, time would not uncover.
> Defying a search by father and mother.
> Where could they be the family wrangle?
> Twilight Zone or Bermuda Triangle!
> All astounded by this disappearance.
> Was their ghostly interference?
> Would there ever be new clues?
> Whatever happened to Paul's shoes?

Poor Theo had a leg badly damaged that summer when he was ran over by a car. The vet was amazingly able to save him and he became the Bionic Cat, with his leg held together by metal pins. He did take the slow motion stuff to a new level; he was the world's laziest cat!

In October Vera achieved a lifetime ambition and passed her driving test. She'll never admit how many tries she had, though perhaps not quite as many as Theo had lives. As I'd promised she got her new car, a little white Fiat Uno, E810 HST. She was so pleased and the freedom of our new-found mobility changed our lives. We even dreamed of moving house; we could stay a little out of town. That would be a long time happening but for now we just enjoyed the new things we were able to do and the places we were able to go and see.

Global Warming was a term we all heard more and more and it reminded us that we were now car owners. There certainly appeared to be a need for education about the effects it was having on our good earth. All the noble intentions in the world are nothing without actions and we only hold this world in trust for those who follow. We dare not let them down!

Dad had struck up a nice friendship with a woman named Isobel. She had devoted herself to looking after her mum; she worked at the hospital with Dad and they were becoming very close. We all took to her and perhaps this was the final piece of the jigsaw for Dad in putting his life back together.

Stan had become very depressed in hospital, I suspected every corner of his mind was tortured by the reality of the prison in which his shattered body now held him. False hopes were raised when he was moved to the Special Unit at the City Hospital but we all really knew there was no way back for him. Poor Lil, equally devastated, her life in tatters, her mind in turmoil, found it all too easy to turn to drink for comfort and a misguided neighbour was all too handy to help her do so. In a tragic case of misdirected anger it was Vera who bore the brunt of all her mother's frustrations and sadly a rift again developed between them. Amid bitter accusations, there would be no time for the hurt to heal on this occasion. Lil a sad lonely woman, Stan lost and alone, the scene was set for tragedy.

Remembrance Sunday, 11th of November 1990, Lil passed away. Our grief would be mingled with some anger at what had gone before. A barely comprehensible note scribbled on the back of a torn envelope advised us of her last wishes and we carried them out as best possible. To me she would always be a younger woman, the tigress defending her children. Stan was well aware of all that was happening and his eyes reflected the grief he could not let out as we tinkered over a game of dominoes. Clearing forty years of life from their house, seventeen of them holding some of her own fondest memories, must have been an emotional moment for Vera.

Stanley Fraser, as strong willed as ever, made his own choice to slip off this mortal coil on the 18th of December 1990. We knew it had all been too much for him but as always he had decided what he wanted to do, and that was to be with Lil. The doctors knew he had chosen to let go and discussed this with Vera—they would not prolong things. So Vera's parents had gone; she had loved them, perhaps I could have known them better but we would all miss them.

It took the world five months to walk the road to war and on the 17th of January 1991, Desert Storm was unleashed in Kuwait. The Americans quickly advanced and the whole country appeared to be in flames as the retreating Iraqis set oilfields ablaze. Before the month was out the conflict was over but little seemed to have been achieved. It was as if the school bully had himself been given a bloody nose and told not to be a bad boy again. Saddam Hussein was out of Kuwait but still held power in Iraq; the awesome force of Desert Storm had swatted the fly away but left it unharmed. More pain and suffering seemed assured for the future.

The arrival of Vera's new car set in motion another burst of activity at Chateau Robertson. She wanted to be able to park it off the road, so Dad, with me very much his unskilled second man, set about turning our front garden into a driveway. It took two attempts for us to complete the version that she was most comfortable with but in the end we made a fine job of it. As the world opened up to us I fell under increasing pressure from Vera to join the ranks of drivers. It was something I'd had no interest in at any time but I finally succumbed. Andy at the Farburn School of Motoring was teaching Leanne and Paul, and I reluctantly joined his band of pupils.

It was on the anniversary of Lil's death that I passed my test. We sat at home that night, celebrating with a bottle of wine, but we couldn't prevent thoughts of both Lil and Stan and my mum from flooding back into our heads. Thankfully the happy memories always outweigh the bad ones.

Faster than an eyelid blinking, sups the king of whisky drinking.
Known as Stan and not as Charlie, a servant of the cream of barley.
Once I saw him at a party, finish two bottles rather smartly.
Mere mortals would have fell to floor, Stan the Man just wanted more.

Famous at his local pub, the only member of a club.
That drinks its whisky by the bottle, one a day is just half throttle.
I hope his glass will never finish, nor his drinking powers diminish.
May he last for many years, glass in hand and saying, "Cheers!"

Leanne ran into a taxing little problem early that year when she started to
have double tax deducted from her wages and received letters from the tax
office demanding that she give them full details of her second employer.
Leanne was always a hard worker but even she couldn't cope with two full-
time jobs. With little or no help from the taxman we finally narrowed it
down to Lisa next door having left school and started work. The fact that
two Miss Robertson's with the same initial and the same postcode were now
in full-time employment had completely flummoxed their computer. Problem solved, no apology from the taxman, shopping spree for Leanne with
her rebate.

Things were racing ahead for Leanne and Stuart and in the spring they
announced their plans to become engaged in August. I was beginning to
learn how to bite my tongue with young Mr Lundie and no doubt he had
his strategy for dealing with me too. The joy that Leanne showed made it all
worthwhile and we were genuinely pleased for them.

We set of that summer for a holiday on the West Coast with Fort William
as our base. Dad and Isobel came with us and we had a lovely time but Dad
always gave the impression that five minutes away from home is far enough
and it was time he was getting back. We saw them off on the train at Perth
at the end of the first week and set off for a second week at Crieff with Ray
and Lilian. Dad had that 'thank goodness' glint in his eye as the train pulled
out.

The car was such an advantage and that second week we explored Perthshire fully and fell in love with it. We both thought it might be a great spot to
retire to but for now Vera spent the week searching out Leanne's engagement
presents.

From the days of my 1984 invincibility my bowls game had crumbled to
such an extent that I was on the verge of giving up playing. Having almost
entirely lost the ability to deliver a forehand shot, I amazed myself by reaching the club Championship final at Polmuir. I even staged another vintage
comeback in the semi-final to defeat George Strachan 21-20 after trailing 4-
17. I lost to that wily old campaigner Dickie Irvine 21-16 in the final, no-one
was going to beat him with only one shot in their locker.

There was a narrow escape for we Scots late in the year. We narrowly failed to get past England in the semi-final of the rugby World Cup; I can still see Gavin Hastings miss under the posts at 6-6. That left the door open for England on home soil to deliver more huge helpings of 1966 and all that. The Australians saw them off in the final so it was back to re-runs of 'they think it's all over.'

A thirty-nine year old Jimmy Connors entered the US Open courtesy of a wildcard entry but went all the way to the semi-finals before losing to the eventual champion, Stefan Edberg.

Paul started the year with a bang; it was however a most unwelcome one. He arrived home in the small hours with his pal Kevin, drenched in blood; he'd had several stitches put into a wound on his head. As they'd walked past the despised poll tax office on Crown Street a fool in a crowd of late-night revellers had launched a bottle at the window. His aim was as misguided as the detested tax, exit Paul to hospital, well done Kevin for looking after him so well.

There were three highlights for Paul that year although I think two of them were more appreciated by other people. Dod Bennett had put together a fine side at ABC and the team played their hearts out for him. They finally got their hands on some silverware on a still June evening at Heathryfold. Dod, a fine junior footballer in his day, would have relished the location. The boys delight showed it was all for him as they ran out convincing winners. The tear in the corner of his eye said what it meant to him. The team didn't carry on after that season; Paul signed for Sunnybank and in pre-season was off to Wales to play for them in a tournament there. I'm sure he took a little satisfaction in declining an offer to re-sign for ALC when ABC folded. ABC might not be the best side he'd ever play for but Dod Bennett was one of the best men he'd pull on a shirt for.

A summer trip to Norway, a flight to the distant Lofoten Islands. No, it wasn't Vera and I planning our holidays, it was Paul off on an exchange trip with the Norwegian Mail Service. Six young cadets were chosen, based on their training reports, supervisor's comments, and time-keeping and sickness records. Paul had been lucky enough to be one of the six selected and off he went in the late summer for that super trip.

In October Vera and I received a letter from Royal Mail advising us that Paul had been chosen as their 1991 Cadet of the Year. We felt it was a very nice touch by them to write directly to the parents and we proudly attended the presentation night at the old Post Office headquarters in Crown Street.

There were landmarks too for Vera and me, our twentieth wedding anniversary and my fortieth birthday. There were lots of anniversary presents for us from Leanne and Stuart, Dad and Isobel, and Paul and there was a strange sadness that only one of our parents had lived to see this day. On my fortieth we had a nice evening with Cath and Dave; the kids had all chipped in to buy me a super zoom camera. Vera made sure I didn't feel too old and bought me U2's *Rattle and Hum* album. I was getting old though; the track with BB King, *When Love Comes To Town*, was my absolute favourite.

And so twenty years had slipped away for Vera and me. I hope my little tale is capturing in honest words the essence of our years together, in sad and happy times. If in reading you have brushed away a tear, always remember life will ever be about the laughter and the tears.

We were due for an unexpected anniversary present too; the Hydro were privatising and staff would be able to purchase shares at discount prices. This was another legacy of Thatcherism that was going to shape what we could achieve in the years ahead and perhaps let us keep dreaming a dream a size too big for our boots.

A Church of Scotland minister was up in arms at plans for topless dancers to appear at the Union Hotel in Turriff and *Bob's Your Uncle* was peak-time Saturday night viewing on the telly. No Vera, twenty years of marriage still hadn't brought us face to face with the permissive society!

War in the Gulf may have blinded us to the arrival on the political scene of a much more dangerous type of leader. Boris Yeltsin had come to power in a cameo of the lone student in Tiananmen Square, a hero against the tanks. He was at once a drunkard, a power seeker and a man adept at the shenanigans of the dark side of politics. He stood at the head of a super-power sinking in a sea of corruption. Where would it all end?

I met Paul and a pal in town one evening; they'd obviously had a few drinks, both underage too! It did amuse me when his pal turned out to be none other than Martin Davidson, son of my teenage pal and fellow underage drinker, Syd Davidson. Martin looked so like his dad—but would he ever manage to drink six pints and then scoff nine mince pies in a pie eating contest, all before going to the dancing? Mind you Syd never did that on the night he met Martin's mum!

Central heating was added to the list of upgrades at Arnage. My dad, Jackie and I had one super night out recalling old times from Park Street and Vera and I drove out to Alford to visit Annie and Bob. They were pleased to see us but at once quite distant; our lives were simply running different courses and we just seemed to lose touch after that summer. Dave Leitch had a new lady in his life, Andrea, whom we met for the first time at a night out at the Northern Golf Club. We four got on very well and this would be the first of many nights out during the firm friendship that was to develop between us.

Dad and Isobel moved to a new house on Errol Place and I finally escaped the horrors of the Police Control Room and became the Albert Steptoe of Queen Street at Lost and Found Property. The kids were working and able to fend for themselves and Vera was doing well at the Hydro. We discussed it long and hard and decided we could afford to take the £3500 drop in my salary for me to make the move. We never once regretted the move, often regretted the loss of earnings but at least we had a life together again. The new job turned out to be one of those perceived by the bosses to be a little bit Mickey Mouse but in reality had quite a lot to it. Best of all, Lost and Found was a ball of string with a hundred loose ends; the bosses didn't want to know and left you alone to get on with it.

Our year could not have started in worse fashion; one minute Leanne, Vera and I were talking about her future plans and the next all hell broke loose and Leanne and I were having a stand-up row. I can't even remember what was said but I bet that Stuart's name was in there somewhere! Before Vera could calm us down, cases were packed and Leanne was off out into the dark winter night. Minutes later, or it seemed just minutes, we were off looking for her to bring her home, but she was gone. I took the next day off work and went to Stuart's mum's house., Leanne was there; I made my apologies to everyone and home we went. I would never let this happen again, my daughter's love was more important to me than any doubts I might have had. She and Stuart had made their choices and their plans and I knew that I had to accept being just a small part of them or risk being left out of Leanne's life altogether.

She trudges off in falling snow,
Disappears in darkness and snow's whirl.
This cannot be the way to go,
We must go out and find our girl.
The way she went we cannot tell,
Find nought but sadness in the snow.
We need to know she's safe and well,
And make her see she need not go.

In morning calm I find the place,
Where she has gone to dry her tears.
There's sadness written on her face,
I do my best to soothe her fears.
Her life is not mine to live,
That I know and well accept.
Her future choices I will give,
My clear support and full respect.

Dad and Isobel made the best choice of all in 1992 when they decided to marry. He could still be his fiery old self at the drop of a hat but Isobel seemed to have a way with him, and if anyone could keep him calm, she could. They decided on a quiet wedding on their own and made a romantic trip to Gretna where they were married on the 29th of July. He would keep his memories and little secrets that would always belong to only him and my mum but it was nice to see him happy. He now had a chance to spend his autumn years with a loving partner.

Vera and I went on a summer expedition to Austria but in the end we found it was closed when we got there! Austria is really geared for the skiers and lovely place that it is, it just wasn't what we expected. Vera was thrilled to fly for the first time and I was delighted to enter and win a local tennis tournament with a Dutch lad I'd met. He turned out to be a ringer, a tennis coach who owned his own sports centre back home. We'd beaten his brother in the final and we had a super night at their mountain top five-star hotel to celebrate our victory. All expenses courtesy of the Dutch lads! The Krimml Waterfalls were beautiful but it was only after we got back to the hotel that I realised I'd forgotten to put film in my camera and had been snapping away on empty the whole day.

We made a marathon day trip to Venice, which was a wonder to behold but it was almost too hot even to walk around. We chose to appreciate it from a local riverbus at the lira equivalent of 50p a head instead of the tour operator's rusty old boat at £16 each. The trip up the Grand Canal was breathtaking. A journey we planned ourselves turned out to be a joy as we travelled on an old steam train, the Giselabahn, through beautiful mountain scenery to the picture postcard town of Kitzbuhel. A cable car ride and a boat trip at Zell-am-See, where we needed to be towed back to shore after our engine cut out, were other memories. All in all Austria proved to be a bit of a disappointment, the place was beautiful but the prices eventually ate away at our 'enjoy yourselves at any cost' spirit.

A long Perthshire Weekend seemed the best way to finish our holiday and so we stopped at Crieff on the way home. Ray and I had our usual Saturday night, pool and a few pints at the Station and then a few more pints at the St Johnstone Club, where he worked part-time. We were well oiled as we headed home, but Ray assured me he knew a shortcut. In the years since I've searched for the field he led us across but I've never found it. Lying looking up at the stars in a pile of cow dung was not my idea of fun and did no good at all to the lovely new suede jacket I'd bought especially for the holidays. Mind you, I should have known better than to take a shortcut with Ray—he once took us on a drive to Falkirk and we ended up spending a lovely day in Dunfermline!

Being homeowners had been a financial struggle; all the improvements had drained our savings and from being £80 a month SSHA tenants in 1988 we were now paying £250 a month for a £23000 mortgage. Not to forget Maggie's poll tax! The whole crazy spiral culminated in September with Black Wednesday; when interest rates hit 15% the whole country was bankrupt anyway. Britain withdrew from the Exchange Rate Mechanism and floated the pound. Interest rates were slashed immediately and an economic recovery sprang out of this near disaster. The Queen told us of her 'annus horribilis' but what did she think was happening to the ordinary people?

The break up of Yugoslavia was beginning and a horror was about to descend on the Balkans that would bring war throughout the region and reports of atrocities and ethnic cleansing, the like of which had not been heard of in Europe since the concentration camps of World War Two.

Bill Clinton became American President and along with all the troubles around the globe there had been race riots in Los Angeles. In truth it was a year when it seemed hard to find a quiet corner anywhere in the world.

In the economic calm after Black Wednesday, Vera and I took the plunge and bought ourselves a brand new car. It was a little red Fiat Uno, which turned out to be off the same production line as Stuart's old banger. After three months of continual breakdowns we proved the pen was mightier than the sword. I'd written to newspapers, my solicitor, the manufacturers, the motor trade association and anyone else I could think of. A week before Christmas we were called to the garage and offered a new car, what a relief!

There were two people who could probably have run faster than our first new car, Linford Christie and Sally Gunnell. They both took gold at the Barcelona Olympics but came second and third to Nigel Mansell, our world motor racing champion, in most sporting polls that year. If popularity could guarantee success then the glory days were back at Pittodrie as Willie Miller took the manager's chair.

Paul took the long walk for the first time ever at football when he was sent off playing for Sunnybank. He imposed a ban on himself two months later when, after a brief flirtation with Inverurie Juniors, he decided to hang up his boots! He got his football career back on track and his driving licence in October. After two failures he set off for test number three in his Royal Mail uniform and sailed through. That was me immediately relegated to the worst driver in the house again!

The only test you needed to pass for the incomparable Jim Neave was that you had the heart to play for the colours. Jim ran Grampian CD Football Club and was a character of immense proportions. His extrovert nature and shoulder length white hair gave him a presence that could be quite scary. Anyone who got the chance to know Jim soon realised he was a gentleman to the core. His co-manager was the perfect foil; Ian Simpson was quietly spoken and totally undemonstrative but his passion for football matched Jim's. Paul would cherish the memory of these two men for the rest of his life.

Paul's introduction to football life with CD was typical of Jim Neave, who approached him at work one Friday and in the passing simply said, "They tell me you're a centre-half. We've a game at the Bridge of Don tomorrow, 2pm kick-off, be there!"

Paul and I had developed a nice sporting habit; we played badminton at the Beacon Sports Centre on a Friday and then walked, or in my case crawled across the car park and took a dip in the Bucksburn Swimming Pool. Along with my tennis with Bill it was enough to keeping my ageing bones ticking over. He'd be taking the plunge in much warmer climes that summer as he prepared for his first foreign holiday with his workmates; they were off to Malta.

Today he is the doyen of radio broadcasters but on Leanne's birthday Terry Wogan was doing the last programme of his long running TV chat show. Television's loss would be radio's gain—how could I face the mornings without his mad banter? I was always on the lookout for a nice tune for Vera and I to cuddle up to and Mr Big with *To Be With You* or Del Amitri's *Be My Downfall* would always set the mood. Mind you we never quite agreed about Whitney Houston—her awful, screeching version of *I Will Always Love You* actually drove me from the room when it came on! Vera loved it but had also lasted the whole of the *Basic Instinct* movie, which had lost my attention just before the end of the opening credits. Different strokes for different folks!

Leanne and Stuart announced early in the year that they were looking for a flat, and they moved into a basement flat in Menzies Road on Vera's birthday. We helped as best we could, with a new suite and a bed but I was still at odds with the modern method of living together. Remember Dad, bite your tongue! They seemed happy and a couple of kittens helped give the place a feel of home.

They'd not lived there long when wet-rot was diagnosed in the living room—more expense than they needed I'd bet. I thought it a little strange that Leanne started working part-time in the Co-op at Torry but needs must, as Vera and I well knew from our early days of married life. However before the end of the year they were obviously struggling as a couple and on Christmas Eve Leanne came home to Arnage.

She didn't need a pep talk, just a hug and a good feed by the looks of her! We took her with us to spend New Year with Ray and Lilian. A Perthshire Weekend was just the pick-me-up she needed. We had a hilarious time and the girls all ganged up on Raymond when he challenged them to a peanut fight. Lilian must have still been picking up the peanuts at Easter!

I decorated the flat the following week in the hope that a tidy up would help it sell quicker. At least Dad and Isobel got the suite from Leanne for their house. I hope Stuart got on well with the rest of his life and achieved all his aims— "Ouch, I've just bit my bloody tongue again!"

The flat did sell by March and so all ties were severed. Leanne did ask me years later why I never told her how I felt and I just shrugged. The truth was I did once but I could never risk losing her in the snow again.

Early in 1993 a crime so horrible occurred that I could never fully read newspapers about it, watch television discussions on it or ever understand how on earth it could have happened. A two-year-old was lured away from a shopping mall in Liverpool, brutally murdered and his body left on a railway line. The tragedy of Jamie Bulger is just as appalling all these years later. The chilling facts that unfolded following his death were that the killers themselves were only children, two boys, both of whom were mere ten-year-olds. What sort of society could possibly produce children capable of such a crime?

The privatisation of the Hydro had allowed us to save to buy shares and now they were about to make us an offer we couldn't refuse. As they drove to downsize the High Street shops side of the business and reduce wage bills, Vera was offered a voluntary severance package. The bottom line was an immediate lump sum of £15000 and a frozen pension, payable when she became fifty years old. We thought about it long and hard but we knew that what they were really saying was, "Mrs Robertson, would you like to win the pools today?"

Vera signed up for the jackpot!

She left the Hydro in March and we had a lovely spring holiday at Dumfries before she started her new part-time job at the TSB Bank in Mannofield. We soon discovered that we hadn't won the pools and Vera took a full-time job at the bank. Their subsequent take-over by Lloyds Bank opened up the door to more savings in shares and a much cheaper mortgage rate. Like me Vera hadn't found the job of her dreams but time would tell that financially we had made the right move.

When a heart-breaking story is properly captured on film the result can be a humbling experience and such a film was *Schindler's List*. The capture of that spark of humanity shining out of the deep dark pit of despair that was Nazi Europe, was at once humiliating, then inspiring and ultimately uplifting. Man's inhumanity to man is timeless but one small act of kindness is the most precious thing we have to give each other.

I was involved in my own story connected to wartime Europe and it was entirely a happy tale. At a rally in Aberdeen, protesting at the Government's plans to start disbanding the Highland Regiments, an old soldier had lost his campaign medals. They were handed in to me at Lost & Found. Thankfully he had made a loss report to the office and I had his phone number.

A call established they were his; he lived in Crieff and was a retired dentist. We'd be in Crieff the next weekend and he was happy for me to take them down to him. We arranged to meet at 'the boat.' I knew exactly where he meant, outside the Station in what might have been a goods yard in the days of the railway, a yacht had been under construction for more than a year.

Come the Saturday we arrived at 'the boat' and climbed aboard. The yacht was a labour of love and he and his wife planned to sail to the Caribbean when it was complete. With the exception of the keel, amazingly made in a mould from some type of concrete, he was doing all the rest of the work himself. The interior was beautiful and he shocked us by telling us that most of the fittings had come from B&Q! He was delighted to see his medals again but didn't get much boat building done for the next few hours. We knew how glad he'd been to get them back when we struggled to clamber back down the ladder in the mid-afternoon. Yo, ho, ho and a bottle of rum!

Leanne was twenty-one in the summer of 1993and had picked up the pieces again. Vera and I had done all we could to help her through a difficult time in her life, but there was someone who had done as much as anyone to mend her broken heart. I hadn't met him but Vera, as mothers do, knew all about him. I was about to meet that third man in life who I would always hold in the highest esteem. Keith Fordyce was his name and his part in my story would have a long way to run. He seemed to be right for Leanne and he was easy to get to know and like.

In our family Paul has always been the lucky one and here's the proof. His first season at CD had gone well and older hands like Alan Rhind, 'Sammy' Masson, Sandy Robertson and Ernie Reaper had looked after the young lad. They were a fair side for a third division outfit, had reached their League Cup final and a win in their last league match would see them promoted.

The promotion dream was ebbing away—one man sent off, 2-0 down and ten minutes left on the clock. Who'd believe what happened next? Three goals in ten amazing minutes and it was mission accomplished. They were a great bunch of battlers; Jim's never-say-die spirit and Ian's steely nature ran through the whole team. Two weeks later came the Cup final at Stoneywood against Blackburn. They were trailing 1-0 when veteran winger Doddie Poulson scored two amazing goals; he has never admitted to this day that they baffled the opposing keeper because they were both hopeful crosses caught on the wind! Even the very best sides need a little luck and maybe Paul was the talisman they'd been looking for?

We spent our first weekend with Dave and Andrea at their mobile home on the Silver Sands Holiday Park at Lossiemouth. Our friendship was deepening all the time and we now added many wonderful weekends on the Moray Firth, filled with good companionship, to our memories. They would soon marry too and like my dad and Isobel they chose a quiet trip away together to tie the knot. They remain our firm friends and in truth I think more of them like family than friends.

Paul was bound for a Spanish holiday in Tenerife that year but Vera and I planned an island trip a little nearer home. As part of her fortieth birthday celebrations we were heading for the Channel Islands. We loved the place, the weather was gorgeous, and our hotel room had a huge balcony. It was all I could do to drag Vera away from her sunbathing. She swore the Elvis versions were better, but I belted out ZZ Top's *Viva Las Vegas* and UB40's *Can't Help Falling In Love With You* on the jukebox at the local pub every night. We even won a prize in their quiz night, skills honed in our many battles with Ray and Lilian. A night at the movies to see *Jurassic Park* was great fun and the walk home, hand in hand in the moonlight afterwards, along the sands at St Helier was a lovely moment.

Two great success stories began in sport when Pete Sampras won his first Wimbledon title and Fergie's Manchester United took their first Premiership championship. *Mr Blobby* had the Christmas number one but hopefully he wouldn't be starting a long reign at the top!

A ray of hope appeared in the Middle East when, after years of conflict, the PLO and Israel finally agreed to recognise each other. At the White House in September Yasser Arafat and Yitzhak Rabin formally shook hands on an agreement that we anticipated would at least give peace a chance. South Africa too moved forward in hope and the day before Leanne's birthday had announced that all-race elections would take place the following April.

We had a lovely weekend late in the year at Crieff when we went to see a super folk duo, Gaberlunzie, at the Conservative Club. They did a superb version of Frankie Miller's *Caledonia*; I've always fancied Frankie's song would do as good a job as an anthem as *Flower of Scotland*. All the chatter between Vera and Lilian was about the rumours of a rift in Charles and Di's marriage. Who cared? Not Ray and I, we were puting the world to rights and a good bottle of malt to the sword.

Paul ended the year on a low note. He'd bought himself a car in September, a sporty metallic grey Fiesta XR2i. A spin on an untreated snow covered Union Street on the way home from a night shift in late November caused an awful lot of damage. Thankfully he was completely unhurt, it would sort but it was impossible to convince him of that for a while. A week later, still very much down in the dumps, he travelled to Dundee and let himself be sucked into a sending off during CD's Scottish cup-tie. It turned out to be a great trip, the boys did hold on for a victory and Paul was as happy as the rest of us after a few beers!

1994 began with the Balkans in turmoil and war in Bosnia a certainty. Our world always offers despair and hope in equal measure and so we rejoiced as Nelson Mandela became President of South Africa and spoke of his hopes for the peaceful future of his rainbow nation. We saw the death of Labour leader John Smith; his successor Tony Blair would change the face of left-wing politics forever.

On our trips to Crieff we'd noticed a change in Ray, who seemed to be falling into poor health. His main problem then was the onset of chronic arthritis, which was beginning to affect his arms and he often had to wear wrist supports when driving. We felt that they needed to move out of their static caravan home into a house, but they seemed happy where they were and not too concerned.

If you chose 3, 5, 14, 22, 30 and 44 as your lucky numbers on the 19th of November you'd have changed your life forever. The bonus ball was 10 and so the National Lottery was born and became a fixture on Saturday night telly. Those awful lottery shows are still being churned out every Saturday and we all still dream the impossible dream.

Vera and I set off on a Wallace Arnold bus trip to the Black Forest that summer and if we'd been lottery winners we couldn't have booked into a better hotel. The city of Freiburg was our base and there was a city centre redevelopment programme in full swing. An international conference cen-tre and five-star hotel were the centrepiece. We were the guinea pigs for the staff; they'd open to real customers the next year!

I was lucky to make it to the Dorrint International—I travelled south from Scotland in a West Ham top and incurred the wrath of Man U fans at every motorway services stop. They were on their way to Wembley for the Charity Shield final and my suitcase was firmly locked in the boot of the bus; Vera had dressed me that morning, women know nothing about football!

The swimming pool in the hotel was in the style of a Roman villa, the lifts talked to you, the hotel had its own teletext channel and the toilets flushed when you waved your hand over a sensor! How on earth the lifts understood a couple of teuchters from Aberdeen I've never worked out.

We made a marvellous trip to Basle in Switzerland by train on our own and had a wonderful day. When we got back the hotel was swarming with armed policemen, which was a little scary, but we later discovered the German Government was spending the night there. It had been a great experience but far too much overland travel.

One of my special favourites from the movies died; Burt Lancaster had been a joy through oh so many favourite movies of mine since childhood days; he had sadly been the victim of a massive stroke, like Vera's dad. The *Birdman of Alcatraz* had been one of his great movies and by coincidence another prison story, the *Shawshank Redemption*, was a big hit that year. Burt would have been perfect as that film's hero, Andy Dufresne.

Sport lost two great men when Sir Matt Busby and the brilliant cricket commentator Brian Johnston died. Was it not Brian who was responsible for the immortal line, "The bowler is Holding, the batman's Willey!"

Paul had well and truly joined the ranks of the battlers at CD, he'd even scored a fifty-five yard wind assisted goal against the Bobbies and they were on the promotion trail again. Their fighting spirit was typified in their North of Scotland cup run that year. One of the early ties was a bruising encounter with Woodside, no soft touches themselves, which ended in a 2-2 draw. The replay took place in a howling gale and Paul snatched the winner two minutes from time to put us through. A twenty-five yarder in a 2-0 quarter-final replay victory over Kincorth was perhaps Paul's personal highlight of the season but Jim Neave would have settled for the 0-0 draw we'd achieved in the first match at Kincorth. They'd had legendary success in amateur football, and Jim, who had taken one of his early sides there and been on the receiving end of a cricket score, savoured the moment. We fell foul of Gary Forbes' excellent Hilton side in the semi-finals but it had been a great run for a second division side.

Promotion was an outside possibility but hinged on winning our last seven games; the cup run had put us miles behind with our fixtures. The first five victories were secured in typical battling fashion but with the season now running into mid-June, the last two matches were against the already crowned league champions Dyce; it looked a tall order. A 6-2 victory against an under-strength Dyce on the Tuesday kept the dream alive but they were at full-strength for the final match on the Saturday. The whole team was outstanding, Paul had perhaps his best game defensively of the season and we ran out 4-1 winners. The night out was a cracker; the lads certainly knew how to celebrate!

On the 14th of April, Keith and Leanne announced they were going to move into his flat in Northfield Place as a couple. He as much as anyone had helped her through hard times and although we worried, we had a sense that it was the right thing for them to do. Leanne had a health scare when her doctor put her for tests to check out the possibility she was diabetic; things came back all clear.

Our heads were far from clear when they announced on the 4th of August 1994 that she was expecting a baby. She suffered a lot of health problems through her pregnancy but that special miracle was on the way again. It was theirs to live through and Keith's mum and dad, Kath and Ian and Vera and I would have the new sensation of enjoying it as expectant grandparents. Wet Wet Wet had been telling us that Love Is All Around and for all of us it truly was!

Life brought us double tragedy,
Its sorrow we would know.
Then over God's good earth,
The winds of war did blow.
I nearly lost my daughter,
Found sadness in the snow.
Yet broken hearts were mended,
And from love life would grow.

To infinity and beyond!

Nineteen ninety-five was going to be the year we'd wish away and we all knew the reason why; the miracle of life was going to happen and we just couldn't wait for its arrival. No-one was hoping for the arrival of the big day more than Leanne; she had an awful time during her pregnancy! She had two spells in hospital with dehydration problems when the doctors just told her and Keith that baby was keeping all the goodness for itself. If only they could have given Leanne a pill that contained what was in the drip they put her on. It had her perked up within hours!

New life was well on the way but in his sixty-sixth year my dad was about to experience the horror of being told his days were drawing to a close; but thankfully in the end the medics got it entirely wrong. It was difficult to understand or believe what the ward sister was telling me when I was called into her office. Dad had been in for a biopsy and now they were telling me he had cancer of the gullet. There was an operation they could do but it would severely affect his quality of life and the prognosis was months rather than years. When I returned to his bedside he knew by my face that I'd been told and his pain and shock mirrored mine.

This began a year of torment for my father until he was sent to begin a course of chemotherapy prior to a planned operation. He had shaved off all his hair, rather than have it fall out but was in for a shock that would probably have made it fall out anyway. The clinic wouldn't start his treatment; his notes apparently did not clearly indicate where the treatment was to be directed! There followed an unbelievable chain of events, which I can never forgive the NHS for.

Dad went back to the specialist and suddenly the diagnosis was no longer cancer but a condition that can show the same symptoms, Barrett's Oesophagus! That was the good news, they told him. Good news! They had put him through months of despair and a man of lesser inner strength might perhaps have sought an easy way out. I did speak to the Consultant but there was never an apology for the distress my dad had been caused. Of course it was great news and we were all overjoyed but how on earth could it have happened in the first place?

As Vera and I waited to become grandparents a final rite of passage into adulthood was to be made by our own youngest child. Paul reached his twenty-first birthday and he seemed to have had a wonderful time getting there. He had inherited the steel of his grandfathers, his mother's sense of fair play and was often, like me, just plain daft. That daftness was never better illustrated than when he arrived home well oiled at 4 am one morning. His excellent *Rab C Nesbitt* impersonation was weirdly interspersed with a strange desire to constantly chant the name of the Italian footballer, Roberto Baggio, but his Italian accent was more Inspector Clouseau than parliamo Italiano! I'm always reluctant to tell tales about Leanne or Paul because invariably the saga of my tartan y-fronts will be re-told and grossly embellished—enough said!

CD were in their first Division One season and although it was a hard struggle they pulled clear of relegation in the end and lost a cup-final to champions Dyce in May. Paul was involved in an entirely accidental clash with Kincorth's Andy Gove towards the end of the season. Andy was a legendary striker and totally fearless. His diving header in a packed penalty box was perhaps too brave. Andy got the ball but a flailing boot caught him full on the face—his injuries looked serious. I was amazed to see him less than two weeks later turn out for Kincorth in a league decider, wearing a mask that was more *Phantom of the Opera* than football. Their long run as Champions came to an end in a 2-0 defeat by Dyce but Andy typified the spirit that had made them Champions for so long.

By the start of the new season Paul would be playing for both CD on a Saturday and a Sunday amateur side that his pal Steve Gormley had started running, Northern Bar. It was all far too much football, I thought. If all this football was leaving him any time for the ladies he wasn't letting on to his mum and dad. A young girl called Mandy had came to stay for a couple of weekends after they had met on holiday the previous year, but that seemed to have gone the way of most holiday romances.

Baby, boy, youth, man.
Blink an eye if you can.
Snot-nosed tubby little son.
Full grown man of twenty-one.
Painted clown in school revue.
Centre half at six foot two.
Flying over handlebars.
Icy spills in motor cars.
Little girl an alien person.
Lusting after Elle McPherson.
From boyhood then to manhood prime.
A dad's best gift, a little time.

Paul's birthday coincided with the 10th year of *Comic Relief* when the hope was to push the total monies raised since 1985 through the £100 million barrier. It was red noses all round for everyone. They were soon being worn on sad faces as England took the Grand Slam decider 24-12 at Twickenham. Rugby would however provide a marvellous platform for Nelson Mandela's emerging nation, as South Africa became World Champions.

A paraphrase of an old Ralph McTell song was running through my mind on the 11th of April 1995. He'd sang, *It's A Long, Long Way From Clare To Here.* I mused it had been a long, long way from there to Clare! My life's journey had now arrived at the birth of my beautiful granddaughter, Clare Fordyce. At 3.38 am, weighing in at 8lbs 3ozs and amazingly born into the Queen's Cross Maternity Ward, a touching reminder of the long closed birthplace of her mum and I.

Leanne and Keith could now set off on the wondrous voyage of discovery that the next twelve years or so would bring, that special time when we mere mortals can aspire to be gods, at least until they find out what the moon's made of! In the half-light of the ward that evening, all the proud grandparents were there. Leanne looked exhausted whilst Keith looked so proud and yet so comfortable as he nursed their daughter in his arms.

So began our lives as grandparents, and Leanne and Keith's life as mum and dad. Leanne had visitors all the time and was showing Clare off at every opportunity she got. I didn't get to do much cuddling because I'd torn my calf muscle playing indoor tennis the day before she was born. Vera had a mystery illness just weeks after the birth and collapsed at home; it was the beginning of two years of problems that would eventually end in a diagnosis of epilepsy.

Nothing however could stop us enjoying those special times. Vera got her photo of the four generations, Dad, Leanne, Clare and me, as soon as she could and we opened up Clare's own building society account. Clare spent her first night with us when she was just three weeks old—Vera was in heaven, I was terror-struck! Leanne and Keith were so comfortable about sharing Clare with their parents and I didn't remember being that way. I was so much younger when Leanne had been born and was sorry if I'd kept any love out of her life.

Clare was such fun for us all and later in the year she displayed her talent as the world's number one raspberry blower, a talent well learned from her father I'm sure! She was however a little wary of Paul in the *Pink Panther* suit he hired to go and see the Dons win the League Cup final with a 2-0 win over Dundee, to date the last time a piece of silverware came home to the Pittodrie trophy cabinet. Paul had long since converted to being a Hibs fan and I'm sure the Pink Panther suit was the only way he could smuggle himself into the game.

Willie Miller had left Pittodrie and Roy Aitken was now at the helm. Roy had won a trophy and saved us from relegation but had also paid £1 million pounds for Paul Bernard, surely one of the shrewdest bits of football business ever, for Oldham! Eric Cantona had karate kicked himself to a two week jail sentence when he lashed out at a Crystal Palace fan, who got his five minutes of fame in the papers.

All I said claimed the fan was, "Off you go Mr Cantona, it's an early bath for you!"

Yeah right! Would any football fan ever question a player's ethnic origin or parentage?

I'm just not designed for the working life, I've endured it since I was fifteen but rarely enjoyed it. We were being roasted through summer in a portakabin in the front car park at Police Headquarters whilst our new office was being built; a break was overdue. Vera and I planned a summer holiday in Cornwall; we changed cars just before the trip and bought a little green Micra.

Cornwall was lovely and everything in Newquay seemed to be open twenty four hours a day. The highlights of the holiday were the non-stop glorious weather and our temporary membership of the local British Legion. The Legion had entertainment every night, cheap booze and bingo, which we kept winning, and it was great fun. The downsides were trying to watch the awful *Waterworld* movie and taking a ride on a giant twister on my forty-fourth birthday. Vera and I worked our way through the colour spectrum as first I went, green, yellow then white but managed not to throw up and she then, from the safety of the ground, went red laughing and then blue as she started to choke on her chuckles!

It was a year for dodgy movies and the historical twaddle served up in *Braveheart* and *Rob Roy* was more than I could take. A Volkswagen TV advert had made a hit of an old Coasters number the year before and it's title said it all, *Sorry But I'm Gonna Have To Pass*.

Our world of joy was not shared by all and although a peace agreement was reached in the Balkans by Serbia, Bosnia and Croatia, a huge NATO force would be required to implement it and the conflict looked certain to erupt in Kosovo and perhaps even Macedonia.

We had a sad moment attending the funeral of Vera's Uncle Alan in Dundee. In the midst of the sadness it was nice to see old friends and relatives. Dave's mum and dad, Stan and Iris were still marvellous for their age and Stan was still a show stopper with his wonderful baritone voice at any of the family parties we were invited to. Dad and Isobel were having problems with drunken and noisy neighbours at Errol and as he went through his health scare, we battled with the council to have them move to sheltered housing.

Big Frank Bruno finally became a world champion of sorts by defeating Oliver McCall on points for the WBC version of the crown. Miguel Indurain joined cycling's five-time Tour de France winners and in the process became the first man to win it five years running.

Vera and I were both adding to our own collections that year. Her passion was Wade porcelain; it was Biggles books and old children's annuals for me. Right at the start of Paul's football season a nice £450 win for Vera on CD's sweeper set us off on a spending spree. Leanne loved to trawl the car-boot sales with us and of course there was always Clare to spend some money on!

£450 wasn't going to help us fulfil our dream; a three bedroom detached villa at Dyce cost £75000 and we were still no nearer buying a house like that than ever. It was incomprehensible to read of Nick Leeson losing £17 billion on the Japanese futures market to ruin Barings Bank, when we stood just a few thousand pounds away from realising the dream of a lifetime.

Oasis had their first number one and would soon be telling us they were better than the Beatles; and perhaps they were. I hope the youngsters had as much fun finding out as I'd had through the Sixties. Robson and Jerome were still crucifying old Sixties numbers and getting to number one in the process! My Sixties' school, empty for many years, was reduced to a charred shell after a huge fire ripped through the old Aberdeen Academy.

Love Can Build A Bridge was the number one single in aid of Comic Relief and we were a family devoted to one wonderful child with oh so many around the world still in the grip of pain and poverty. At Christmas I thought of Clare, of many Christmas days long past and of many yet to come with her and hopefully other grandchildren! We spent a lovely Boxing Day together with Paul, Dad and Isobel and Leanne, Keith and Clare. It was sad to hear that Dean Martin had died on Christmas Day and everyone allowed me the pleasure of listening to a few of his tracks as we all settled for a quiet family evening. Well as quiet as Clare would allow!

Early the next year we had a little victory as Dad and Isobel got news that they'd been allocated a move to sheltered housing at Murray Court on Great Northern Road. Things had got out of control at Errol; the police had been called out and I had to go over one night during a spot of bother. The council had actually moved homeless drunks into flats occupied by pensioners—it was like allowing a fox to live in a field of sheep! They were both so happy when they moved in; there was a twenty-four-hour warden, a security entry system and Dad loved the view across town from his top floor flat. At the end of April we had a joint celebration at the flat, their house warming and our Silver Wedding anniversary.

Three parents lost, two children grown, a beautiful granddaughter, these things and so much more all seemed to have happened in the blink of an eye but we'd reached twenty five years of marriage with no regrets. Vera loved her beautiful bunch of flowers from Clare and we spoke together of days gone by and days yet to come.

When something happens that ordinary folk can't conceive of in their worst nightmares, then all words fail. No more to do or say than feel a part of the deep shame that sometimes just being a member of the human race can bring. How small and insignificant all the daily woes became, how fragile our hold on humanity.

For children of Dunblane we weep.
A monster put them all to sleep.
As parents of these angels cry.
The nation grieves and wonders why?

Our own baby was fast approaching her first birthday. She had developed just a little bit of a temper but still had us all on a string. She used almost the same method of propulsion as her mum but instead of paddling her legs from side to side she somehow managed to push them out in front of herself and drag herself along on her bottom. By the end of May she was nearly walking, and it was maybe too soon for Leanne. At the beginning of June she and Keith told us she was expecting once more. If she were as poorly in pregnancy this time around she'd never be able to keep up with Clare on the rampage! The wee soul would pull herself up against the arm of a chair and shout 'Ta-ta' as she tottered off across the room, usually to end in a crumpled heap three or four paces away.

Leanne and Keith had planned a wedding with Clare as a flower girl but with another baby on he way they decided to move things forward and set a date for the 13th of August 1996. Leanne was no better this time than she'd been with Clare and was back in hospital once more, the amazing drip did the trick once again! They should sell that stuff in the pubs, I thought.

On the big day, Leanne was the calmest of us all. I was appointed official photographer but Keith never lets me forget that I turned up like an extra from an episode of *Randall and Hopkirk Deceased*. I thought my off-white suit was super cool! All the lads had a dram for their nerves in the Kirkgate Bar before the ceremony at the Registry Office. Clare was even more relaxed than her mum was; she slept right through it! The evening at the Ferryhill House Hotel was superb, a great meal, super company. It all was a day to remember.

Bill and I were still having our tennis nights but as my bowls game had crumbled I'd long since given up playing with him and his brother Ian at the Indoor. The standard in the First Division was way beyond me now and I was a hindrance to the team. It had taken me two years to pluck up the courage to tell Ian I wanted to pack it in and he'd been too much of a gentleman to tell me I was rubbish. I was back playing with my pal Davie Pattillo and his dad—I was still rubbish but luckily they were gentlemen too!

Life often doesn't work out the way you plan. Bill and Nancy had been great pals of ours but they had split up a few years earlier. We met the new lady in Bill's life, Allison, towards the end of that year. She was a lovely girl and it was a pleasure that we all got on well in each other's company. Bill was the undisputed champion of *Trivial Pursuits* nights and it was Allison who introduced us to the Student Shows at His Majesty's Theatre. How on earth Vera and I had never been to see one before I'll never know. The kids were superb in them. I think the first one we ever saw was called *The Scaffie's*

Revenge and it was hilarious.

Bill and I went to the CD golf outing at Keith that year. Paul was slowly recovering from an ankle injury and had been out of football for almost two months but he did manage the golf and more importantly was fit to phone his mum to come and take me home from the King's Bar that evening. Well we had kicked the day off there at 7am and at least I hadn't challenged anyone to a race!

Keith was always there for Leanne during her difficult pregnancy and Vera and Kath were always willing to take Clare for a weekend. Not only was she all over the place, she was now a chatterbox too. I saw plenty of her; I could easily pop up to Leanne's at lunchtimes. Clare loved you to read to her and I began to think that *101 Dalmatians* was actually an instruction as opposed to the book's title. She had a talking book edition of *Jungle Book* but the wee smarty-pants always pressed the sound effect just before you got to that part of the story. Her scolding of Tom for his treatment of Jerry was a joy to behold as she watched them on telly and she just loved *Rugrats* and *Toy Story*.

She had two games she loved to play. We'd all be given the command 'Eep!' and as we all pretended to be instantly sent off to sleep she would strut around the room in fits of laughter. And a mysterious, invisible monster lived upstairs in our house—she would painstakingly track it down and then thrash the life out of it with her plastic tattie masher!

She had a failed attempt at being the monster herself and decided a towel wrapped over her head would add to the horror. She just couldn't understand why she couldn't see a thing with it on and got so annoyed, emerging in floods of tears time after time.

The wonder of the Olympics that year was one Michael Johnson who claimed both the 200 and 400 metres gold medals with his amazing upright running style. In contrast to Michael was there ever a more graceful mover than Steffi Graf? She won her seventh Wimbledon singles title and was such a joy to watch you could sometimes forget all about the tennis! The villain of the previous year, Eric Cantona, was now the football writer's Player of the Year.

Vera was on another decorating marathon and Leanne's old room was to become her upstairs sitting room. We started in August and I just got finished before Christmas; nobody had warned me that marrying Vera would be like getting a job for life painting the Forth Road Bridge. I called on a pal to provide the centrepiece of our efforts though and she was delighted with the beautifully Artexed ceiling in our living room.

The over-exertions of Paul's two-pronged assault on the football world had not been the cause of his ankle injury. That was down to a horrendous over the top tackle. It happened of all days on his birthday and in effect the ligament damage put paid to his season. One of my last acts of the season would be to fall down the hill outside the storeroom at CD's Upper Westfield pitch, hotly pursued by the goalposts that the lads and I had been carrying!

The Northern Bar as always finished runners-up in everything to Quinn's, later to become Moorings Thistle. Stevie Gormley had done a fine job with the team but deserved more than having to suffer me and Barney Battles doing our karaoke version of *Lipstick On Your Collar* at the end of season bash. CD would finish fourth in their second season in the First Division but amazingly it would be the end of the road for Jim Neave and Ian Simpson.

Paul was in the dressing room after their last match of the season and was one of only a handful of players who re-signed for the next season when Jim and Ian offered the lads forms. They'd taken the club to four successive promotions, cup success and a high finish after two seasons in Division One. What more could the lads be looking for? Jim and Ian decided very soon afterwards that the club would become defunct. It was a sad end to a marvellous story. Paul did eventually sign for Glentanar for the new season but it would be a long time before I felt his heart was really in it again.

Bill and I added a new string to his sporting bow when he joined me for a game of badminton and we decided to extend our summer tennis sessions into regular games of badminton over the winter months. He'd never played before but soon got the hang of it and it kept us ticking over all year round. I met up with a group of old boys late in the year as I had a re-union with Ian Davidson, Billy McAndrew and all the other lads from our youthful days of drinking at the Continental.

I'd annoyed Vera by tormenting her about being so wound up about who would win *Stars In Their Eyes*. Who needed a Marti Pellow soundalike anyway? When I laughed as I caught her crying during the episode when Raquel left *Corrie* I was in serious trouble and branded an unromantic so and so. I took up the challenge to prove her wrong and get back into her good books. It would be our twenty-seventh Christmas together and I made it my mission to get her twenty seven presents under the tree. She loved it and I was her pal again, although I still had to wash all the dishes after lunch. On my own too—Paul was wiped out with a bad cold!

Where would it all end over the troubles in Northern Ireland? The IRA cease-fire was broken, as bombings were carried out in London's docklands and in Manchester. Fierce rioting broke out in the province and we wondered what had happened to the hope of last Christmas when crowds had sung Christmas songs and carols in Belfast.

Vera and I had a super double holiday that summer, a week in a cottage near Harrogate at a tiny village called Burnt Yates. Then we spent the second week at Conwy in North Wales. The magnificence of York Minster was awe-inspiring and we joined the Legion again in Wales. We had great fun at both places and if we'd had Paul's travelling expenses the world would have been our oyster. Royal Mail were moving out of their Crown Street HQ and Paul was off to their new base at Altens. Some staff were to be paid a one-off payment in compensation for their additional travelling expenses to work. Paul was initially excluded from the offer but a letter of appeal I helped him with did the trick and he got his little windfall.

Charles and Diana went their separate ways and divorced. She was at once the darling of the Press and our celebrity-obsessed society. If I lived to be a hundred I'd never want for a moment to live the kind of life that they had.

Scientists were cloning sheep that year and I fancy they did a wee bit of overtime to give us the Spice Girls. They all sounded like a flock of sheep baa-ing in double time to me! In fact the boffins may have done a double shift just to make sure there were enough bovines in the choir and knocked out Baddiel and Skinner for *Three Lions* too.

Good music was put to a beautiful purpose when *Knockin' On Heaven's Door/Throw Those Guns Away* was recorded in memory of the innocents murdered at Dunblane.

A sad memory of 1996 was seeing my boyhood hero Muhammad Ali struggling to light the Olympic flame in Atlanta. He was now fighting the toughest opponent of his life, Parkinson's disease, and his courage in that battle would match any he'd ever shown in the boxing ring.

Another year was in a hurry and it came to an early climax on the 5th of February 1997 when our second granddaughter, Shannon, was born at 10.40am. Our little girl tipped the scales at 9lbs 8 ¾ ozs! The first time Vera and I saw her we were amazed at how much hair she had; it was jet black. She had the same soft bottom lip that her mum had when she was born and her dad's eyes. No doubt she'd soon have us all attending to her every whim just like her big sister and we'd be pleased as punch to make sure she had as good a start in life as Clare. Two granddaughters, I'd maybe need to change from football to hockey as my favourite sport in a few years!

One week later I was at Leanne's for lunch and got my first shot of feeding Shannon; by the end of the month we had both the monsters for a sleepover together. Clare was being just a little naughty and kept on repeating "Oh shit," any time her grandmother said it as she rushed to tend to Shannon's slightest movement or whimper. Clare was too clever for her own good and Leanne had her off to a 'terrible two's' nursery just before her actual birthday; she just needed the stimulation of other people and was very curious about the world.

Vera was developing a habit of changing cars more often than she used to change her living room suites. The kids were the only excuse she needed; the Micra would be too small for travelling around with them both and so it was on, to a Renault Clio for us. A nice five-door job that did make it a lot easier to get the kids' things in and out, I must admit. Of course there was one other kid in the family we'd forgotten about, and I was called upon to do the holiday run to Glasgow Airport once again as Paul and his mates set off yet again for Tenerife. Vera said I was mad and I said the run would be good for the car!

My other regular phone call was the biannual one from Dad and Isobel to change the time on their video recorder after the clocks had changed. Twice a year I showed them what to do, twice a year their heads nodded and Dad said "Fine, no problem," and twice a year Isobel phoned to say he'd lost his rag trying to set the time.

A more serious regular occurrence was beginning to have too much of an upsetting effect on our daily lives. Over the previous two years Vera's 'turns,' as we called them, had become more frequent and more severe in their nature. After one particularly bad one in April we sought the help of our family doctor. Doctor Anderson of the Oldmachar Medical Practice was a lovely man and set things in motion for Vera to see a specialist. By July she'd had all her tests and a mild form of epilepsy was diagnosed. There were drugs that could control the situation but initially Vera just didn't want to take them. By the end of the year, after more problems and a long discussion with Dr Anderson, she started taking the medication and things would be reasonably under control until one desperate dark day; but thankfully that was seven years in the future.

Since the halcyon days of the Big Three and the particular greatness of Jack Nicklaus, the world of golf had been looking for a hero and one came to the fore in amazing fashion. Like Nicklaus he came with a fine pedigree as an amateur champion; Tiger Woods simply strolled away with the US Masters to fulfil his vast potential and set off on the quest to try an emulate Jack's achievements.

Every time we saw Shannon she looked more and more like her mum. However the wee soul was not having the happiest of starts to life and her health was often a worry. Before the year was out, both she and Clare had come down with the chicken pox and then there were fears that Shannon had a clicking hip. Leanne and Keith were then also told that Clare had asthma; they were at their wits end but the worries would pass and both the kids would thrive in the years ahead.

There were still laughs to be had with the bairns and none better than Clare's sudden desire to eat boiled eggs. She visited us one Sunday afternoon, demanded and ate four before she was satisfied. There was one little problem attached though—she started breaking wind rather frequently.

As she ran around the living room I questioned, "Did you fart?"

In that time-honoured way of small children, who thrill at any achievement they make, she proudly answered, "Yes I did!"

I suspected Keith Fordyce had put her up to it, he was the biggest stinker I'd come across since Alan Reekie!

In August the world was stunned when Princess Diana was killed in a mad car dash across Paris as she sought to escape the attentions of the Press. The amazing outpouring of public grief that followed her death was astonishing and in death as in life, every moment of her story was feasted on by others. The heart-rending delivery of *Candle In The Wind* at her funeral service by Elton John certainly brought a tear to the eyes of millions. Sad as her death was, she was given an almost saintly status that was in truth undeserved.

The world *did* lose a saintly woman when Mother Teresa died; she had devoted her life to the care of starving children in Calcutta. In their different ways both of these women would be greatly missed and their memories would grow with the passing of the years.

With a bigger family to house Leanne and Keith started to look around for a larger place to live. Throughout the summer we all hoped that the simple solution would be for them to buy our house and Vera and I could perhaps achieve our aim of a wee bungalow. It was not to be and at offers over £68000 a house at Potterton, which Vera really liked, was still just out of reach. It was such a disappointment to tell them that we couldn't afford to move and in the end they had to pay a little more than they'd planned. The good news that came out of it was that they moved in just round the corner from us to a nice semi in East Main Avenue.

There are no doubts millions of people remember where they were during Diana's funeral service. I was alone, driving down the deserted Aberdeen to Stonehaven road with the radio on as Elton sang. It was eerie; there was not another vehicle or person in sight. Life as they say must go on; this was the day that Keith had planned for their house move, and I was on my way to his mum and dad's house at Newtonhill to help load all the stuff they had stored there onto his dad's lorry.

Shannon may have been poorly at times but she loved to hear her own voice and by the time she was only months old she would deliver marvellous tales in babyspeak that kept us all smiling. Put a video of the *Big Friendly Giant* on and she'd shriek her head off. Leanne managed to get a job working part-time at a local shop, the cash was handy but she could shriek as loud as Shannon could when she came home after a particularly hard shift. Poor Keith! She also decided to take on a job calling on houses to update the voter's roll. I seem to remember Keith doing a lot of canvassing on that one too. What a nice man, I hope she appreciated him!

It was the Cotswolds that year; the area was beautiful and the weather was all we could have hoped for. The cottage and pool were great; Cirencester was a great base, there was plenty to do and lots of super places to see within easy travelling distance. Lilian and Ray had managed to get a council flat in Crieff and had moved out of the Holiday Park. On the way home we spent a few days with them and agreed that the flat really seemed a good move from the point of view of Ray's health. He and I had gone out, on the Saturday afternoon, for a game of pool and a few pints at the Station. The local Highland Games were on and suddenly a host of pipers were in the pub giving us a rousing medley of Scottish tunes. Every single man was given a free dram by the landlord and it was one great memory of many happy, happy times with Ray.

We were gluttons for punishment that summer and travelled from Crieff straight to Lossiemouth for a few days with Dave and Andrea. It was all too much in the end and Vera and I trailed home to Aberdeen after a hectic holiday that saw us both glad to get back to work for a rest. How on earth I've any memories of that few weeks at all I don't know, too much time spent with too many good chums who were only too happy to fill us up with far too much liquid refreshment!

On our anniversary we were off early to the polling station, and before the day was out it was becoming apparent that Tony Blair and his New Labour would be sweeping to power with a huge majority. The last few years of Conservative rule had witnessed a high tide of sleaze and corruption claims and the country was certainly in a mood for change. Would his huge majority drive Mr Blair forward to change the face of politics and Britain as he promised or would they simply find it easy to slip into the Tories still warm slippers?

The tragic murder of Scott Simpson shocked all of Aberdeen; the poor wee lad's death brought such a warm and tender response from the people in his own community and across the city. He had fallen victim to a monster and the lives of Scott's parents had been ruined. Yet at this moment the loving side of human nature was around for all to see. In the midst of his tragedy you could still see what a wonderful place our world could be, if only!

Scotland walked the road to devolution in 1997 as we voted for our own Parliament at the same elections that swept Tony to number ten. Another tier of civil servants, highly paid politicians and little real change was all we seemed to be getting. It was two years before the parliament became a reality and then they started to drip feed us details of how much the parliament building was going to cost!

We had been told for years how difficult the hand-over of Hong Kong to the Chinese would be but in the end it all went smoothly, the Chinese were targeting a share of the world economic pie and weren't silly enough to pass up a ready made financial centre!

Leanne's best pal Fiona joined the mums in May that year when her son Scott was born and with Leanne beginning to make plans to become a child minder, a visit to East Main was best made with a pocketful of sweets and a storybook. That was for Vera really, my visits were best made with a lawn mower and a paintbrush. Leanne had the biggest garden in Mastrick, Keith had an asthma allergy to grass and I had the fastest flymo in the west! We had new neighbours at Arnage too; Joss and Valerie and their young daughter moved into 71 but spent months doing it up and we didn't see too much of them. They owned the house for almost three years before they split and sold up but we really didn't get to know them all that well.

Paul's football life at Glentanar did not start well; they were immediately involved in a bottom of the table battle and a couple of months into the season he decided to have a break from it all. I think he was still missing the fun of playing for CD. By January he had got himself back in the mood and although the boys tried hard it was a season doomed to end in relegation. In contrast Northern Bar were going from strength to strength and although still second fiddle to the Moorings, their season ended with promotion to the Sunday Amateurs top division. One of Paul's best ever displays was in a 2-1 cup final defeat to their arch-rivals at Woodside. A Man of the Match award was scant reward for the efforts he put in that April Sunday. Never one to dwell on misfortune Paul ended up celebrating back at the pub with members of both sides. Someone must have hit him over the head with his Man of the Match award because he arrived home after midnight and introduced us to his invisible friend Fred but only our cat Theo could actually see and talk to Fred!

Vera and I were never out to too many functions, but the chance to see some old pals at an AA reunion at the Transport club seemed a great idea. Sadly we ended up in the middle of a bar room brawl as the whole affair went pear-shaped. In honesty not one member or former member of staff was involved in the fracas, it was some guests who decided to rearrange the place settings. Vera had her bag stolen early in the evening but we'd spotted the culprit and recovered it amongst limp excuses and apologies. Heb Nicoll and I ended up protecting our wives as fists and furniture flew everywhere. The whole company was ejected from the club and a great idea was sadly ruined.

On Clare's second birthday we had a smashing party but Keith, Paul and I made our excuses later on. We were off to the Northern Bar with the King of Quizzes, Bill. I couldn't believe we only finished third but I was suspicious of the queues at the public telephone after every round of questions. We would never consider cheating but strangely Paul disappeared after every movie question. Towards the end of the quiz I thought I saw Paul across the road from the pub—it couldn't be? I stood up and went to look out of the window, it was him but he wasn't just across the road, he was inside the Blockbusters Video shop!

Vera saw her favourite stage musical for the first time that year and loves it still, *Blood Brothers*. We'd gone to see it with Bill and Allison and finished off the night in grand style at the Continental where an impromptu jazz session by an old fella on the band's piano simply brought the house down. Vera took the opportunity to tell Bill that I was on my last warning at the tennis. I'd now torn my left calf muscle and this she warned would be my last comeback, one more injury and the racquet was history. Eight years and countless injuries later I'm still dressing up like an escapee from King Tut's tomb to chase tennis balls and shuttlecocks.

Paul had gone on holiday to London for a week but his mate Neil was posted missing after a day; later Paul discovered he'd decided to just go home. The missing Neil hadn't spoiled Paul's week and he'd loved London. Neil wouldn't be the only thing that would go missing for Paul that year. He borrowed our car to go to a match in October; the weather was incredibly warm for the time of year and three hours later he told his mum he'd really enjoyed his walk home in the sun.

"Oh that's great, son," she observed, "But where's the car?"

He decided to stay with Glentanar and with pals and workmates like Hoppy, Lugs and Toughie in the side they soon shaped like promotion candidates. He even managed to come off the subs bench on one occasion as a replacement in goal for Hoppy who'd taken a bad knock. Best game of Northern's season was a pulsating 3-2 victory over the Gray's Inn in a super cup-tie at Sheddocksley. The booze-up back at the Gray's afterwards was pretty pulsating too but at least I was only 100 yards away from my own front door.

Roy had outstayed his welcome at Pittodrie and we were about to enter our 'manager a year' period as we moved from Roy to Alex Miller, Paul Hegarty and then Mr Ebbe Skovdahl himself. The direction of the club was a complete mystery through this period and an R Kelly song I'd heard that year just about said it all, *If I Could Turn Back The Hands Of Time!*

Vera and I had one big movie favourite, a superb drama of the days of slavery and the trial of a group of slaves who broke free on the high seas and sought that which we all too often take for granted, freedom. *Amistad* was a movie, which told a great story, made you think, made you cry and in the end made you happy. Now what else does a film need to do?

A real life sadness occurred just at the end of the year, one of those silly moments that gets out of hand. Vera and I had gone to spend Boxing Day with Dad and Isobel; we were all having a lovely time. I barely remember now but I think a programme came on the telly about Princess Diana. Vera and Dad had a little disagreement about her or the programme or something, I forget. Dad had ever been a man on a short fuse and suddenly he was in full flow, we all got our characters and our planned holiday for the next spring was rubbished. I didn't say much, called Keith to come and take us home but for once I felt Dad was the one who needed to apologise. He never did and perhaps sits now and wonders how it all started himself. Time passes, a week becomes a month, a month a year and still today, the rift has never healed. After all that had gone before in ours lives we were stupid enough to allow it to come to this. A fleeting meeting years later gave no real chance to heal the hurt and now loving memories are tainted with bitterness. I should have the strength to solve this problem; I think often of how to do it and now somehow I just can't take the first step.

Yet I must take it before the next step becomes the saddest step of all.

We did make one great discovery in 1997 and that was to find that New Labour were even more right wing than Mrs Thatcher had been!

Tony was a crusading politician and we had a crusading cop at Grampian Police, Dr Ian Oliver was the top man and one of his little schemes was to introduce random drug testing for staff. I was called completely by chance on two occasions within a month. As the only addiction I'd ever had in my life was for Creamola Foam I couldn't help but think that if we had cash to spend on the drugs problem, then why not direct it to the most needed areas. Oh well they did say he was going to be the country's next Drugs Tsar, whatever that meant? The Doc was as remote to me as Tony Blair, but I took no joy in his demise as he was exposed over clandestine meetings in the woods with a lady friend. Many people much more in the know than I was at work held him in the highest regard and as modern scandals go it all seemed something and nothing.

Leanne had passed through all the checks required of her to become a child minder. It was strange; I'd never thought of her in that role but she managed it very well. Although it gave her the opportunity to earn her living at home and be with her own kids at all times it was clear to see that it was hard, hard work. She and Keith both worked to make it a success and those attitudes were making their marriage a success too. Keith was as comfortable with other children as he was with his own and had great patience with them, although somewhat less with inanimate objects. Don't ask him to set up an easel, he'd wrecked Clare's last Christmas almost before it was out of the box and always approached DIY problems by applying the drop test first!

At forty-six years of age and under threat of enforced sporting retirement from Vera, I made a sporting comeback. Keith got me involved in one of his works football matches and I even managed to score a goal in the 5-5 draw. As I had asked to play at left back to keep me well away from the action I was delighted at my scoring exploit and Keith immediately nicknamed me Branco after Brazil's overlapping full back. I was more overweight and out of breath than overlapping and outstanding but it had been great fun. I'd play a few more times with Keith and his workmates, especially at five-a-sides. Vera just shook her head and checked that all the insurances were fully paid up! Bill was dafter than me and had never stopped playing football; when I started playing regularly in his works five-a-side team Vera gave up her protestations and bought me a new pair of football shoes for my birthday.

There would be no more comebacks for possibly my favourite singer of all time; Frank Sinatra died in May and the world lost a rare genius. Frank could have sung your message list and still made it seem like the most beautiful lyric you'd ever heard. Vera and I had our own little tribute to him and cuddled up with a couple of bottles of wine and watched *Robin and the Seven Hoods* and *High Society* on the video.

Northern Bar had lost so many times to the Moorings that Stevie Gormley had to go and spend one weekend a month sitting on their manager's mantelpiece. The spell was finally broken early in the season when they defeated them 2-1 after extra-time in cup-tie. Paul missed this historic occasion as he'd signed up for a morning's overtime at Royal Mail! He did notch up another hat-trick a few weeks later and not long afterwards invested £1000 in a new computer. Presumably he needed it to keep track of his growing goal tally! Joking aside, it was a super year for me watching the football and I can't imagine how much Paul must have enjoyed being out on the pitch. Glentanar clinched the championship with their own amazing finish to the season and

Huntly's dramatic collapse. Paul was a member of the Royal Mail team that lifted the Scottish Cup; Dundee, Fife and Glasgow were amongst the scalps they took and I've got the photograph of Martin Tough in a Celtic strip to prove it! Northern finished second in everything and Paul was as pleased as punch when he lifted Glentanar's Player's Player of the Year award.

Keith provided me with another highlight in spring that year; he'd been coaching Shannon and I was as proud as punch as she made her first clear stab at calling me Granda. The girls sorted us all out in the days ahead. Kath was always hoovering and became Grandma Noo Noo after the character in Telly Tubbies, and my name sounded like a doll's so I became Granda Sindy. Meanwhile, to avoid confusion, Vera and Ian were tagged in that simplest of ways that only children can use and were known, no less affectionately, as Other Granda and Other Grandma.

A really special holiday lay ahead for us that summer. We hired a large cottage with a swimming pool at Diss and set off there with Leanne, Keith and the kids. The weather was fine most of the days and it was lovely to enjoy such a lot of time with the girls. Keith and I even managed to sneak away to Carrow Road and watched Norwich City play a pre-season friendly against Tottenham Hotspur. That week ended with Vera's forty-fifth birthday and by coincidence Kath and Ian were just arriving to spend their own holiday in the area. They watched the kids that evening and Leanne and Keith took us out for a lovely meal for the perfect end to the day and our holiday week.

We set off from Diss for our second week at a cottage in the Lake District but discovered that the brochure had been a little bit economic with the truth. Basically it said head north and turn left for the Lake District at Penrith—curiously our instructions said turn right! The cottage was tidy but way too small for four adults and two children. We had to make a round trip of twenty-two miles to get to the starting point to go anywhere else and the weather turned absolutely vile. By the Thursday we had all had enough and decided to beat a hasty retreat back across the border and head home.

We did salvage one special memory from our Lake District disappointment when we took the girls to Lowther Leisure Park. They were both spellbound at the little circus, especially the trapeze artists. Clare was at first very scared of the *Punch and Judy* show and then as bold as brass and shouting as loud as anyone else before the show was half way through. Shannon just wouldn't come off the Noddy car on the merry go round and if Clare dragged me to the top of the helter-skelter once she did it a hundred times.

Clare and Shannon were the focus of attention for the whole family and we took a photo of them to a local artist and asked if he could do an oil painting of them, Vera, Paul and I planned it as a Christmas present for Leanne and Keith. The result was more than we'd hoped for; he had Shannon to a tee and captured her long dark hair beautifully. Clare grew on you and amazingly it was as if he'd guessed how she'd grow; she became more and more like her image in the painting over the next eighteen months or so. The kids themselves displayed some artistic talent and turned up one Sunday to assist me hang the last roll of wallpaper in the kitchen. Vera wasn't on a new decorating offensive, just a little tidy up for the kitchen, phew!

It was a trip down memory lane for me as I joined Keith and Clare when they went swimming; Shannon would come too but often seemed to get just too cold to be enjoying herself properly. The cold didn't seem to bother her in December when she and her sister arrived to play in the snow in my garden. She was just beginning to become a chatterbox and told me their snow had been all messed up and they needed some more to play in!

American President Bill Clinton became the first to be impeached for over one hundred years. His high crimes against the state appeared to revolve around not whether he'd had an affair with a young female assistant, but rather that he'd encouraged her to lie about the matter under oath. In the late twentieth century the furore just seemed to make him more popular in America than ever. He was a godsend for satirical programmes and comedians in need of cheap one-liners. The joke was on us; what a character to have in the role of world's most powerful man!

Hope sprung eternal in Northern Ireland and in what seemed like the most positive move ever towards peace the Good Friday Agreement was reached. It was a confused deal, which included the release of convicted murderers and saw no surrender of arms. People like me watched from afar and prayed that from the confusion peace would arrive but there was little doubt that it was the gun, bombs, death and suffering that had driven the peace process this far.

The big news on the football front was that Glentanar were hoping to make the huge step up to Junior football. It was a tribute to all the players who'd helped them win the Second Division Amateur Championship that the club gave them the opportunity to establish themselves at the higher grade. They were an ambitious club and had a superb pitch and excellent facilities at Woodside. They made their bow on the Junior stage in a Grill League Cup match against East End on the 8th of August. They lost a close encounter 2-1; Paul had missed a lot of pre-season training whilst on holiday but came on as a sub for the last half-hour.

It was great fun to watch, I just hoped the step up in grade didn't mean too much of a change in attitude. Football at the highest level was now permeated with cheats, I felt: players diving for free kicks and penalties and feigning injury at the drop of a hat only to miraculously recover seconds later. What had happened to the beautiful game? Money had happened to football and the ridiculous amounts involved for both players and coaching staff had, for me, taken the game away from its roots, and the working man. I fancied that my supporting days would be over when Paul hung up his boots, unless I had a grandson of course!

By September the boys had clocked up their first win in Junior football with a 2-1 victory over RAF Lossiemouth. The big time was catching up with them and there were already rumours of manager John Irvine leaving the club. John was then and still is one of Paul's favourite characters and best friends in football, so he wasn't too happy when John did eventually leave. By November Gary Forbes had taken over as manager and the drive to push the club onward and upward was well and truly on. That same month Paul grabbed his first Junior goal and although the team wouldn't be winning a championship that year they acquitted themselves well enough and went on to finish in a comfortable mid-table position.

Travelling was the big fun of the Junior games and the company on the touchline, of lads like Barney Battles and Roger Rushton, was superb. One early trip the Glens made was to play St Joseph's in Dundee. That was an experience—the local pub was intimidating enough but the match was a battle royal and after a 3-3 draw the lads clinched a 5-4 win on penalties.

Vera and I were still on our travels to Crieff and Raymond and Lilian were as good company as ever although Ray often seemed to be very tired and always very cold. I'd discovered Lucinda Williams's album, *Car Wheels On A Gravel Road* and as Vera invariably slept on our runs through I could play it to my heart's content. In one of our *Trivial Pursuits* nights Ray was especially miffed when we all dissolved into fits of laughter as he announced that Fatima Whitbread was the last British woman to lift Olympic track gold. The more we laughed the more confused he became.

"I know she's won the World Championships and is one of our best ever athletes," he said in considered tones, "Why is it so funny to say she won the 100 metres at the Olympics?"

A chorus of laughter all round and we echoed as one, "Because she's a javelin thrower Ray!"

We were just thinking what a quiet year it had been when, after a November footballing lesson from Kelty Hearts in the Scottish Cup, Paul had stayed at home to help me floor our loft. It was after midnight before we got finished and we were just heading off to bed when an almighty crash rang out from what seemed to be just in front of the house. We gathered ourselves together and ran outside just in time to see a big red car zigzag off down Arnage Drive. Eunice's garden wall had been totally demolished and our driveway gates had sustained a fair bit of damage too. The culprit was never traced but at least I was able to fix the damage to our property myself. Poor Eunice had a major rebuilding job to do and the wall looked in imminent danger of collapse for weeks after.

The big movie of the year was a flop for me as Leonardo diCaprio, looking all of twelve years old, impossibly romanced Kate Winslet on the doomed *Titanic*. The special effects were what the film seemed to rely on to carry it through and it somehow missed out on the depth of story that such a tragedy needed to be given.

Paul scooped a big £600 quid win on the fixed odds to end his Christmas shopping worries and we spent a lovely Christmas Day with all the family, except my dad and Isobel and I hoped they'd had a lovely time too. Paul must have kept a fair bit of his windfall for a big Boxing Day night out. It was Mum who heard his 2 am fumblings at he front door and proceeded to investigate. From my bed I heard their brief conversation.

"Paul, come inside, where are your keys?" demanded mum.

"Don't worry mum, I haven't lost them, they're in my pocket!" a somewhat tipsy Paul reassured her.

"Bed!" commanded mum.

We were at the ebb of a century and it was a time to look around and see where we were and what life had brought us. The best part of half a century had led me to a wonderful marriage; Vera was the fixed point in my universe and in times of trouble all I needed to do was seek her out, and like the North Star she would lead me to safe haven. My daughter had brought me not only her own loveliness but the joy of two beautiful granddaughters. For good measure she had thrown in a husband, Keith, whom I had liked from the first time I met him. I could say no more of him than that, were he my own son, I would have been a proud man. My son and I were friends; there was no more I could ask of him. I hoped that my father and I would be reconciled and it would have been nice to see my sister again; but life's not like that and even the happiest of lives have their skeleton's closet.

Early in the year Bill and I got a side together to play Keith's works team. The historic clash took place at Balgownie and Paul played at centre half for our eleven. He and I would have many sporting memories to treasure but to have played football together, if only the once, was a great one for me. Keith's boys brought their own script and won the match 3-2. If we hadn't dragged Paul out of his bed after a night on the town I dread to think what the score might have been. The pitch was a sea of mud and my legs were aching after ten minutes; how I managed the whole ninety I'll never know. My boots were well and truly hung up after that but it wasn't such a bad way to say farewell to the beautiful game.

Paul got as close as he ever had to a steady girlfriend; Gina was a student in Aberdeen and for a while they went out a lot together. Gina had some problems in her own family and once again distance would come between Paul and a girl. She needed to go home to be with her family and they would soon go their separate ways. I've never been convinced that absence makes the heart grow fonder. Love builds from closeness, it thrives on the occasional fight, it always wants to make up, it feeds on laughter, it enjoys a cry and most of all it loves lovers to be together. Paul was a good man and lived life to the full, the good woman for him would be just around the corner and he would meet her in love's good time.

My great pal Bill told me in spring 1999 that he and Allison planned to marry. They tied the knot later in the year on the 9th of October. It was their special day and I was proud to be a very small part of it. Bill, in typical fashion, made a superb speech at the reception and it was good to be amongst so many dear friends at that moment. I felt as proud of and happy for Bill that day as I would have had he been my own brother. He and Allison have gone on to achieve that special gift of love, a wonderful life together and they both deserve it. At risk of spoiling a great friendship I'll reveal a secret from the Stag Night. Bill, after the tortures you endured at the Fantasy Club, you'll be my hero for life!

Conflict and the slaughter of innocents in Kosovo was now out of hand. In March NATO began the bombing of Serbia. An organisation that had been set up to prevent war was now waging war. By summer thousands of NATO troops were on the ground in Kosovo and as with all wars the way out was now the most difficult thing to see.

We were returning to old haunts that summer and had booked a cottage in the Cotswolds again. We were in for a big surprise when we discovered that we were only a few hundred yards from where we'd stayed a couple of years before. The area was still as beautiful a spot as you could hope to see so we were not disappointed.

Work is the engine that drives our lives. Love it or hate it, the rewards for it dictate all that we can do and achieve in life. Like most people I never felt I was quite being paid my worth and for once in my life the bosses agreed with me, although it was very reluctantly! From early in the year through to June I fought a losing battle with an ongoing job evaluation process and eventually took my appeal directly to the Deputy Chief Constable Peter Wilson. I'm convinced that he swung things in my favour. The mere fact that such a high-ranking official requested my case to be reviewed seemed to move mountains and the outcome was in my favour. I've shared my working life at Lost & Found with some super people and was dismayed that my good fortune was not fed down through the ranks to Sheena Thomson or Val Cadenhead. They would not enjoy my good fortune despite their own, perhaps somewhat less vigorous appeals.

Alex Ferguson was made a Freeman of the City of Aberdeen in 1999 and there were many who wished that his brief return to the city might have been longer. The glory days were long gone from Pittodrie but for Fergie the magic moments rolled on. His Manchester United side became the first side to lift the treble of Premiership, FA Cup and Champions League. Their amazing victory over Bayern Munich would have been as good a place as any for the Ferguson fairytale to end.

We were voting for our own Parliament that year but personally I'd have given my vote to anyone who promised to ban boybands. Mind you Westlife did strike back by coming up with a number that even I liked, *Flying Without Wings*. My secret's out, I became a fan of Shania Twain and then discovered a guy whose music was magical and whose story was so interesting. Jessie Winchester had fled to Canada to avoid prison after refusing the draft during the Vietnam War. A respected writer who shied away from performing live himself, his songs had been covered by many top names. He was a complete mystery to me but I'm grateful to DJ Tom Morton for introducing me to his music. Jessie's album *Gentleman Of Leisure* went straight to number two in my personal all-time chart, just behind *Beatles For Sale*.

Glentanar consolidated their first Junior season with a creditable mid table finish and there was much to build on. The next season started in fine style when they defeated Sunnybank 2-1 in a Grill League Cup-tie. 'Bank were one of Aberdeen's great Junior sides and had been the first from the city to win the Scottish Junior Cup way back in 1954, it was a proud moment for the Glens. They would finish the season in fourth place in the league but the club's ambition would see the eventual break-up of the squad that had come through from the amateur ranks as they pursued their aim to climb ever higher up the soccer ladder. I became a little more involved with the club too and took on the job of writing the match reports on their home games for the *Green Final*. My signature was to always try and mention one of Paul Masson's super tricks. 'Bates,' as the lads called him, was a special player to watch and like all really good players seemed to do everything at half speed. Paul Robertson's season finished early; he'd been struggling with a cartilage problem on his knee. It would take the surgeon's knife to find the cure but it signalled the end of his tilt at Junior football. After a lengthy enforced lay-off he decided to give up the extra commitment that Junior football required and would eventually return to the amateur ranks playing for his old boss and great mate, John Irvine.

Keith and Leanne had been married for three years and with Keith about to be promoted at work they were doing really well. Leanne was making a real success of her child minding and always had plenty of money to buy wallpaper and paint, which was bad news for me! Vera and I watched the kids on their third anniversary to let them go out for a meal. The girls were becoming a real handful, racing, jumping, drawing, singing, they were ready to try anything but sleeping! Shannon had left most of her health worries behind her but Clare gave us all a scare when she was taken into hospital with suspected glandular fever on Christmas Eve. Thankfully she got home for Christmas Day at Keith's mum and dad's and was looking more her normal self when we saw them on Boxing Day.

One health scare saddened all the family, when Raymond was diagnosed with suspected skin cancer; at times it seemed as if all his problems were worsening at once. He was his usual quiet self but it was becoming clear how worried Lilian was about him and it was difficult to feel we were being of any help from one hundred miles away.

Aberdeen doesn't have a great history in the golfing arena but our own Paul Lawrie took the Open Championship unexpectedly after a play-off. It was sensational stuff as Lawrie saw off American Justin Leonard and Jean van de Velde. We'll never forget van de Velde's escapades in the Barry Burn with the Championship seemingly in his grasp after 72 holes. Lance Armstrong claimed his first Tour de France triumph after a personal victory over cancer, he would prove to be the greatest cyclist of all time and become as near invincible as any man in any sport ever has been.

A chance meeting with an old pal from primary school introduced me to some more new music. Bobby Burns tapped me on the shoulder and from memory I instinctively ducked; Bobby had been best fighter at King Street, remember! This time it was handshakes and hugs all round, he'd done well in the finance business and told me he was retired and back home for good. He'd always loved music, had his own band and planned to concentrate on that. A couple of days later he called into my office and gave me a CD of some of his stuff. Vera and I loved it and Bobby and Frank Robb are now joint number one in my local artists chart! They'd be joint number two of course if I had a Bobby Vincent CD.

Vera was on the trail of a new car again; the Clio was too grey! We decided to take a chance on a Hyundai Accent, brilliant white in colour, and a cracking car it turned out to be. In September what we all wanted to see was the much-vaunted eclipse but it turned out to be a damp squib in Aberdeen and for a few minutes the world simply became the colour of our old Clio. Paul eclipsed his previous best by phoning from Spain on the second day of his holidays to say he'd lost his bankcard. He'd lasted almost four days on his two previous Spanish sorties. He'd woken us up at 2 am to get his mum to cancel it and then woke us again at 4 am to say he'd found it; sadly it was no longer any use to him, mum had cancelled it as requested!

Paul returned from holidays and embarked on a house-hunting programme. We helped him as much as we could but somehow it felt strange that Vera and I were now coming full circle and would soon be left on our own. The great joy was that Leanne and Keith were so close by. Happily Clare and Shannon, as we wished, thought of our house as their own and would call at any time they wanted and usually tell us and their mum how long they would stay too!

As the Millennium drew to a close I fancied that the concern over human rights and the sense of being of the individual were the great strides forward that man had made. Yet sometimes the sense of self can blind us to the hopes and fears of others and become plain selfishness. As a new age dawned I prayed we'd just get the sharing right this time around.

The Millennium Bug that would bring chaos to computers around the world never materialised, there was no Armageddon, no earthquakes or firestorms. We spent the first hours of the New Century with our loved ones, Leanne, Keith, Clare and Shannon. We spoke on the phone with Lilian and tried to comfort her over Ray's failing health and then later that day had a lovely party at Dave and Andrea's. Paul was off on the Millennium celebration trail, our world was as ever it had been and we were thankful for that.

Vera dragged me into the 21st century and set me up with a Visa card and a Debit Card at the bank; I was a member of the plastic pal club at last. I got my own back and bought her first mobile telephone; what with her little health scares now and then it seemed a really good idea. I soon added Leanne to the directory of mobile phone users and amidst great protestations of their pointlessness, Keith and I were both on call before the end of the year.

Ray's poor health was not the news we wanted to start off the year, but by the end of the week he'd been allowed home from hospital. I chatted with him on the phone and he sounded so much better—but the devil was smoking again! We managed to get down and see him in February and although he looked poorly I think he was happy for the four of us to have a nice weekend and do all the usual things together. Lilian was in a terrible state when he was taken back into hospital in May. His cancer was still the main worry but he was his usual stoic self when we visited him in hospital. From the day his health problems started I never once heard Raymond Baird complain or seek sympathy from anyone, he was that kind of man. Towards the end of the year we went down to Crieff to do our usual swap over of Christmas presents; Ray had undergone some surgery by then and it was a shock to see him. He was as positive as ever and confident that the plastic surgeon would be able to do wonders for him in the months ahead.

My troubles were nothing in comparison but in March I tore the large lumber muscle in my back. I'd been experiencing a lot of stiffness after tennis and badminton, especially in my back. I thought a trip to the physiotherapist might do the trick, it certainly did! The exercises she recommended floored me completely, the first time I did them, I was in agony and laid low for two weeks. Maybe at forty-nine years of age I'd be best just to put up with being stiff after a tough game.

We'd been doing a fair bit of house hunting with Paul to no avail, when I happened to notice an advert for first time buyers to participate in a Scottish Homes partnership with the builders R B Farquhar, at a new development on Sunnybank Road. Paul was keen and we got his application in; by the end of March he'd signed on the dotted line for the first home of his own. Things moved apace and the building was almost complete by the end of August. Paul was determined to get everything just the way he wanted it before he moved and just like his sister he had a plan—I should have smelled a rat! Through November I was painting rooms and helping him get things just so. Mum was his ally in interior decoration and in honesty the place was perfect when he moved in during December. We did the move on a Saturday and I sensed just a hint of sadness about him when we finally got finished. Leanne obviously thought that now I was back in training it would be best to keep me active and Keith and I were soon on varnishing duties at East Main where they'd had all their downstairs doors replaced.

Clare was five years old, I phoned her on her birthday and got told off for not walking round the corner to speak to her in person! We were all at her birthday party in the evening and had a lovely time. Convincing Clare to share all her presents with Shannon was the only little problem that arose the whole evening. Keith's sister Elaine and her husband Dave were there, they'd recently gone to Sri Lanka to be married and Kath and Ian had accompanied them. They had taken their wedding video along for us all to see and they'd obviously had a wonderful time but Dave certainly looked a worried man when they went on that elephant ride through the jungle!

I remembered the awe of making my first run across the top of Constitution Street to do a message for my mum at the Co-op baker when I was four or five years old. Leanne could see Arnage Drive from her front door and we could see East Main Avenue from ours. If Mum and Grandma stood at their front doors, Clare was never out of sight from one house to the next! Still I bet she enjoyed the thrill of her trips back and forth to collect her favourite videos or pass on a little message. Summer trips to the Banchory funfair with her and Shannon were huge fun and they were both such a joy to have around. Every kid wanted *Tracy Island* that Christmas and we managed to get one but it was Keith who needed rescuing when the day arrived. Poor Keith could never linger too long in our house without a breath of fresh air; the cat hairs just set his allergy off in minutes. On Christmas Day he was especially bad and in the end we uprooted the whole party and adjourned to East Main Avenue to carry on the festivities.

I finally thought I'd lost contact with the music world when Eminem came to the fore. My generation had been shocked when P J Proby split his pants on stage but I struggled to understand the musical roots of a man dressed in an ice hockey mask, wielding a chainsaw and swearing his way through poor poetry instead of singing. I was the one out of step, the world is for the young and the young must do things differently!

I have never seen the sense of drama that surrounds sport better displayed than it was in the Sydney Olympics. The stage was dramatically set for native Australian Cathy Freeman and she rose to the occasion in sublime fashion. Her victory in the 400 metres final gave Australia so much more than a gold medallist. The Irishman Roy Keane had been the beating heart of Fergie's wonderful Manchester United side yet had missed their Champions League glory through suspension. In any side of the era Keane would have been the first name on the teamsheet and deservedly became both PFA and Football Writers Player of the Year. Michael Schumacher had tasted the glory of world championship victory before but now began his imperious run of success with Ferrari. Great champions seemed to abound that year and who would deny the claims of Steve Redgrave, five-time Olympic Champion, to rank alongside the greatest of them.

Our view on the new century would need to be updated and the 'monsters,' Shannon and Clare, sagely advised us that it was time to get a wide-screen television. Oh well, if worldly-wise three and five-year-olds think that we better get modernised! I wonder if *Toy Story 2* and *Bedknobs and Broomsticks* really will be more exciting now?

Changes were afoot at Arnage Drive. Joss and Valerie had split up and they had their house up for sale. In his last few weeks there Joss seemed to go just a little wild and we heard more of him in three weeks than we'd done in three years. They'd been nice neighbours and with his life falling apart it was perhaps understandable. Number 71 sold very quickly and the couple who moved in next door, Alan and Linda, were a joy to have as neighbours. We didn't know it then but we would be on the move ourselves quite soon and I just hope they never thought their arrival had influenced us.

The day after Bill's fiftieth birthday we challenged Keith's works team to a five a side match at Goals, they were far too good for us but it was fun to dust the mothballs off the football shoes for an hour. Allison had Bill well and truly fooled with a surprise birthday party and his many, many dear friends were all there to share the moment with him. The advancing years weren't diminishing his thought processes either, he was still a nightmare to play at *Trivial Pursuits* and had oh so cleverly married a girl who was every bit as good as him!

Paul was on the comeback trail at the football and I really think he might not have bothered if it had been with any one other than John Irvine. John was running the amateur side Glentanar Reflex and Paul decided he could maybe help out his old friend and keep himself fit in the process. Paul's life had changed enormously and was about to take that wonderful turn that makes life worth living; at Christmas time he met his special person, Elaine McConnachie.

Two thousand years of history had passed and my involvement had been no more than the blink of an eye. Yet how special, precious and extraordinary the making of my own little footprint on the sands of time had been for me. Treasured memories too many to mention, the love and friendship of so many wonderful people, the sheer wonder of living through amazing times and I had been given the miracle of life and in turn had given it to others. There are no ordinary lives; we can all indeed be special!

The closing of a century,
The passing of an age,
We had seen great moments,
And writ on history's page.
A special gift was given,
With love the only price.
All our lives blessed with it,
Not the once but twice.

The Road to Inisfree

Two thousand and one would be an odyssey that would take Vera and I from one of the saddest moments of our lives to one of the happiest. There would also be an event, which may well have changed the shape of the world forever.

The sadness began with a New Year's Day telephone call. Just after the bells we had spoken with Paul who was enjoying the first Hogmanay party at his new flat and taking all the credit for the pot of soup his mother had made for him. No sooner had we put the phone down than Lilian called to give us her best wishes for the New Year. When I spoke with Ray his voice was almost inaudible, he broke into a fit of coughing and eventually had to hang up. It wasn't a good sign, but when we travelled down in March he looked very well and as near his normal self as he'd been for the last year. We managed our usual night of pool at the Station and enjoyed a pint of Belhaven light together. By August his skin cancer had returned and although he made a huge effort to make things as normal as possible that weekend we could see how ill he was and how heavy a toll his illness was taking on Lilian.

Over the months that followed we kept in close touch by phone but could tell from chats with Lilian that all was not well with Raymond. On the 8th of October on top of all his other ills, Lilian phoned us to say Raymond had suffered a stroke and been rushed to hospital. Sad memories of Vera's dad came flooding back for us all. We would travel down at the weekend to be with Lilian but the awful news before the week was out was that he'd suffered another stroke and the cancer had spread through his body. We arrived at Crieff in the early evening and the three of us sat speaking of Ray; we would all have been having a wee dram in normal times but we never did that night.

Just before 1 am the hospital in Perth called Lilian and asked her to attend there. The three of us went through and sat with Ray for his last few hours. He died at 4.30 am on the 13th of October 2001. Lilian was there for him in those last few hours and perhaps now can treasure those moments. I knew Vera was so sad over Raymond, hurting for her sister and thinking of her father too. For me it was a duty rather than a choice, I didn't want to see this fine man and great friend struggle to draw those last few breaths, indeed as he struggled I wished this life would let him go, but now I know what I really wished him was peace.

Lilian was heart-broken but cheered when Leanne, Keith and Paul all made the trip through to see her the next day. Lilian and I went to see Raymond for the last time the day before his funeral and I prayed that like me she was happy to see him look so peaceful after all the pain he'd been through. Ray had a lovely service, a good turnout and we all had a lovely tea at the Lovat Hotel afterwards. When we got back to Crieff I said to everyone I was going to have a dram at the Station, one for the road for Ray. We all went and somehow it just seemed the right thing to do. We'd lost a quiet, gentle man. Lilian's life would never be the same again and Vera's life and mine would be all the emptier for his passing.

Vera and I had celebrated our Pearl wedding anniversary, half a lifetime together and we hoped, much more to come. We took a cottage in the Potteries for a week, in a wee village called Barlaston just outside Stoke. On our special day I surprised her with a platinum and diamond ring during our meal. As we drank our champagne she was in tears but what the other smiling diners didn't realise was that she wasn't crying tears of joy, she was upset because I bought the ring a size too small!

If this was a time of love it was fitting that we had finally decided to take the road to Inisfree. Our favourite film is *The Quiet Man* and Inisfree is the village that Sean Thornton returns to in Ireland to try and rebuild his life. We didn't want to rebuild our lives, we just wanted to put the last brick in place. If we ever managed to get our dream home it would be called Inisfree and we hoped against hope that this would be the year to live our dream. We'd discussed things with Vera's boss at the bank and with our upper limit at £85000 we went searching for the cottage from *Random Harvest*.

The sale signs went up in September at offers over £49000 and we felt we were reaching for the sky. Events overtook us at an amazing speed; by early October we had an offer of just the asking price, which was quickly increased to £51000 and suddenly it was decision time for Sid and Vera. We had looked at places at St Katherine's, Newtonhill, Blackburn, Inverurie, Potterton, and Udny Station amongst others. We were on our way home one Sunday from another disappointing viewing at Ellon. We hadn't yet seen a house as nice as what we had made of Arnage and we were beginning to panic.

"Turn in here," shouted Vera, suddenly, "There's houses being built!"

I'd almost missed the turning into the Blackdog but yes indeed there were, Alan Grant (Grampian) Ltd. was developing around forty at a site there. The show house was a very nice semi-detached, not quite the house of our dreams but better than anything we'd seen so far. At £84500 it was just at the top of our price range, and we were tempted. During a chat with the sales girl, Emmie, she mentioned that they had permission to build four bungalows on an as yet undeveloped piece of land. My reaction was that they'd be way too expensive for us. As she showed us the proposed plans we were falling in love with the idea; and at £92000, including a sun lounge, the smallest style might just be a possibility for us.

A hasty meeting followed with Derek at the bank—yes we could stretch that far, yes we'd sell and yes we'd put down our deposit on Inisfree! There was a snag of course; Inisfree was still just a piece of paper, and our buyers wanted entry as soon as possible so where would we live? Enter Leanne, Keith and Paul. They all offered to put us up. We could live at Leanne's for the whole time the house was being built and just to give everyone a break we could use Paul's flat during the weeks he was night shift—problem solved. Well not quite, where would we store all our stuff? The Shore Porters Society would happily store it all for us but in the end it cost us more than our mortgage had been at Arnage. We were committed; there was no turning back. On the 15th of November 2001 we said goodbye to our old friend at Number 69 and became a pest to our kids for five months until we moved into 59, Hareburn Road at the Blackdog...Inisfree.

When we first saw you, a house of dreams,
But now our lives have other schemes.
Where children grew and games were played,
A wealth of memories we made.
From ten year old to wife and mother,
Our daughter grew as did her brother.
He most times a right wee twister,
And now fine adult like his sister.

David, Susan, chums aplenty,
Childhood days we'd hoped they might be.
Billy, Ruby, Eunice, Harry,
Would Alex and Mabel ever marry?
Cath and Dave were our best chums,
Those boozy nights upset our tums.
Just how many walls can one man scrape,
And not once burst the plaster tape?

The grass we cut the roses pruned,
The stereos bought and videos tuned.
A family growing with Keith and Clare,
Now Shannon makes me lose my hair.
So soon a grandad and a gran,
The ticking clock times every man.
In years to come where 'er we roam,
We'll always think of you as home.

Vera and I were pushing the boat out for our thirtieth year of marriage and had planned three holidays. What better place to go for the summer than back to Germany, a place we loved, and in particular the beautiful Rhine

Valley. Leanne was on house-sitting duties and Paul drove us to Hamilton to board our charabanc bound for foreign climes. A marvellous crossing from Hull to Rotterdam and then on to Lahnstein, a small town near Koblenz; how appropriate that Vera and I had actually been booked into the hotel's honeymoon suite! We couldn't resist a day back in Rudesheim for a trip on the cable car Elvis used in *GI Blues* and the weather just got hotter and hotter. At Lahnstein, on the opposite bank of the Rhine, a lovely castle was lit up at night and glowed an almost soft pink in the dusk. Vera and I would stroll hand in hand along the riverbank every evening.

As always we planned some trips of our own and set off on the train to Bonn; it was 36 degrees when we got there. We found a beautiful little Bier Garten on the banks of the Rhine and sat with a glass of wine and ate Schinkenwurst and Apfelstrudel. As we changed trains at Koblenz that evening for the local train to Lahnstein, the station announcer, in German, advised the local train was cancelled and travellers for Lahnstein should board the intercity express, which would stop there. Vera was reluctant to disembark but I convinced her and we changed trains. Just as well my German was okay or we might have ended up in Frankfurt! The same evening saw us cruise along the Rhine to the Lorelei rock and at one point the boat was swamped by a dark cloud—it was thousands of moths! One final shopping trip to Koblenz the next day and it was off to Zeebrugge for the ferry home. A lovely couple from Dumfries that we'd became friends with, John and Margaret, celebrated their twenty fifth anniversary during the holiday and we gave them a small gift and a card when we stopped at the lovely city of Brugge. We had dinner together on the ferry home and enjoyed a wonderful evening in the ship's ballroom.

Our third little trip had just been a chance to get away from all the worry of planning to move house and in September we'd taken a little cottage at Dalgety Bay in Fife. We hadn't come into money, and they were all bargain basement trips but we thoroughly enjoyed every one of them. The poignant memory of our trip to Fife was that Ray and Lilian came across to spend the Sunday with us. We stopped and had a lovely meal and a dram at a little pub in Crail, it had been a long journey for him and it would be the last time we'd all be together before that awful day just a month later.

Well, well Granda was fifty years old and I was delighted when everyone clubbed together and bought me a lovely Yamaha keyboard for my birthday. I'd always wanted to play a musical instrument and even enrolled in night classes to hone my skills. With so much going on in our lives I didn't make too much progress but I still tinker on it and if pushed can do a mean up-tempo version of *Oh Lonesome Me!* I was a bit apprehensive about my flying lesson but could defer that till a later date. Reading *Biggles* books was one thing; actually flying a wee plane was an altogether different matter! My birthday ended up in the best possible fashion, taken round to Leanne's by the girls for a party and then reading them a bedtime story, twice!

I was resigned to being middle aged and it showed. After more than thirty years of drinking I finally decided that the hangovers were more trouble than it was all worth!

Clare was also in the midst of learning to fly but it was her own wings she was flexing as she worked her way through her first year at Muirfield Primary School. All the wonders and mysteries that lay before her—I envied her! I should have known, you just don't go telling inquisitive kids that your cordless phone is also an intercom to the base station downstairs. Once Clare and Shannon had mastered which buttons to push, sleepovers were a nightmare. They'd be upstairs in bed, Vera and I would be exhausted in the living room and the phone would ring once more.

"Earth calling Granda, earth calling Granda!"

One Sunday we set off to tour around the car boots and took the girls with us. We ended up at Echt and took Leanne, Clare and Shannon in to the local hostelry for a meal; Clare was so desperate to get home and tell Daddy that she'd been in a pub! The sense of growing up doesn't take long to happen.

The world changed on the 11th of September 2001 and perhaps will never be the same again. Two aircraft crashed into the World Trade Centre in New York. The images that shot around the world were horrifying and unbelievable. This act of terrorism was more vivid as it had been perpetrated against the world's most powerful nation, and modern technology brought it immediately into our homes. The dramatic collapse of both towers seemed almost symbolic; we knew Americans would not accept this shameful attack on their nation and as the towers crumbled, so did the world's hopes of peace.

Blame was placed at the door of the Taliban Government of Afghanistan who had allowed the terrorists safe haven and training facilities within their borders. Although America sought and received a degree of UN approval for their retaliation, there was never any question that it would take place. The hunt was on for the leader of the Al-Qaida terrorists held responsible, Osama Bin Laden. The world's war on terror had begun and more than ever I felt that here was a clash of two cultures which might never resolve until one had totally destroyed the other. Was mankind strong enough to provide a more noble solution? The fate of millions perhaps, lay in the hands of the American President George W Bush, and our own nation and our Prime Minister Tony Blair were America's firm allies through all this. Would we walk the road to war together and find the right solutions, but were these the right men to lead us to them?

Paul and Elaine were becoming a bit of an item but we didn't see too much of them. Paul had always had a private side to him that kept parts of his life to himself and we accepted that. Leanne was very different and wore her heart on her sleeve; Mum would always be the first to hear her latest list of woes and life worked for her that way. They were happy in their lives and that was all that mattered to Vera and me.

Paul was in limbo with his football and still struggling with his fitness. We went to Ellon one March Saturday as he did a favour for Jim McLaughlin and turned out for Parkvale Juniors. He had a good game as Parkvale lost 3-2 but was smiling in the car on the way home. Jim had asked him to come along to the training but Paul was still out of puff as we reached Aberdeen, he was happy to leave the Juniors behind. By the start of the next season he'd be fully fit and helping John's Glentanar Reflex in a chase for a league and cup double.

Tim Henman was in the semi finals at Wimbledon again and 'Henmania' was sweeping all before it once more. Tim was a great tennis player but shared his era with many other greats like Sampras, Agassi, Hewitt and Federer. I always thought we expected too much of him and would only realise how good he was after his career was finished—but by then it would be too late to enjoy his wonderful skills for what they were. Tiger Woods won the US Masters in the spring and for a few months held all four of golf's major titles simultaneously. Surely a Grand Slam in all but name, he'd won the first three during 2000! Ronnie O'Sullivan became World Snooker Champion for the first time and might be the next flawed hero on the sporting stage. Who could forget his 147 maximum at The Crucible in 1997, compiled in 5 minutes 20 seconds!

Top class football was a worry to me and I lost interest at an alarming rate. On the few occasions I might still go to a game the intense attitude of the supporters, bordering sometimes on hatred for the opposition, put me off completely. How can you take a game seriously when the so-called experts on the telly all came up with the same garbage to describe the beautiful game? 'Obviously, at the end of the day, it was a game of two halves and we couldn't break forward from our central diamond often enough to get the ball wide to the wing backs for them to stand it up over the far stick.' I was lost!

Shannon and Clare were dragging us back into the world of movies and as *Harry Potter* burst onto our screens the videos and DVD players were working overtime. The much vaunted *Gladiator* failed to do for me what *Spartacus* had done all those years before. How could that scene on the hill be equalled when, to a man, the slave army call out 'I'm Spartacus' in a vain attempt to save the life of their leader?

Kylie was getting into all our heads with the annoying na-na-na lyric of her latest hit but *Queen Of My Heart, Hero* and *Whole Again* were all tunes I could happily listen to. The music at the student show that year was wonderful. We'd gone with Bill and Allison to see *'The Codfaither'* with its hero called Fraser Plaice. The cleverly comic parody of *Mac the Knife* had the audience rolling in the aisles. Ricky Simpson...Willie Miller...Frank Lefevre...Stewartie Milne!

We'd had a little victory that year and finally got a payment from British Telecom for their continual wandering onto our property to access the telegraph pole at the foot of the garden. We sold them access rights for £500 and that was the windfall that helped us off on all our hols that year. Little did we know that after years of fighting with them we'd be sold up in months. Vera did it again and late in the year we changed from our Accent to a Micra, the logic this time was that we didn't have a house to put a new suite into!

Two sad little moments came towards the end of the year. We spent a weekend at Lilian's as I decorated her hallway; she was still hurting so much. We visited the spot at the garden of remembrance where we'd scattered Ray's ashes and laid some flowers. Through her tears she showed us where she intended to have a commemorative plaque placed for him. Just before Christmas I attended the funeral service for Bill's dad Jack, it was a privilege to pay my last respects to a very, very nice man.

Lilian still had time to think of others and got a wonderful present for Paul's Christmas when she successfully bid for a signed West Ham top that was being auctioned for charity on Radio Tay. He was delighted and his mum and I got it properly framed before Christmas Day. Lilian spent Christmas with us and a sad yet amazing year drew to a close.

I'll never fly again in anything less than the size of a jumbo jet. I'd put off using my flying lesson voucher as long as possible but eventually Biggles Day came around. Our aerial reconnaissance of the Blackdog allowed me to take some pictures of the house being built and on the round trip to Peterhead I was given a brief shot at the controls. We were almost home when the stench of aviation fuel became simply too much. The instructor passed me the paper bag and at once opened vents, which let fresh air stream in. My annoyance overcame my desire to retch and I asked him why he hadn't opened them before. I'd looked okay to him so he hadn't bothered! I made it back without recourse to using the bag.

On the 1st of April 2002, not prophetic I hoped, Vera and I gave our solicitor a cheque for £31000. We'd gone to our absolute limit, sold Arnage and cashed in most of the shares that we'd saved so long and hard for and were set to run a £61000 mortgage for Inisfree. We prayed it would be worth it and hoped that we had done the right thing. On the 5th I set off first thing in the morning to accept the keys from the Site Manager and let the carpet fitter make a start. Poor Keith was rushed into hospital with a burst abscess in his throat and so of all things Leanne had the worry of him and the turmoil of Paul and I trying to move all our stuff from her house on the same day. We had stuff stored at Paul's too and new goods to pick up from Powerhouse; by late afternoon we'd got it all shifted, Paul put the hire van back and Vera and I settled for our first night at Inisfree. It was eerie as ours was the only house completed, there were no streetlights and it was pitch black when we looked outside. When we stood at the front door we could hear the roar of the sea from the nearby beach. It had been a long wait but we were home, we had arrived at Inisfree!

The rest of our goods and chattels wouldn't arrive for a few days from storage at Shore Porters, I couldn't get any more time off and Vera did a great job to see everything into the house herself. Happily Keith was home and well quite soon and the gang came across to see the new place. Leanne had often come with Vera and I on our regular weekend visits to see the construction advance stage by stage but Paul had chosen not to have a look until Mum and Dad were settled in. A few days after we moved in Elaine and he came across to have a look see. They were both very impressed and happy for us. Elaine's new Volkswagen Beetle suitably impressed us, it was a lovely car and Vera just loved the blue colour. Oh no, I could sense a change being planned!

The mystery was—what had happened to Shannon and Clare? Nothing, Mum was just calming them down for a week or two to let us settle in. They made their first sleepover before the end of the month. Poor Theo had spent our homeless days with Paul at Sunnybank and he was struggling to come to terms with becoming an outdoor cat again. He went missing for a week but did return and the girls were both delighted to see him. He was now an old man and didn't take kindly to being dressed up in pink ribbons, so he was off on his travels again not long after the kids arrived. We were under instructions to phone them at home as soon as we found him again. He returned, we phoned, everyone was happy! Although we'd bought a new house there was going to be much to do at the Blackdog and Vera and I would have a lot of hard work ahead of us.

The first piece of DIY I ever did at Inisfree was to hang a framed ten pound note above the vestibule door. I'd remembered our wedding night of thirty-one years before and had fulfilled a promise to myself to make something of our £10. A detached bungalow just a little bit out of the city, within walking distance of a beautiful beach. We'd made a long journey together and got to our destination through sheer hard work. I could have only got there with Vera's help and my only regret was that we'd not had all this when Leanne and Paul were kids. I was certain their hearts were filled with happy memories of Arnage and Clare and Shannon could now build memories of Inisfree.

The old Queen Mother died and whatever my personal opinions of the Royal family, she had been a true icon of my life and times. Those life and times were becoming rather worrying, with the war on terror, global warming and our own country seemingly awash with drugs that were destroying so many lives. Sadly so many of the victims seemed to be the young and I worried what sort of world my granddaughters would inherit. At least some scientists didn't think it was all gloom and doom; Australian boffins told us that the level of CFC's in the atmosphere was falling and the hole in the ozone layer over Antarctica was shrinking and would close completely by 2050. It won't matter to me by then but hopefully we were getting things right for the future.

The global village concept didn't seem to be producing the wonderful world that many had hoped for. Islam and the world's most powerful Christian nation were locked in conflict and in Britain we were swamped under a tide of illegal immigrants from all corners of the globe. Economic migration had been a part of world history since mankind's story began but with ever growing populations and ever reducing resources where would it all end? It was still the sharing that we didn't do and if the affluent couldn't give the poor a share they would simply come and take it, it was human nature.

The awful murders of Holly Wells and Jessica Chapman appalled the whole country. As a father and grandfather who could see pain and suffering of children all around the world I found it hard to comprehend why we simply didn't do away with the piece of vermin who had committed these repulsive crimes. Ian Huntley would spend years having attention lavished on him, when he deserved no more than we might pay to an insect accidentally squashed underfoot. Oh what a world of contradictions! Our hearts went out to the families of those poor babies.

Keith solved our first big problem at Inisfree—nobody wanted our council tax, I couldn't give the money away. From his privileged position in the corridors of power he discovered that we didn't exist, there was no number 59, Hareburn Road—no Inisfree! I enjoyed myself with a couple of funny letters to the Assessors Office and although they were determined to make us number 30, they finally agreed that we could keep number 59, the address to which they'd been sending all the correspondence telling us we were number 30! The postie avoided a headache and we started stumping up our cash.

Cash disappeared as fast as the turning tide at the Blackdog and never more so than when we were trying to do something with our huge back garden. The builders had left us a beautifully fenced in wilderness and a pal from work, Sandy Smart, took on the job of turning it into a place we could enjoy. Over the summer, with me as his right hand man, Sandy laid patios and turf; the garden was transformed into a haven of peace and privacy for Vera and me. With the fencing already built I had to barrow seven tons of rubble out to a skip at the front of a house. Pushing a loaded barrow up the wooden planks was a nightmare. Clare and Shannon were across at weekends helping me.

They'd chant, "One, two, three go, Granda!" as I struggled up the planks one more time.

The two of them just loved rolling in the skip as I tipped yet another load of soil away, if Leanne could have seen them I'd have been in big trouble! Sandy was worth every penny we paid him and more, he saved us an awful lot of cash and the finished garden helped transform the look of the whole house. I took great satisfaction in it all myself as Sandy had encouraged me at every turn to help with as much of the work as I could.

A lot of work was required at Pittodrie too and we moved on to the partnership of Steve Paterson and Duncan Shearer in the quest for a hint of former glories. A 3-0 defeat to Dunfermline in their first game didn't augur well for the future. At least Europe's golfers were back to winning ways and I spent a great day at Paul's flat watching them regain the Ryder Cup with a superb victory in a close encounter played in the most sporting fashion.

Shannon was five years old and would soon be starting school, at her little birthday party it was wonderful to see Keith's Grandma and Granddad joining in the fun. Leanne reached her thirtieth that year but I'm sure the kids would keep her young; sane would be another matter! When we popped over with her presents Clare was talking in French and Shannon was telling us all about her coming move to the big school. Apart from talking French, Clare was going through that talking to herself stage, but did take time out to show us her new joined-up writing. It was better than mine was already!

Leanne and Vera now had marathon telephone calls and would simply forget to come off the line. Shannon joined in one evening but she was only phoning to tell us that she'd lost her first tooth! They were both fast growing up and it was never more noticeable than when they came for a sleepover, they were now putting *us* to bed before midnight! Sheena Thomson had been my colleague and friend for over ten years and I've never worked with a more decent, hard working person. We got on very well together and shared lots of laughs and not so funny times at Lost and Found Property. Sheena was devoted to her elderly mum who'd had a long struggle with various ailments in the last few years. It was a sad day when she called to say her mum had died and if ever a loved one had given everything to another then it was Sheena. In a touching gesture Sheena gave Vera and I two little Wade candy dishes that her mum had owned; she knew Vera loved Wade and said her mum would have wanted them to go to someone who appreciated them.

Paul was well and truly back in harness with his football and John Irvine had put together a tidy young side. For the first time ever Paul was in a team with a prolific goalscorer and at twenty-eight was himself now one of the auld heids. Davie Scott could rattle in the goals but what a lazy player he was; like so many I'd watched over the years Davie could have played at a much higher level with just a little change of attitude. An old friend from CD days provided Paul and me with a lovely memory; I'd actually forgotten all about it but Paul rang me just in time for us to make it to Jim Neave's retiral do. All the old faces, including Ian Simpson, were there; it was great fun and a grand night.

With a final flourish to the season the boys lifted their League Championship and put the icing on the cake by winning their divisional cup at Stonehaven with a late winner deep into injury time to give them a hard earned 2-1 victory over Quayside Electricals. Paul was Captain on the night and an old pal of mine, Richard Forbes, was doing the official photographs for the Amateur Association. He sent me copies of the team group and Paul accepting the trophy, life is ever about our memories. In truth Paul had hobbled through the second half of the season and a recurring groin injury was causing him all sorts of problems. He was a surprised and happy man when the committee voted him their Player Of The Year at the end of season bash a few nights later.

The kids were always telling us about another blockbuster but *Lord of the*

Rings was more for Clare and her wild imagination. Shannon would watch *Ice Age* with her sister but often became bored after a few minutes and head off into her world of dolls, chattering endlessly to all her little charges. The world of wonder of their own imagination is a special place for children. The Oscar ceremonies became a triumph for black acting talent as Halle Berry became the first black woman to be voted best actress and Denzel Washington claimed the best actor prize.

Music had a sort of country flavour for me that year; it must have been the move to the Blackdog. I introduced Vera to Charlie Lansborough and enjoyed new albums by Alison Krauss and Beth Nielsen Chapman. Bill and I were still turning back the years at the tennis and even managed a victory over his workmates Kevin and Ally. Ally Cameron was simply the best tennis player either Bill or I had ever encountered. It was a pleasure to play against him and one win a year against Ally would be enough to make our season a success.

Vera was still having some problems with her health and the good old Lloyds TSB moved her to one of their busiest branches. Not only would she have to struggle through the worst traffic jams every morning but also she'd have the added stress of more pressure at work. We decided to take a stand and appealed to her bosses. They saw sense and moved her across to Torry several months later; at least she got a moment to draw breath during the day. The Park and Ride scheme eased our travel problems and a lovely house warming party in July seemed to set the seal on our move to Inisfree.

The wisest move we made was to change our mortgage late in the year. We didn't change our lender but we reverted to a full repayment mortgage and were lucky enough to cash in our endowment before the effects of war in Afghanistan and all the other effects of 9/11 had bitten too hard into the financial world. We were able to reduce our mortgage to £52000, keep our repayments much the same and began to see a few thousand drop off our total debt every year. Only one big problem remained at the Blackdog; it must have been one of the wettest years on record and there was water everywhere. Poor Dod and Lindsay out back of us actually had water lapping at their back door. The builders were extremely slow to respond but eventually claimed to have repaired some field drains to solve the problem. It certainly seemed to work but then we've never again had a year of rain like that first one at the Blackdog.

In August we made a trip down to see Lilian and took the kids with us. They thoroughly enjoyed a visit to the Blair Drummond Safari Park and Lilian was so happy to see them. She still didn't have her troubles to seek, as the pet shop she'd run for a friend for many years was being closed down and in October she lost one of her cats. The cats had been like children to Raymond and she, and it was almost too much for her to bear.

One day I read of the death of a man from the early days of my working life; Danny Stroud, Managing Director of John Cook and Sons. I'd been one of his office boys when Vera and I met. His obituary told of how he'd risen from the post of office boy to run the firm. He'd obviously been nobody's fool and I smiled and guessed he must have known about my fish bonus all the time!

Lilian spent Christmas with us and so did Paul; my impossible find of the Barry J Huggman football reference book just blew him away. Elaine popped over from her mum and dad's later on and they headed off for a quiet night together at Paul's. It was Leanne's on Boxing Day and between our presents and Lilian's it was all we could do to get everything in the car. The kids put it all into perspective when they left everything lying about the living room floor and spent their evening playing with a wee plastic game of noughts and crosses which had popped out of a cracker!

Dave Leitch was our first ever first-foot at Inisfree; he was tall and dark and I was willing to take Vera's word for it that he'd once been handsome, they'd known one another since she was three! He came into our house as a dear friend and that was good enough for me. We spent a lovely evening over at Northfield with Dave and Andrea and Stan and Iris, such a nice way to start any year.

Gloom and doom ushered in the New Year as America and Britain and a vague coalition of other nations prepared to launch a land offensive against Iraq. The agenda was regime change and the removal of Saddam Hussein, who was refusing to surrender his weapons of mass destruction. Winning a war against Iraq appeared to me to be a reasonably certain goal for America and her allies but winning the peace appeared even then to be an impossibility.

I was involved in a little health scare myself and attended hospital for a Barium Enema; the procedure was just a little too intrusive for my liking but it needed to be done. In the end it was worth going through the embarrassment to set my mind at rest. I was suffering from a mild form of diverticulitus but it was nothing that good dietary habits couldn't keep under control.

A good pal at work, Jim Boyle, lost his fight against cancer; it was so sad as only two years had passed since he'd lost his wife to the disease after her heroic fight against it. Our dear friends Stanley and Iris Leitch both suffered ill health. Stan fell and broke his hip and as is often the case, the consequences of such an injury for a man of his age would de extremely debilitating. Within weeks Iris was rushed into hospital for an operation on a stomach aneurysm and an ovarian cyst. The doctors told Dave and Andrea that she was lucky to be alive but she made a wonderful recovery in comparison to Stan.

Paul and Elaine took off for a weekend in London early in the year and by late spring had made the decision to move into his flat as a couple. We were really pleased for them both but Vera was surprised that Paul had ever managed to get himself organised enough! Elaine was a lovely girl and we were sure they'd do well together. They announced their engagement on Christmas Eve, which was the third anniversary of the day they'd met. I was able to get Elaine onto my daft Christmas present list that year and a copy of the Dons Cup Winners Cup Final match programme against Real Madrid, signed by captain Willie Miller and goalscorer John Hewitt, would keep me in her good books for a while.

I had another memory to add to my list of football moments when Keith, who'd only taken up refereeing the year before, was given the North of Scotland Cup Final, to be played at New Advocates' Park. He had a good game in the middle but the torrential rain spoiled the quality of the football. Mintlaw scored a comfortable 4-1 victory over their local rivals Invercairn. Of all things Keith forgot to get a copy of the match programme for himself—that was typical of him. Luckily he was able to have mine. Leanne often spoke to her mum about her worries for her kids, the education they were getting and all the other difficulties that modern life was throwing at young families. We knew that she and Keith were wise enough to do the right thing and both their families would always be right behind them in whatever they did.

They told us that a young man called Roger Federer was going to become the finest player that tennis had ever seen and from the moment he won his first Wimbledon title in 2003 the experts certainly looked as if they were right this time. Thierry Henry was weaving a special brand of magic at Highbury for Arsenal and would be voted both Players and Football Writers Player of the Year for the next two years. I made a sporting comeback and joined Belhelvie Bowling Club. It was close to home and I hadn't been out on the grass for years, so being a member of the side that won the Benachie League was a wonderful return to the outdoor game for me.

The road to war was quickly travelled and in no time the end came for Saddam's regime. The search was now on for the weapons of mass destruction that we'd been told were such a danger to us all. It seemed the harder the coalition looked the more difficult they became to find. Surely our leaders had not taken us to war on a false premise? The absolute horror of it all was the vacuum that normal life in Iraq appeared to fall into; after Saddam there was nothing and the building blocks for the future were nowhere to be found.

I'd had a great life so far and hoped that both Shannon and Clare would enjoy the same gift. Their sleepovers were a delight for Vera and me, between hair pulling and exhaustion that is. Clare had a few fainting spells but was checked at the hospital and the doctors were happy enough, just all part of growing up we supposed. They were both coming along just fine.

Granddaughters cry and granddaughters smile,
Granddaughters puzzle you all of the while.
They're never between just good or bad,
They're only ever happy or sad.

Granddaughters twist and granddaughters turn,
Granddaughters never have money to burn.
They're either just saving or just gone and spent,
All of the savings money you lent.

Granddaughters praise and granddaughters moan,
Granddaughters' smiles soon turn to a groan.
They're happy simply because they're not sad,
And good every moment that they're not bad.

Granddaughters hug you granddaughters give you a kiss,
Granddaughters are all a most special miss.
They're in your thoughts when you're apart,
And never an inch away from your heart.

I had to thank Tom Morton for yet another musical discovery and think I bought myself three Blind Boys of Alabama albums in a matter of weeks. I amazed Vera by buying Pink's latest single *Trouble;* the sheer energy she put into her performances reminded me of Lulu in the Sixties. Emmylou Harris came up with my album of the year and I listened to *Stumble Into Grace* over and over. The students didn't let us down either and came up with possibly the best show I'd ever seen, *An American in Powis. You're in Torry* to the tune of *That's Amore* was a not to be forgotten highlight.

It was head in hands for Paul and me in May when West Ham were relegated from the Premiership with 42 points, a total that would have safely kept them up in any of the five previous seasons. Glentanar got back in swing for the new season and won the Rusty Nail's pre-season tournament in August. How would they cope at the higher level?

Well a few months later Paul had a little black mark against him when, for the first time in his career, I saw him simply lose his head. Off he went after throwing a punch at an opponent—fortunately, like most of the Glen's forwards that day, he missed! The fists were flying again a week later when their Scottish Cup-tie against a disgraceful outfit from Dundee ended in a riot. The referee lost control completely and the game was abandoned with seconds to play. I'll never forget poor Davie Farquhar being assaulted by two or three hooligans masquerading as footballers. Both sides would be banned from the competition but the referee really should have made a proper report of where the blame lay.

Bob Hope, the comic hero of my youth became a centenarian, and sadly one of the great singers of the Sixties, Bobby Hatfield, made his final bow. Global warming was here with a bang as summer temperatures in Britain soared through the 100 degrees Fahrenheit barrier for the first time since records had been kept. In those lovely summer days Vera and I could be found scouring country lanes for any old stones we could find to lay out our little rockery in the front garden. We managed to find all we needed—I just hope we never took away any that we shouldn't have!

Bill and Allison were on the move and had become very keen on a nice house in Newtonhill. It was a lovely move for them and so handy for both of them for work. Bill surprised me and became a gardening convert in no time at all.

The main family event of 2003 was Vera's fiftieth birthday. She went over to Leanne's for the day, mainly to see how Clare was after her check up at hospital. The fact that Clare was fine made her day and all the girls went out for lunch together. She loved all her presents and had enjoyed her day. I'd kept my secret as well as I could so she was completely taken by surprise when we got to the Northern Lights on the Saturday evening for our quiet meal! Her face was a picture as she found, Leanne, Keith, Clare, Shannon, Paul and Lilian waiting to join us. We had a really nice evening and all went back to Inisfree for a little get-together. My jokey little present for her was a special Wade moneybox of a Tetley tea man whose theme seemed most appropriate: 'Fifty Years With Sydney.'

We were thankful for a huge stroke of luck just a month earlier. On the way home from a weekend at Lossiemouth with Dave and Andrea, we came as near to disaster as we ever had in our lives. Just outside Keith a maniac had overtaken a line of six vehicles without noticing we were dead ahead on the southbound side of the road. His frantic attempts to brake sent his car into a sideways skid directly towards us. I was up on the grass verge and was certain we would collide. His vehicle momentarily straightened, passed us and then skewed sideways again; how we lived to tell the tale I'll never know.

Our dear pet, chum and cuddly toy that occasionally moved was having problems. Theo seemed very stiff in his movements and was always giving out little screeches, which sounded very much as if he was in some sort of pain. He was still mobile for his age and happy to be outdoors most of the day when we were at work. He was however an old cat and we would keep an eye on him and have the vet check him over just to make sure he wasn't suffering any pain.

Oh no here we go again, England Champions of the world. In a great competition in Australia the disciplined England side under Clive Woodward took the world title after a pulsating extra time win over the hosts. Johnny Wilkinson was immediately given god-like status and Clive Woodward was being touted as the next England football manager. The English side thoroughly deserved their victory but thankfully none of the television commentators came up with a punch line as good as 'They think it's all over.'

Vera and I ended the year with a very quiet night; I gave Paul and Elaine a run to Hoppy's wedding reception at the Westburn Lounge. The weather turned absolutely awful and the rain and gales put paid to the big Union Street party that had been planned. In our cosy bed Vera and I snuggled up and thought what a good year it had been.

2004 was a year when everything paled into insignificance for me in the light of one terrible afternoon on the 27th of June. Just sometimes, a day comes along that chews you up and spits you out. We'd had a nice evening at Doug Robertson's fiftieth birthday party and Vera was planning to have a wee bit of a lie-in and follow me round to Paul's. He and I were racing on with finishing the fencing in his garden. She called me for a lift around midday; she didn't look at all well but insisted in walking round to Asda for something nice to have with our cup of tea. She seemed to be gone forever. I'd later learn that she'd blacked out in the shop. No sooner had she arrived at the house than Elaine called me in from the garden to say Vera had taken ill. I thought it would just be another of those 'wee turns' for me to deal with, but oh boy did I get that wrong. What followed was the worst half-hour of my life; God knows what Vera went through! At one stage I was certain she'd stopped breathing as first she had a really violent seizure and then went absolutely lifeless. Paul called an ambulance but could barely speak, and I sensed that, like me, dark thoughts were racing through his head. I took the phone and with the calm assurance of the control room operator I somehow managed to get her back. The sense of relief was immense but suddenly she lapsed into another violent fit. Poor Elaine was distraught and Paul and I were never so glad when, at that very moment, the paramedics arrived at his front door. She was coming round once more as they knelt beside her and chatted to her. She was admitted to hospital for observation and Leanne, Paul and I had a long wait at the hospital before being told she was to be kept overnight. We three drove home through an amazing thunderstorm to get Vera an overnight bag and in all the turmoil I returned to the hospital without her drugs. On the second trip I got the kids home and was left alone with just my thoughts.

Most important of all Vera was now in safe hands and nothing else seemed to matter much at all. It was a long time before I could say the words but that day I had feared the worst for Vera. It was a long and lonely night for me and as I lay in bed I thought of all our parents but mostly I thought...'Good night my love, I'll see you in the morning.'

Oh the darkness is here; it's coming again.
Am I losing my darling, my wife and my friend?
I'm holding you tight, please don't slip away.
I know in my heart, today's not the day.
There's a lifetime of love, for us both still to own.
But it's not meant for me, to live on my own.
Oh the darkness is here but it will go away.
And with me my darling, in this life you'll stay.

The outcome of this dreadful day was a review of Vera's medication and since that time the change seems to have done the trick. She was required to surrender her driving licence for a year and that turned out to be a much bigger problem than we had first thought. It even set us to thinking about moving house again! Happily we did get back to normal as the year progressed and Vera became her old self again. We were all just thankful that she was getting better.

The little things in life seemed so unimportant but as the year had started, one of them began driving us mad. Our central heating was constantly breaking down and it would take the whole year and £900 of repairs to find the fault. Luckily for us we had a contract with Scottish Gas and they were brilliant throughout the whole saga. We had a mystery at the Blackdog when heavily bloodstained clothing was discovered near the beach. The mystery was solved when the police traced a man who'd attempted to commit suicide, had happily survived, but been too distraught to alert the emergency services.

We decided to do our bit for the planet and were determined to stick to our New Year resolution to recycle as much waste as we could; it reduced the rubbish we put out every week by two thirds! We did have a lot more rubbish in the house but that was courtesy of Top UP TV. We added it to our Freeview package but as always discovered that the more channels you have the more rubbish there is to watch. Still it was fine to have a wee bit more choice and Vera and I could watch *Dad's Army* repeats all day!

That beautiful blue car of Elaine's had preyed on Vera's mind and on our anniversary I took her out for a meal and somehow ended up at the Broadfold Garage signing up for a brand new Suzuki Ignis, blue of course! I hate to think how much money we've wasted on cars over the years but it's always been about what we could afford every month and not the price of the car. I had to admit the Ignis was the best motor we'd ever had.

Paul and Elaine quickly went house hunting after the announcement of their engagement. They looked at a place beside us but decided it was just a little too far out of town. They got their hearts set on a place at Newburgh Crescent and in the mad state of the housing market ended up having to pay well over £110,000 for a house that was on the market at offers over £89,000. It was scary stuff and Vera and I thanked our lucky stars that we had made our move at just the right time a few years earlier. Paul certainly had a stressful time through his thirtieth birthday—the bank had messed up his insurance and for a while it looked like the profit he'd made from his flat was going to be eaten up in the claw-back deal with Scottish Homes. In the end we got them to agree that they were looking for £5000 too much but they still got their pound of flesh. Happily Paul and Elaine got enough not to spoil their plans either. The big move happened in April and, after a five-hour delay for the keys to be released, we finally got started. Paul, Elaine's dad Charlie and I were exhausted by the end of a long hard day.

Very early in the year, amidst all the trouble on this planet, George Bush announced American plans to build a space station on the moon. Perhaps that would be a better vantagepoint to look for the elusive weapons of mass destruction. Official enquiries would be set up to discuss why we thought they existed, why we couldn't find them and eventually why it didn't matter if they ever existed because the main concern always was that they might have existed. Oh ma heid! The Madrid bombings in March were enough to make us aware that there was a war to be fought and an enemy to be defeated, but surely we could have been trusted to accept that as a fact without all the undue scaremongering. A man whose life was lived in the conflict of the Middle East died late in the year; Yasser Arafat had been a hero to many and a murderer to others. As the horrors raged on in Iraq an irreparable hurt and a never ending hate was building up on both sides. Would their God or ours have the power to heal the scars or build the bridges of peace for the future?

My very dear friend Sheena Thomson retired and for me it changed my working life forever. Sheena and I were both of an older school and I felt that after thirteen years I was past my sell by date for Lost and Found. We'd had some laughs, Sheena and I, and dealt with some strange things. The ceremonial casket with the ashes inside: happily we traced the relatives. A 20-foot kayak, a pneumatic drill and a ship's anchor. I said to Sheena that I was certain I could make out the faded words Mary Celeste stamped across it. Then there was the lovely old lady who came looking for a set of teeth.

"When did you lose them?" I asked.

"Oh I didn't lose them, I haven't worn teeth for twenty years. It's just that I have a wedding on Saturday and was hoping you might have a pair I could borrow for the photographs!" she explained.

We did and she was delighted, I just hope she took them out before she kissed the groom!

Leanne and Keith were hoping to move on too but Vera and I knew how things were for them, two young kids make it very hard to make many financial plans other than to look after them. They had both worked so hard and given their children a wonderful start in life, we were very proud of them. Leanne was studying to add some qualifications to her child-minding skills and hopefully this would serve her well in the future. Keith was a professional man and no doubt his job still had much to offer him in the years ahead. They would achieve their dreams in good time and if they had as much fun as Vera and I had getting to the end of the rainbow then they'd be a happy pair.

Europe retained the Ryder Cup and how fitting that Colin Montgomerie, Scotland's finest golfer of the modern age, should hole the winning putt. A marvellous athlete from Morocco, Hicham El Guerrouj finally claimed the Blue Riband 1500 metres gold medal at the Athens Olympics and for good measure doubled up with gold in the 5000 metres. In 2004 my own sporting life was blessed with moments that I'll never forget as long as I live. As my enthusiasm for bowls blossomed once more I started to play in the Scottish Police Bowling Association matches; the trips were great fun and the lads great company. I was surprised to be selected to travel with the Scottish team that would play in the Indoor Home International Series in Belfast. I was certain I'd just be along for the ride but the surprises kept coming. I was picked for the first match against Ireland and with the team winning 6-1 we were unchanged for the battle with the auld enemy. England were seen off 5-2 and a similar scoreline against the Welsh saw us lift the championship. I'll never forget the Scottish lads, to a man, singing down the English team as they launched into *Swing Low Sweet Chariot* at the hotel later that evening. Everyone in the bar applauded our passionate version of *Flower of Scotland*. I made it into the outdoor squad later in the year at Newcastle but it was only an injury that gave me a place in the last match against England. We lifted the title once more and those four appearances for Scotland are a cherished memory for me. Sporting success is fleeting, and as it had been in 1984, so it was again. My game just didn't stay competitive at that level and I withdrew from police competitions the next season. I still enjoy a game but no longer aspire to its highest levels.

Leanne had a lovely spread laid on for Shannon's seventh birthday party but sadly the wee imp didn't show up. She was a stroppy little madam that night and wouldn't speak to anyone! But then life's like that at seven, adults can be such a pest when you're trying to play games! Clare took a touch of fever later in the evening and we all set off home just a little early to let Leanne and Keith get her settled. I'm sure I heard Shannon shout yippee as we all said goodnight at the front door! I got the girls interested in badminton and they both showed great promise. Clare was her usual self and had to become instantly the best badminton player in the world. She nearly did and after a few weeks we could manage a fifty-stroke rally and Shannon wasn't too far behind. We did even better with the girls doubling up but I was exhausted, there was no way of knowing where they'd hit the shuttle. If we ever matched the 400 runs world record that Brian Lara had just set in cricket I'd need an oxygen mask!

Clare was nine years old and it often amazed me how grown up she was beginning to look, but the child hadn't quite disappeared yet. A limerick she'd written was printed in *The Beano* and there was a marathon phone call to tell us all about the skateboard she'd won. All Clare's phone calls were marathons, she wouldn't ever hang up and you always had to ask to speak to Mum so that you could then put the phone down. There was something else that Shannon wouldn't put down either—the lid of my talking police officer cookie jar. She just couldn't resist the challenge of opening the lid and pinching a piece of chocolate before the cop said, "Stop, stay away from the cookie jar!"

Paul started the year under suspension after his fresh air shot, the ban that would end before he knew it. John phoned late Saturday morning to say he was playing, Paul reminded him he was under suspension. He had watched their match the previous week being abandoned because of the weather, which meant there was one game of his enforced absence still to run. John advised him it was a pity he hadn't stayed until the end. The referee had only taken the teams off for a few minutes until the snow stopped and the game had actually finished. Suspension served and a mad dash to Hazlehead ensued. The boys flirted with the fringes of promotion before the end of the season but in honesty another season at the lower level wouldn't do them any harm. At one stage they played a golden oldies back four of Richard Murray, Paul, Martin Tough and Gary Lees, who'd played that same roll for Glentanar Juniors just a few years before.

There would be a hard season ahead for the team but my footballing highlights were off the pitch in 2004.

Elaine, Paul, Vera and I had a great night out at the Rusty Nail where Glentanar held their end of season horsey night. Paul's madcap antics brought the house down. I asked Vera if she thought he was just like me when he'd had a drink? She screwed up her face for a moment and then explained the subtle difference.

"Well nearly," she said, "Paul is completely nuts but he can hold his drink. You're completely nuts but with a drink in you couldn't hold your trousers up if you weren't wearing a belt!"

"Thanks Vera!"

Jim Neave hit the jackpot for me; the one thing missing from Paul's footballing rogue's gallery was a Grampian CD team photograph. Jim found one for me and a pal at work enhanced and enlarged the image on his computer. That was Paul's surprise Christmas present out of the way again!

Two British girls had such differing experiences in the Athens Olympics; Kelly Holmes scaled the heights and won two gold medals over 800 and 1500 metres. Poor Paula Radcliffe plumbed the depths of despair as she was forced to pull out of the marathon, a race for which she had started firm favourite.

Elaine and Paul were busy puting their own stamp on their house and their new fitted kitchen was really lovely. I thought the only thing I had left to put my stamp on was birthday cards but Vera decided that what we needed was a dining room. Up to the loft went my computer and keyboard as she converted the smallest bedroom. How would I ever perfect all those David Gray numbers in a freezing loft?

Elaine and Paul also had some wonderful news for the family; they planned to marry the following July and Clare and Shannon were to be flower girls. A new home to mould into shape and now a wedding to plan. Was that a grey hair or two I could see on Paul's head? Luckily for him Elaine was so well organised he didn't have to buy one single bottle of *Grecian 2000*.

Vera and I managed a week away at a cottage in the Brecon Beacons; the couple who owned it were lovely and had us through for an evening with their friends. The pool was very relaxing first thing every morning and our trip down a mine in South Wales was really memorable. £1.20 pence a pint in the Labour Club at Merthyr Tydfil was pretty memorable too! We had put Theo into a local cattery whilst we were away on holiday and although I'm sure he was well looked after, our summer was going to end in sadness. He was ill from the day we got him back and in the end the vet said there was no alternative other than to have him put to sleep. He was just an old cat and plumb tuckered out. I hope we'd given him as much love and friendship as he'd given us these last fifteen years. You'll be sadly missed old fat cat!

We spent an October weekend with Lilian when her grief was still never far from the surface; life's hard on your own and as she got older I'm sure that fact became more obvious to her. At least she had her new job and outwardly was the brash, positive woman she'd always been, but inside she was a broken hearted softie.

My good pal Harry Park and I had joined the Boilermakers Club. Harry and I had been workmates, drinking pals and bowling teamates for years and it was always fun to socialise with him and his better half Eileen. We went to a super Halloween party at the club but the disco weren't playing my stuff. I was on both sides of the musical divide then but he didn't have any Leann Rimes or *Dry Your Eyes Mate* by the Streets. *The Lord of the Rings* was back with another blockbuster and I just loved it when the kids came across to watch it; the action sequences were fantastic.

As we all enjoyed our Christmas and New Year holidays news broke of a disaster of such magnitude that it was difficult to believe the scale of death, devastation and destruction that had been wrought. The Asian Tsunami had been caused by a massive earthquake off Sumatra; that tidal brought death to many countries and hundreds of thousands lost their lives. The world launched a massive aid operation but it would be years before all the damage could be repaired and the suffering caused to millions was just incomprehensible.

Here's to the future here's to the past.
Here's to dreams that didn't last
Here's to tomorrow here's to today.
Here's to dreams that always stay.

Here's to a girl here's to a boy.
Here's to a life they filled with joy.
Here's to mum's and here's to dads.
Here's to memories far too sad.

Here's to joy here's to sorrow.
Here's to thinking of tomorrow.
Here's to laughter here's to tears.
Here's to memories of past years.

Here's to despair here's to love.
Here's to blessings from above.
Here's to hope here's to hate.
Here's to besting the hand of fate.

Here's to life here's to death.
Here's to every wondrous breath.
Here's to beginnings here's to ends.
Here's to dear departed friends.

Here's to legend here's to now.
Here's to our wedding vow.
Here's to tonight here's to forever.
Here's to a life we'll spend together.

I had secretly broken a promise to myself, I'd vowed I'd never try to make my children live my dreams for me but I had lived my football dreams through Paul. Perhaps he's always known that but I'm glad I did and my life has been all the richer for it. The marvellous people I've met and shared triumph and defeat with roll off the tongue. John Johnstone, Dod Bennett, Jim Neave, Ian Simpson, Stevie Gormley, Barney Battles, Bob Charles and John Irvine, the list is endless. I can only apologise to all the wonderful people whose names I haven't mentioned and who have warmed the touchline with me over the years.

No football story would be complete without naming my best team ever, 4-4-2, so here goes. It has to be the fearless Michael 'Hoppy' Hopkins in goal. Richard 'Lugs' Murray at right back, such a wonderful spirit and great striker of the ball. Paul Robertson at centre half, you always had the heart for the game and did what I told you, never pulled out of a tackle and played with your head up. Alan 'Rhino' Rhind at sweeper, thanks for teaching Paul all the tricks I couldn't. Ernie Reaper at left back, the CD singers on the bus trips convinced me...there's only one Ernie Reaper! Chris Pelicos in right midfield, if anyone tackled harder than Chris did I've never seen them. Sandy Robertson and Ian 'Sammy' Masson sharing centre midfield, what an engine for any side. Paul 'Bates' Masson in left midfield, every side needs a genius. Davie Scott up front, I know you'll score goals and you can be as lazy as you like with the other ten guys in this side. Colin MacRonald up front too but in a free roll, I've already got a genius but there's no harm in having a magician too.

223

I'd like to thank every other player who has shared the field of dreams with my son for the absolute pleasure they have brought me over the years. There has to be one major apology too, and that's to Martin Tough. Martin, I've checked the teamsheet several times and can't understand why your name is not on it so I've decided to make you my Player of the Decade, 1990's that is—you'll never last out this one with your hamstrings.

2005 would be the year I finally moved within the police organisation and it was off to Bucksburn as a Registrar in the Disclosure Unit; hopefully this old dog would be able to learn new tricks. I was just getting too old for the hurly-burly at Lost and Found and couldn't take the public any more. I maybe didn't think of work with as much fondness as I might but Grampian Police had been a good secure employer for me.

Shannon and Clare were growing oh so well but sometimes growing up has its scary moments. Clare was attacked by a gang of kids outside Mastrick Library, not the sort of thing you're ready for just before your tenth birthday. We all had a scare over Shannon too when she was taken into hospital with pneumonia but after a really terrible few days she was home and on the mend. It was a worrying time for Leanne and Keith. Vera and I had a lovely trip to Edinburgh Zoo with the kids and Clare was snap happy with my digital camera—she forgot to take her own one! Vera shared her fifty-second birthday at home with Leanne, Keith, both the girls and me. The vouchers and cash she got from Elaine, Paul and Lilian would set her up for a rare old shopping spree too.

Pope John Paul II died and it seemed that sainthood would be the future recognition of his life of virtue. The Irish comedian Dave Allen had perhaps blasphemed somewhat in his lifetime but his wry humour would be sadly missed. There was no doubt that we'd never see the likes of the wonderful acting talents of John Mills again. We'd certainly never laugh as much as we had with Ronnie Barker; this prince of funnymen would be a great loss to a world seemingly filled with so much hurt.

Tony Blair made it back into power yet again after a May election but somehow New Labour had become a tired bunch, devoid of any ideas that might stir the minds and imagination of the country. Locked into the awful aftermath of the war in Iraq, there seemed little room for manoeuvre to allow them to paint a bright picture of the future for the nation. The threat of terror just wouldn't go away either and the London Underground and bus bombings in July brought not only tragic loss of life but made it clear that we had not won the hearts and minds of the Nation of Islam. The world certainly stood at a crossroads. Then as if there wasn't enough pain in the world a huge earthquake devastated northern Pakistan; the death toll quickly rose to 20,000 and it was feared that would rise much higher. The wonderful side of humanity as always showed through and aid poured in from around the world.

I briefly spoke with Dad and Isobel and they both seemed well enough within themselves. We exchanged phone numbers and I called him a couple of times but somehow we were both unwilling just to throw our arms around one another and let bygones be bygones. We have to do it before it's too late in this world and if he can't I must, I will!

Vera and I were happiest at home, our new little LCD widescreen telly made our bolthole in the sun lounge just perfect and the bank's valuation of our house at around £150000 was comforting and made us very proud of the journey we'd made through life together. Age was beginning to tell though, and for the first time ever we forgot to turn our clocks forward. We didn't realise until we wondered why they were selling booze in the supermarket at half past eleven in the morning on the Sunday. I had a silly thought and dreamed of writing a book; I'd had a try at building a family tree but found it boring. Just thinking of old times was much more fun but how many of us have uttered those famous words, "I could write a book!"

Bill and Allison had an addition to their family when the got themselves a wee Westie called Fergie. I'm sure Bill was taking him on all those walks to keep super fit for the tennis. Bill had joked about it at his wedding but now we really were forgetting the score during our tennis matches. One thing is clear in my mind, after more than twenty years neither of us has ever questioned the other over a line call nor have we ever thought there was a need to. Dave and Andrea were back at Lossiemouth after a season without a caravan there. They loved their little bolthole and it was a pleasure to once more spend some great weekends there with them. One of them wasn't so good for poor Andrea, who had a knee replacement operation, but less than a week later was mine host for a long weekend stay. Concerned for her well being, Dave and I did the dishes together for the first time in years, or was it ever? At least she had Vera to help her properly.

Jack Nicklaus finally pulled alongside Muhammad Ali in the greatest sportsman of all time race along Union Street. How fitting that he birdied the final hole of his final Open at the home of golf and how typical that he wanted to share that wonderful moment with so many others. Jack and Muhammad would dead heat across the line in the end and they and many others have filled my life with so many unforgettable sporting memories. In truth they never stop coming and if anyone tells you cricket is boring just show them the videos of the 2005 Ashes series, that will be right at the top of any poll for the greatest series of all time. Three bowling finals were a delight for me and although I lost two of them it was nice to have played well through the season and the friendship on the green was the most important thing of all. The worst aspect of the sporting year was Keith being assaulted by a player and even worse the club committee telling lies to try and shield their man from punishment. A decent man like Keith leaves his home two or three times a week to ensure twenty-two other guys enjoy themselves and gets a belt in the mouth for his trouble; whatever happened to sportsmanship?

If I could have written a love song for Vera I would have called it *You're the One I Love* and luckily a man who could write songs did it for me—thanks David Gray. I'm still listening to the two best albums of the year; Willie Nelson was an old friend and his reggae album, *Countryman,* was a delight, especially his duet with Toots Hibbert on *I'm A Worried Man.* The discovery of the beautiful music of Lynn Miles was a delight and her album, *Love Sweet Love,* was one of those I could listen to over and over again.

Paul and Elaine had done a huge amount of preparation for their wedding and in the end they got the wonderful day all their hard work deserved. In the run up to the wedding it was a pleasure for Vera and me to meet Elaine's mum, Joyce; we had both briefly met her dad Charlie before. They were a lovely couple. Joyce was suffering from multiple sclerosis and on meeting her we were filled with admiration for the way she bore her illness with great dignity and bravery, but best of all for me she was a funny lady and loved a laugh.

Paul and I started the day of his stag party with a great game of badminton and then it was off to the pub for the cup final. Keith joined us as all the boys met up in the Rusty Nail for the evening session and John Irvine supplied the special touch when he arranged for Jim Neave and Ian Simpson to turn up as surprise guests. Keith and I slipped away and let the young lads head for the city lights later on, but I was tipsy enough to need a taxi home.

Elaine and Paul made a lovely couple on the 2nd of July 2005 and the whole wedding at the Palm Court Hotel was a wonderful affair. Charlie looked so happy as he arrived in the horse and carriage with Elaine, who looked simply beautiful. Her mum and dad must have been so proud of her and I'm certain she was every bit as proud of them for the special day they'd given her. Joyce was a joy at the wedding and Paul, Charlie and Richard all made super speeches. Clare and Shannon were very pretty in their outfits—sorry Shannon was pretty and Clare was smart! The evening reception was great fun and Vera, Leanne, Keith, the girls, Lilian and I had a great time. If my wee daft idiot made an appearance I can only apologise and say to Elaine, Paul and the rest of the family that, like me, he will love you all for every moment of every second of every minute of every hour of the rest of your lives.

If my life has been ordinary it has been lived in special times and I have shared the world's stage with special people. Clare would start her own list of such memories when she won a prize to go and meet the world's' most famous children's author, in person, at a book reading at Edinburgh Castle. J K Rowling was the author of the *Harry Potter* stories and Clare adored them; this would be a special moment for her to carry in her heart through the years to come. Just stop and think, we all have them and I hope you have enjoyed reading about some of mine.

When I was young my family thrilled to an old radio programme called *Desert Island Discs* and I wanted to end with a variation on that theme. I imagined I was alone on an island and could chose only one book to read, one film to watch and one song to listen to whilst I was there. The book would be *Animal Farm,* which cynically leaves you thinking that nothing ever really changes. Yet in the suffering of the animals and the fate of Boxer, we know that the abiding redemption of the human condition is to keep trying to change things for the better. The film would be *The Quiet Man,* which is a comedy, a love story and a tale of how right always wins through in the end. What a wonderful place this world would be if only that were true. The song I'd listen to would be *The First Time Ever I Saw Your Face* by Roberta Flack and I could forever be dancing with the girl in the red mini dress I met all those remarkable years ago.

A million thoughts have moved across my mind as I have written my story. If I am mistaken in any remembrance please forgive me. Memories are your own truth and though not necessarily everyone else's, they are the true tale of your own life.

I wrote this book for you, Annie because although we lost one another somewhere along life's highway, I still treasure all of the times we had together.

I wrote this book for you Clare and Shannon because you are my Tardis to the future and will let your own children read it one day. A day will come when you'll hold a grandchild in your arms and they'll smile or cast a glance and you will think of me for a moment. Look around, I'll be there whispering I love you!

I wrote this book for you, Mum because all of what I am and what my life has meant has come from the moment you gave me the miracle. One day we'll read it together.

I wrote this book for you, Dad because life just beat the shit out of you as you tried hard to give so much to others. I should have loved you better and I wish I'd been a tough guy for you.

I wrote this book for you Paul, because you are my son and my friend and I treasure the fact that we have never exchanged harsh words in our lives. It also proves that my memory is maybe just a little better than you thought...so there!

I wrote this book for you Leanne, because you were my first opportunity to give the miracle and in return you gave me immortality. I've never stopped loving you since the first moment I saw you. If I made you cry one cold winter night I'm so, so sorry.

I wrote this book for you Vera, because you know me warts and all and yet still love me. I just wish I'd had the skill to make my words perfect, so that you would have felt you could hear the theme music from *Hanover Street* as you read every line and turned every page.

A sadness when a dear friend died,
And once again a family cried.
Then happiness filled every thought,
Elaine and Paul had tied the knot.
Life's for living no rehearsals,
It comes with triumphs and reversals.
Love is life's enchanted token,
With love hearts are never broken.

Until tomorrow.

The End

Also from PlashMill Press

A Boy's Own Offshore Adventure   *by*   *Brian Page*

Price: £11.99   ISBN: 978-0-9554535-1-9

A Boy's Own Mining Adventure   *Brian Page*

Price: £11.99   ISBN: 978-0-9554535-3-3

Silver Threads   *by*   TOM RALSTON

Price: £9.99   ISBN: 978-0-9554535-5-7

Poaching the River   *by*   *Rod Fleming*

Price: £11.99   ISBN: 978-0-9554535-0-2

THE TOBACCONIST   *by*   *Jennifer Dalmaine*

Price: £9.99   ISBN: 978-0-9554535-2-6

Free Carriage!

Carriage anywhere in the world is free when you order direct from PlashMill
Press. Please see our website for terms and conditions.

www.plashmillpress.com